What Schools Can Do

SUNY Series, Teacher Empowerment and School Reform

Henry A. Giroux and Peter L. McLaren, Editors

What Schools Can Do

Critical Pedagogy and Practice

Edited by
Kathleen Weiler
and Candace Mitchell

State University of New York Press

Published by
State University of New York Press, Albany

For information, address State University of New York Press,
State University Plaza, Albany, N.Y., 12246

Production by M. R. Mulholland
Marketing by Bernadette LaManna

Library of Congress Cataloging–in–Publication Data
What schools can do: critical pedagogy and practice / edited by
  Kathleen Weiler and Candace Mitchell.
    p.   cm. — (SUNY series, Teacher empowerment and school
  reform)
    "The articles included all originally appeared in the Journal of
  education, which is located at the School of Education at Boston
  University" — P. vii.
    Includes bibliographical references and index.
    ISBN 0-7914-1127-3 (alk. paper). — ISBN 0-7914-1128-1 (pbk.:
  alk. paper)
    1. Educational sociology—United States. 2. Education—Political
  aspects—United States. 3. Education—United States—Philosophy.
  4. Curriculum change—United States. 5. Educational change—United
  States. I. Weiler, Kathleen. II. Mitchell, Candace. III. Journal
  of education (Boston, Mass.) IV. Title: Critical pedagogy and
  practice. V. Series: Teacher empowerment and school reform.
  LC191.4.W48 1992
  370.19'0973—dc20   91-30790
                                                                   CIP

10 9 8 7 6 5 4 3 2 1

Contents

Acknowledgments

We would like to take this opportunity to thank the numerous individuals who have in various ways contributed to this book. The articles included all originally appeared in the *Journal of Education,* which is located at the School of Education at Boston University. We would thus first of all like to thank Joan Dee, Associate Dean of the School of Education, for her continued generous support and encouragement of the *Journal* over the years. In addition, we want to thank Jim O'Brien, who has contributed a great deal more than his formal position as copy editor of the *Journal* might indicate. His insight and critical engagement with the issues raised in these articles as well as his considerable talents as an editor have been invaluable. For more than a decade, the *Journal of Education* has been a leading voice in the critical study of education. This commitment is due in large part to the encouragement and support of Henry Giroux, who first became involved with the *Journal* when he joined the faculty of the School of Education in 1978. His energy and high standards of scholarship, as well as his support of a generation of graduate students, provided leadership and direction to the editorial board and established the *Journal* as an international forum for the exploration of critical issues in education. We also want to thank the editorial board members of the *Journal.* The success of the *Journal* over the years has rested on the commitment and involvement of this editorial board, which is composed of graduate students at Boston University. And finally, we want to thank Priscilla Ross, our editor at SUNY Press, who has supported this project from its inception.

Candace Mitchell
Kathleen Weiler

Introduction

The essays in this volume bring together disparate voices of critique. We hope they will challenge readers to see educational issues in new ways, to explore not only the workings of power and culture in schools as they now exist, but also to engage in educational practice to create better schools for the future. In a society dominated by individualism and narrow forms of rationality that serve to mask and justify inequalities, the political and social critiques of those who have been excluded and who are now speaking their own truths is vital in encouraging resistance and change. These essays raise a multiplicity of voices and debates about where we are, why we are here, and the kind of futures we can struggle to achieve. Education in the United States since the nineteenth century has been marked by periodic panics over questions of national identity and purpose. In times of crisis, reformers and critics have turned to the presumed inadequacy of education as the source of social and political ills. Incompetent teachers, inappropriate curricula, unwieldy bureaucracies, and racially or culturally 'deprived' students have all been blamed for each period's perceived weaknesses in political, economic, or cultural spheres. In the past decade, this tendency to blame education for national decline has, if anything, increased. Through official reports, national studies, and popular polemics, a conservative rhetoric about the 'crisis in the schools' has come to dominate contemporary discourse about education. Schools and teachers have been blamed for the declining economic health of the nation, for continued unemployment, crime, and a perceived decline in 'moral standards' among the young. At the same time, there is a marked retreat from a commitment to education as a civil and moral right for all children and an acceptance and even encouragement of what is in effect a two-tiered system of education in this country. This attitude of both blame and neglect of public education has been accompanied in the early 1990s by a conservative campaign to silence critical voices and demand conformity to the authoritative writings of a canon of 'the Western tradition.' Education may indeed be in crisis, but it is a crisis over resources, power, and voice. The authors of this volume, who are loosely associated with what has come to be known as "critical pedagogy," address these questions from a stance of both critique and visionary hope.

Critical pedagogy links education with an analysis of politics and economics, and takes as central the belief that schools are places where social analysis and the empowerment of students can take place. Their work continues a long critical tradition in U.S. education. In the early decades of the twentieth century, social philosophers such as John Dewey, W.E.B. DuBois, and George Counts presented a vision of education as the means for individual growth and for social change. In the late 1960s, critics began to develop an analysis of education in the United States that carried on the radical tradition of such earlier figures as Dewey, DuBois, and Counts. While this critical tradition echoed the approach of these figures, it was also deeply influenced by the development of critical social analysis in other areas. With the growth of social movements in the 1960s, critiques of various aspects of U.S. society emerged: legal and institutional racism was challenged by the African-American-led-civil rights movement; patriarchal practices and sexism were critiqued by the women's liberation movement; the role of the United States in a world system of imperialism and neo-colonialism was called into question by the movement against the Vietnam war and by the introduction of political and social criticism from Latin America, Asia, and Africa; the inequities of the class divisions within the United States were analyzed by a number of neo-Marxist theorists. By the late 1960s, this broad range of critical analysis was influencing teachers and theorists to begin to examine education and schools. A number of first-person accounts of public schools by such writers as Herbert Kohl, Jonathan Kozol, and James Herndon exposed the racist practices and unequal structure of urban schools. At the university level, analyses of the role of leading universities in providing ideological justifications for the actions of the government emerged from the anti-war movement. And fundamental challenges to traditional curricula and dominant institutions were mounted by African-Americans, feminists, and a variety of other unrepresented groups. It was in the context of these multifaceted critiques of the dominant social system that a more fully developed critical theory of education emerged in the mid-1970s.

The critical studies of education that emerged in the 1970s were dominated by reproduction studies of schooling, which argued that schools served the primary role of reproducing an unequal and oppressive social system under capitalism. Studies of education in the United States such as Bowles and Gintis's *Schooling in Capitalist*

America, and European works such as Basil Bernstein's *Class Codes and Control* and Bourdieu and Passeron's *Reproduction in Society, Education and Culture* made the argument that schools, through their organization of space and time, their choice of curricular knowledge, and their valuation of dominant forms of language and culture, were institutions that both justified and maintained class boundaries. Schools thus were seen to teach a 'hidden curriculum' of social control. In Althusser's terms, they were "ideological state apparatuses" which functioned to reproduce the status quo. By the late 1970s, a new group of theorists had emerged who focused on students' resistance to these dominant forces. These studies asserted that students' own actions had to be considered in theorizing the role of schools in capitalist societies. Most influential of these analyses of resistance was no doubt Willis's study of British working-class boys, *Learning to Labour.* Thus, from an early concern with the 'hidden curriculum' and the role of schools in reproducing oppressive social relationships, critical educators moved to consider the possibilities of student resistance and curriculum transformation. These studies led to increasingly sophisticated and complex forms of analysis. Gramsci's formulation of hegemony and the possibility of what he called "good sense" or critical understanding on the part of social actors provided the foundation for a vision of education as both active and political. At the level of radical practice, the work of Paulo Freire inspired teachers and students to seek ways of teaching for social transformation and liberation. By the late 1980s, the term critical pedagogy came to be applied to the work of a number of theorists in the United States working from this complex intellectual tradition.

The term 'critical pedagogy,' like other labels, implies a more static and bounded category than is in fact the case. As the articles in this volume will attest, a wide range of perspectives has come to be included under the broad rubric of critical pedagogy, but all of the work described as critical pedagogy shares a stance of critique and an interpretation of pedagogy in its wider sense as including curriculum, social relationships in the classroom, and the ways in which the classroom reflects the larger social context. Recently the concerns of theorists associated with critical pedagogy have broadened, reflecting the intellectual ferment in the 1990s and, in particular, the development of more complex feminist, postmodernist, and postcolonial theory. Although there had been debates and conflicts among the theorists of critical pedagogy over questions of interpretation and practice, the theorists of the 1970s and early 1980s shared an underlying set of assumptions or paradigms grounded in traditional

Marxist and neo-Marxist thought. This led them to frame their analyses in terms of class and class reproduction or resistance. With the growth of educational theory written by feminists and people of color, these theorists' predominant focus on class came under increasing criticism. White male theorists associated with critical pedagogy were called upon to address the implications of their own positions of privilege in gender, race, or class terms and to consider the ways in which they also implicitly made privileged and universal claims. This critique of critical pedagogy as a form of discursive practice and system of truth echoed various forms of postmodernist analysis, particularly the work of Foucault. Postcolonial and postmodernist theory and the critiques by feminists and people of color have called into question claims to a unitary and transcendent truth that underlay earlier critical studies in education. Feminists and people of color in particular challenged the exclusive focus on class in analyses of the social relations of schooling or dominant forms of knowledge. These feminist, postcolonial, and postmodernist challenges have led critical educational theorists to reexamine their own assumptions and the ways their own thought could be examined as discursive practice. These challenges have led to tensions and conflicts within critical pedagogy, but at the same time they have led to a rich interchange and revitalization of the ways in which power is conceptualized as operating in schools and curricula, and in particular a much more complex understanding of the ways in which students and teachers are both subjected to and subjects of what we call education.

All of the essays in this collection appeared first in the *Journal of Education,* a journal which has provided an important venue for critical studies in education in this decade. The *Journal of Education,* published through the School of Education at Boston University, is the oldest continuous educational journal in the United States. Throughout its history, it has reflected important trends in educational research and theory. Its present concern with critical pedagogy, however, dates from the late 1970s, when Henry Giroux joined the faculty of the School of Education at Boston University. In Giroux's six years at Boston University, he encouraged critical research and scholarship among his graduate students, was central in bringing leading educational theorists to speak at Boston University, and was instrumental in encouraging the editorial board of the *Journal* to consider publishing special issues from a critical perspective. In 1980, Giroux edited a special issue of the *Journal* on the hidden curriculum. In the early 1980s, the *Journal* published special issues on topics such as literacy and ideology, schooling and work, and gender and class. Giroux's position at Boston University ended in 1983, when his application for tenure, which had been unanimously supported by the School of Education and the All University Wide Tenure Committee, was denied by Boston University president John Silber. Giroux's career at Boston University itself is a reminder that all intellectual work is political and that struggles over ideas are also material struggles. Although Giroux was forced to leave Boston University, the *Journal* has continued to act as a forum for critical pedagogy.

In selecting these essays from the *Journal*, we have been guided by a principle of including a variety of perspectives—including feminism, cultural politics, and discourse—to explore the theoretical bases and practical implications of a critical approach. While all of these essays can be included under a broad umbrella of critical pedagogy, in the sense that they examine existing structures critically and challenge dominant assumptions about education and schooling in the United States, they present a wide range of concerns and perspectives. Most of them are critical of the early exclusive focus on schools as means of class reproduction. Rather, they focus on the ways in which schools and curricula have reproduced racist ideology and assumptions, the ways in which patriarchal assumptions have defined both school practices and research in education, and the openings that exist for teachers to use students' own cultural worlds as the source for an oppositional pedagogy. At the same time, they build upon the earlier critical studies of education of the 1970s and, in particular, reflect the continued influence of the pedagogy of Paulo Freire. Many of these essays are also deeply influenced by post-modernist social theory as well as by feminism or antiracist theory. Of course, the term *postmodernism* itself is highly contested and has been applied in a variety of ways to developments in architecture, literary criticism, philosophy, and popular culture. Postmodernism in the broadest sense can be seen as a movement in Western thought and art that challenges the idea of universal truths or "master narratives," as they are sometimes called. But as Hal Foster points out, there is a basic contradiction between what he calls "a postmodernism of reaction" and "a postmodernism of resistance."[1] It is this sense of postmodernist critique as "resistance" to accepted truths and unitary dominant versions of social reality that underlies many of these essays. In this sense, these essays provide a critique not only of dominant forms of analysis or accepted truths, but of the early tradition of critical educational theory itself. We have selected what we feel to be representative essays organized around two themes: theorizing power/knowledge and pedagogies of possibility. By moving from theoretical analyses to examples of curriculum transformation and classroom practice, we hope to provide both a foundation for the analysis of schooling and also alternatives for teaching practice in the direction of democracy and social justice. The organization of this volume reflects this dual focus on critical pedagogy as critique and as work for social change.

The first section, "Theorizing Power/Knowledge," presents essays that provide a theoretical analysis of the workings of power through school practices and knowledge. In many ways the guiding principle underlying all of these essays is set out by Henry Giroux in "The Hope of Radical Education." As Giroux makes clear, radical or critical educational theory begins with the need to question accepted truths and assumptions about education and society. This leads to the stance of critique and a concern with the underlying social and historical processes at work in any educational encounter or school site. But he also makes clear that implicit in the idea of a critical approach is a commitment and a belief that society is a historical construction that is in process, that has changed over time, and that can be changed in the future. In her essay, "A Feminist Perspective on the Relationship Between Family Life and School Life," Madeleine Arnot presents a feminist critique of the British critical sociology of education of the 1970s and early 1980s. She points out that this work, although important in exposing the inequities and implication of state schooling in reproducing class inequities, was deeply flawed by its failure to address issues of gender. Not only were most studies of schooling by critical sociologists of education in Great Britain during this period exclusively focused on boys, but they also ignored the role of the family. While studies focused on the role of schools in reproducing (male) workers, these same studies failed to address the role of schools in reproducing patriarchal family structures, structures which in a shrinking economy assume a dual workload for women as workers in low paid jobs and full-time workers in the home and in child care.

Arnot's critique of critical sociology of education uses its own tradition of political economy to demonstrate the shortcomings of an analysis that fails to address gender. But the terminology and approach she uses echo traditional critical methods and assumptions. The next two essays, Laurie McDade's "Sex, Pregnancy and Schooling: Obstacles to a Critical Teaching of the Body," and Linda Brodkey and Michelle Fine's "Presence of Mind in Absence of Body," use the language and approach of both postmodernist and feminist theory to examine the ways in which power operates in school discourse and in teachers' and students' consciousness as embodied subjects. Both of these essays seek to unravel the silences and materiality of ideology in the way school knowledge separates "mind" from the reality we experience in our bodies. McDade considers the political and ideological struggles around a program for pregnant teenage girls. She argues that this case illuminates the ways in which power operates in schools and the ways in which knowledge of and through the body is denied by dominant school practices. In her description of the effects of a political decision to eliminate this program for pregnant teenage girls, she shows the ways in which struggles over curricula and school organization do symbolic and material violence to those who are oppressed—in this case predominantly poor black and Puerto Rican girls, women of color who are the most oppressed group in U.S. society. In a study of responses to a sexual harassment survey at the University of Pennsylvania, Brodkey and Fine echo one of the themes of McDade's essay, the ways in which knowledge of and through the body is denied—in this case by the victims of sexual harassment themselves. Through an analysis of the written responses to this survey as narratives, Brodkey and Fine uncover the silences and absences in these texts. As they point out, by defining themselves wholly as "mind," these women, who were sexually harassed, managed to take a viewpoint of observer to their own bodies, but with damaging effects on their own ability to study and teach. In all three of these essays, the specific experiences of women and the ways in which patriarchal assumptions are incorporated into consciousness become the basis for critique of the dominant views of what it means for women and girls to be educated and to teach.

The next three essays share similar approaches to the analysis of classroom knowledge. Cleo Cherryholmes uses Foucault's conception of discursive practices to uncover the structuring principles of knowledge in social studies education. Cherryholmes argues that it is important to become self-conscious about the ways in which discursive practices shape and limit what is permissible for us to say. By becoming more conscious of the ways in which discourse operates, we can begin to see the underlying principles and assumptions that structure discourse, and can be clearer about the ways in which we can act to achieve our own goals as teachers. Cameron McCarthy uses a similar analysis of discourse to consider the ways in which the concept of multiculturalism has been appropriated in textbooks and

curricula. He argues that much of what is presented as multicultural
education is in fact simply the addition of fragmentary images or
stories of 'the other' to the margins of the dominant Western narrative
which organizes knowledge in textbooks and other curricular
materials. McCarthy argues that 'Western-ness' as the dominant
organizing principle of knowledge is itself a deeply politicized concept
emerging from struggles over power and resources. Instead he argues
for what he calls an "emancipatory multiculturalism" which would
emphasize multivocality in the construction of curricula. A similar
critique of dominant ideas of what constitutes culture and the
conception of Western values and knowledge is presented by Thomas
Popkewitz in his essay, "Culture, Pedagogy, and Power: Issues in the
Production of Values and Colonialization." Popkewitz examines the
Museum of Modern Art exhibit on modernism and a Teacher Corps
project in three rural Native American communities to consider the
ways in which the normative definition of what is "our" culture is
itself socially constructed within fields of discursive practices. Like
McCarthy, Popkewitz points to the centrality of conceptions of a
normative identity or culture and the idea of the 'others,' who can
be objects of study or who can be given some marginal space on the
edges of the dominant narrative. And, echoing most of the essays in
this section, Popkewitz calls for an interrogation and deconstruction
of the discursive practices that organize and categorize experience
to reflect and reinforce relationships of power.

In the second section, we turn to essays that explore the theme
'pedagogies of possibility.' These essays include accounts of classroom
practices, analyses of conflicting forms of classroom discourse, and
alternative forms of practice. They consider the ways in which
teachers and students come to class as situated subjects with specific
histories, experiences of dominance or subordination, and have
available to them forms of knowledge (popular culture, for example),
and different subject positions that work in complex ways as
resistance or accommodation. In the first essay in this section,
Deborah Britzman uses the experiences of student teachers to explore
the possibilities inherent in the pedagogical encounter for cultural
critique and new discursive practices. She argues that the unexpected,
what she calls "the uncanny" in teaching is precisely what should
be embraced in conscious opposition to pedagogies that "manage
techniques, discipline bodies, and control outcomes." Her discussion
of one example of student resistance that expresses and plays upon
deep-seated racism, violent sexism, and fascism raises significant
questions about what critical pedagogy can mean and how it may be

framed. As Britzman argues, it is not enough to present what we feel
is progressive curriculum; critical teachers must also understand and
explore the ways in which their students (and they themselves) are
historically constructed within an oppressive and unequal society and
speak through the forms of discourse available to them. But, she
argues, a recognition of these complexities is vital as critical teachers
attempt to put their ideas into practice. The second essay in this
section, "African-American Teachers and the Politics of Race," by
Michèle Foster, provides an example of the contradictions and
problems faced by African-American teachers in the context of
desegregation. As Foster argues, these teachers attempted to "fashion
a pedagogy designed to counteract oppression and foster
empowerment" in the face of racist laws and practices. By giving voice
to these teachers, Foster demonstrates that although dismantling
legally segregated schools after Brown v. Board of Education was
essential, it was not enough and that racist practices continue to shape
schooling in the United States. She argues that it is imperative to
attack structural inequalities and to recognize and combat racism
in school practices and organization. Like Britzman, then, Foster
argues for the need to understand and analyze the barriers to equality
as the first step to building pedagogies of possibility.

The next three essays in this section—Maxine Greene's "The
Art of Being Present," Henry Giroux and Roger Simon's "Schooling,
Popular Culture, and a Pedagogy of Possibility," and Marilyn
Frankenstein's "Critical Mathematics Education"—suggest ways of
intervening in schools to build pedagogies of possibility. In "The Art
of Being Present," Greene argues that teachers should consciously
seek aesthetic encounters in their teaching in which "preferences are
released, uncertainties confronted, desires given voice." Echoing
Britzman's argument that critical teachers should take seriously the
role of the imagination and of the unexpected, Greene argues that
art and literature provide ways of presenting a multiplicity of voices
and of challenging accepted and conventional truths. These themes
are continued in Giroux and Simon's "Schooling, Popular Culture,
and a Pedagogy of Possibility." Giroux and Simon argue that popular
culture provides a significant site for the creation of a critical
pedagogy. By taking popular culture as a serious subject for critical
analysis and study, Giroux and Simon argue that teachers can
acknowledge students' own knowledge and meaning making and thus
validate students' own situated subject positions and voices. In
opening up popular culture as an area of serious study, Giroux and
Simon do not propose a simple celebration of mass culture. Instead

they intend both to validate students' engagement in discourse and to call existing truths into question. In "Critical Mathematics Education," Frankenstein uses Paulo Friere's epistemology to consider the ways in which mathematics can be studied in a critical fashion. As she argues, statistics and mathematical "truths" are often used to support and justify existing inequities. By discussing mathematics as a form of human knowledge that is historically constructed and within the reach of students, Frankenstein seeks both to demystify mathematics and to encourage students to understand its present uses and potential for emancipatory change.

In the last essay in this collection, "Writing Pedagogy: A Dialogue of Hope," Anne-Louise Brookes and Ursula Kelly present their mutual exploration of what critical pedagogy has meant to them as teacher-educators. In an exchange of letters, they reflect upon the ways in which critical pedagogy, as expressed in essays like the ones in this collection, sheds light upon their own work as critical teachers. As they attempt to put these ideas into practice, they come to see how difficult and complex it is to move from a theoretical understanding of the world to action in the world. While they see shortcomings in some of the works of critical theorists, they also find support for their own commitment to continue to work for change. It is our hope, reader, that although you will doubtless disagree and argue with various views and claims put forth here, this collection will provide a similar challenge and support for you.

Kathleen Weiler

Note

1. Hal Foster, "Postmodernism: A Preface," in *The Anti-Aesthetic: Essays on Modern Culture* (Port Townsend, WA: Bay Press, 1983) p. xi.

I

Theorizing Power/Knowledge

The Hope of Radical Education*

Henry A. Giroux

The School of Education at Miami University in Oxford, Ohio, is housed in McGuffey Hall, named after the author of the famous 19th century readers and a long time professor at Miami University. As one approaches the building from the West a large statue of McGuffey rears from the shrubbery. The inscription reads:

Wm. Holmes McGuffey
1800–1878

Who while professor in Miami University
compiled the famous McGuffey readers
Which established the social standards
of the great Middle West of the United States.

Eminent Divine and Philosopher
Peer of College Teachers
Inspirer of young men.

On another panel are chiseled the first words from the first lesson of the first McGuffey reader:

Here is John
And there are Ann and John.
Ann has got a new book.
Ann must keep it nice and clean.
John must not tear the book.
But he may see how fast he can learn.

It was both appropriate and ironic that Henry Giroux, a leading spokesperson for radical education in America today, should have his offices in a building named after McGuffey—appropriate because both attained a measure of recognition in the educational world and ironic because one could scarcely imagine two more dissimilar philosophies. When we met Giroux in his third floor offices he commented on the irony. "McGuffey was pretty conservative in his thinking but he was a committed educator. We share that in common." We had not come to talk about McGuffey but to get some perspective on a movement in education that is gaining considerable prominence. So we began our business with a leading question.

Q: *What is radical education?*
Giroux: Radical education doesn't refer to a discipline or a body of
             knowledge. It suggests a particular kind of practice and a
             particular posture of questioning received institutions and
             received assumptions. I would say in a general way that
             the basic premises of radical education grew out of the crisis
             in social theory. More specifically, we can distinguish three
             traits: radical education is interdisciplinary in nature, it
             questions the fundamental categories of all disciplines, and
             it has a public mission of making society more democratic.
             This last point is perhaps the principal reason why radical
             education as a field is so exciting. We can take ideas and
             apply them.
Q: *Almost like having your own laboratory?*
Giroux: Something like that. I prefer to think of it as a public
             sphere. Most disciplines don't have that. As a result their
             attempts to construct a public discourse become terribly
             academized and limited. That is why I find radical
             education so exciting both theoretically and politically.
Q: *How close is the tie between the two?*
Giroux: Very close. We can add that as another distinguishing trait.
             Radical education joins theory and praxis.
Q: *Is radical synonymous with critical?*
Giroux: Yes, I think they have to be. I can't conceive of a radical
             position that is not at the same time, and even in the first
             instance, critical both in historical terms about the ways
             schools have evolved in this country and ideologically in
             terms of the particular kinds of values that operate in our
             schools and in our practices of education. Critical education
             operates on two basic assumptions. One, there is a need
             for a language of critique, a questioning of presuppositions.
             Radical educators, for example, criticize and indeed reject
             the notion that the primary purpose of public education is
             economic efficiency. Schools are more than company stores.

They have the much more radical purpose of educating citizens. Which is why the second basic assumption of radical education is a language of possibility. It goes beyond critique to elaborate a positive language of human empowerment.

Q: *We hear a lot about empowerment these days. How do you understand that term?*

Giroux: It is the ability to think and act critically. This notion has a double reference: to the individual and to society. The freedom and human capacities of individuals must be developed to their maximum but individual powers must be linked to democracy in the sense that social betterment must be the necessary consequence of individual flourishing. Radical educators look upon schools as social forms. Those forms should educate the capacities people have to think, to act, to be subjects and to be able to understand the limits of their ideological commitments. That's a radical paradigm. Radical educators believe that the relationship between social forms and social capacities is such that human capacities get educated to the point of calling into question the forms themselves. What the dominant educational philosophies want is to educate people to adapt to those social forms rather than critically interrogate them. Democracy is a celebration of difference, the politics of difference, I call it, and the dominant philosophies fear this.

Q: *Is your position that our assumptions were at one time sound and became outmoded or were they faulty to begin with?*

Giroux: If we are talking about traditional perspectives, I think the traditionalists have always been wrong about the nature of education.

Q: *How can you say such a thing?*

Giroux: Let me put it differently and say that within the field of education the languages that have dominated have generally been languages that have highly instrumentalized the purposes of schooling by either privileging certain groups of elites who become the managers of society or narrowing the scope of education so severely that schools become mere factories to train the work force. The traditionalists lack a language of possibility about how schools can play a major role in shaping public life.

Q: *But surely the liberal arts tradition has not been*
          instrumentalist in that way?
Giroux: I say that liberal education in any ideal sense of that term
          has always occupied a subordinate position vis-à-vis the
          dominant languages. And that is unquestionably true in
          this country since the 1950s. If we are talking about the
          public schools then the instrumentalist argument is very,
          very powerful. And this has been true from the beginning.
          If we are talking about higher education then it depends
          on what kinds of schools we have in mind. We all know our
          educational system is tiered. Some institutions are voca-
          tional. Others are places of real learning, although
          primarily for the elite. Harvard will never define itself as
          an institution whose primary mission is the promotion of
          industrial growth! It appeals to the life of the mind, the good
          life, and so forth. The higher rhetoric! We can distinguish
          different missions. But if we look at higher education in
          general I argue that the instrumentalist ideology prevails.
Q: *Hasn't the wave of reforms we have had lessened the*
          dominance of that ideology?
Giroux: I don't think so. Most of them have to my way of thinking
          been misguided. What has been the thrust of these reforms?
          Back to basics, merit pay, a standardized curriculum,
          raising test scores, evaluation criteria, and the like. This
          is just another version of the technological fix that ignores
          the philosophical questions. It is quantifying the educa-
          tional process in a belief that the outcome will be some kind
          of excellence or economic competence. All of this suggests
          to me that those who are pushing these reforms have no
          educational philosophy at all. We have to ask what the
          purposes of education are, what kind of citizens we hope
          to produce. To say that test scores are the answer is to beg
          the question of "What do test scores measure anyway?"
                 Here is a story that perfectly illustrates the point. Joe
          Clark, a school principal in Newark, has been touted by
          many reformers as the paragon of what an inner school
          educator should be. How does Clark operate? He marches
          through the halls of his school with a bullhorn and a base-
          ball bat, publicly berating anybody who flouts his authority.
          When students misbehave they must learn the school
          anthem and sing it over the P.A. system. Clark is given
          credit for restoring authority to the school and for raising

the test scores of his students. What that report omits is that some nine hundred students, most of them minorities, have been expelled to roam the streets with bleak prospects. One has to ask: What educational philosophy motivates this kind of action? What sense of learning do students get? How do teachers teach in such a context?

Q: *Has there ever been a time when schools met your criteria?*

Giroux: No, although there is a discernible tradition of dissent and vision that argues for a connection and the imperatives of a critical democracy. It is an important and powerful tradition, particularly during the 1920s and 1930s in this country. But we are not talking about much history here. Prior to the 20th century there wasn't much education of the sort we think appropriate for a democracy for the simple reason there wasn't much democracy.

Q: *Does democracy have to be critical democracy to be genuine?*

Giroux: That's what I mean. Dewey talked about democracy as a way of life that has to be made and remade by each generation.

Q: *The existentialists use the word appropriation to cover all questions of making our ideals meaningful in a lived context.*

Giroux: I like that word. It brings to the fore for me the crucial role of pedagogy and the question of how we learn to become subjects who engage not only our own self formation but the possibilities for society at any given time. How does one come to self-understanding? How does one situate oneself in history? How do we relate questions of knowledge to power? How do we understand the limitations of our institutions, or even of our age? Those are pedagogical questions. Radical educators understand them to be political questions as well. But let's face it, this is a lost discourse. None of the many recent reports about educational reform even scratches the surface of this problem.

Q: *What problem is that again?*

Giroux: The relationship between pedagogy and power.

Q: *Are radical educators a heard voice in the land?*

Giroux: They are an argument on the block, especially since 1976 when Samuel Bowles and Herbert Gintis published their path-breaking *Schooling in Capitalist Society*. I would argue that that book, along with some seminal works in the sociology of education, provided the foundation for a

new language that went beyond the earlier critical
tradition of Dewey and his colleagues. In the last ten years
this influence has become quite evident in what is
published, what is taught and what is talked about at
professional meetings.

Q: *Does radical education draw its inspiration primarily from
          Marxism?*

Giroux: It did. Bowles and Gintis did. But as I look at the work of
          radical educators today I would find it difficult to say that
          Marxism is the primary influence on it. And where the
          Marxist influence exists in education it can sometimes be
          overly reductionist and one-dimensional.

Q: *You mean not good Marxism?*

Giroux: It is more a question of how good Marxism is to begin with.
          We can appropriate a number of good things from Marxism
          but do we want to appropriate the paradigm itself?

Q: *It seems the radical educator has to do just that in some
          sense because Marxism has supplied the principal language
          of critique in the 20th century. Where else would you look?*

Giroux: I would say that to be a radical educator today you have
          to engage the Marxist tradition. And there is no question
          that Marxist discourse dominated in the beginning because
          in the beginning most work in radical education was about
          reproduction theory.

Q: *What is that?*

Giroux: It is a Marxist category which says that the basic function
          of the schools is to reproduce the dictates of the state in
          the economic order. It was a rather simple and mechanistic
          view but not entirely false and it had important conse-
          quences for politicizing the debate about the purpose of
          schools, which is something that the paradigm itself
          completely ignored.

Q: *But are there other traditions?*

Giroux: I myself draw from a number of positions. There are critical
          traditions in feminist literature, in literary theory, and in
          liberation theology that I find useful. But it is hard to put
          a label on all of this. I would like to call myself a good
          working-class, radical American.

Q: *As in populist?*

Giroux: Sure. A critical populist who includes some elements of the
          IWW, Bill Haywood, C. Wright Mills, Martin Luther King,
          and Michael Harrington. In other words, people who speak

to people in a language that dignifies their history and their experience. I don't understand how you can speak to people if you don't celebrate their voices.

Q: *How did you become interested in this field?*

Giroux: I went to college on a basketball scholarship. I started off in the sciences but then the Vietnam War came along and all of a sudden social theory became very important. The more I read the more I became interested in teaching. Not only did I see that as a way to make an impact but I saw teaching as a wonderfully noble profession. And I still feel that way. One of the things I try to impress upon my students is how important the field is.

Q: *What did you do your PhD dissertation on?*

Giroux: It was a study of curriculums. I was interested in the different ways kids learn in schools and the ways in which subject matters get selected for the curriculum. Where I grew up learning was a collective activity. But when I got to school and tried to share learning with other students that was called cheating. The curriculum sent the clear message to me that learning was a highly individualistic, almost secretive, endeavor. My working-class experience didn't count. Not only did it not count, it was disparaged. I was being reproduced according to a different logic. I think schools should be about ways of life. They are not simply instruction sites. They are cultures which legitimize certain forms of knowledge and disclaim others. The language for understanding this phenomenon in some pretty sophisticated ways is now starting to emerge.

Q: *For example?*

Giroux: Take the work being done on ideology and language in schools. It's very rich. If you believe that language actively constructs as well as reflects social reality, that language always develops out of a sense of difference—if something is this it is not that—and that language always embodies particular kinds of values then you can raise questions. You can ask: What is the relationship between what is learned and the pedagogies in place? Where does the language they use come from? Whose interests does it promote? What are its value assumptions? And the like.

Q: *One thinks of inner city schools. It seems to be the case there that the kind of education offered mismatches the experience of those to whom it is offered.*

Giroux: In my mind we have instrumentalized the process of
           education so much that we have forgotten that the referent
           out of which we operate is a white, upper-middle-class logic
           that not only modulizes but actually silences subordinate
           voices. If you believe that schooling is about somebody's
           story, somebody's history, somebody's set of memories, a
           particular set of experiences, then it is clear that just one
           logic will not suffice.

Q: *Not many people believe that.*

Giroux: Well, I'm surprised how many do. Even people of a very
           conservative cast are much more open to the kind of
           argument I am making. They, too, see schools as cultural
           institutions, as cultural frontiers if you will, and not merely
           boot camps for the economy. They see the value dimension.
           Unfortunately, their understanding is not very democratic.
           My point is that learning has to be meaningful to students
           before it can become critical. Our problem is that we have
           a theory of knowledge but no theory of pedagogy.

Q: *Isn't this all pretty abstract? After all, schools are run
           bureaucratically on the principles of delegated responsibility
           and dictated policies. And that seems clearly what the
           majority of Americans want.*

Giroux: But that's another question altogether, although related
           to the first question. The first question is: Can learning take
           place if in fact it silences the voices of the people it is
           supposed to teach? And the answer is: Yes. People learn that
           they don't count. The second question is: What are the
           necessary conditions to educate teachers to be intellectuals
           so they can engage critically the relationship between
           culture and learning and change the conditions under which
           they work? As I put it in some of my writings, we need to
           redefine the role of teachers as transformative intellectuals.

Q: *Would you elaborate on that intriguing idea?*

Giroux: Michael Waltzer speaks of intellectuals as engaged critics.
           They do not operate from an aloof perspective that
           legitimizes the separation of facts from values. They under-
           stand the nature of their own self-formation, have some
           vision of the future, see the importance of education as a
           public discourse, and have a sense of mission in providing
           students what they need to become critical citizens. So to
           give you a somewhat schematic sense of what I mean by
           teachers as transformative intellectuals, I would say, first,

that teachers are engaged. They are partisans, not doctrinaire. They believe something, say what they believe, and offer their belief to others in a framework that always makes it debatable and open to critical inquiry. Second, to talk about teachers as intellectuals is to say they should have an active role in shaping the curriculum. Think of intelligence as a form of currency that enables teachers to have a role in shaping school policy, defining educational philosophies, and working with their communities in a variety of capacities. Transformative intellectuals are aware of their own theoretical convictions and are skilled in strategies for translating them into practice. Above all, finally, it means being able to exercise power. Pedagogy is always related to power. In fact educational theories, like any philosophy, are ideologies that have an intimate relation to questions of power. So learning must be linked not just to learning in the schools but extended to shaping public life and social relationships. The proletarianization of the teaching profession has made educators too dependent and powerless. Does that give you some idea?

Q: *That's fine. Wouldn't you want, for much the same reasons, all professionals to be transformative intellectuals?*

Giroux: To be sure. But bear in mind that the teaching profession alone has the primary responsibility to educate critical citizens whereas we might argue that the first responsibility of, say the medical profession, is healing. Educators have a public responsibility that by its very nature involves them in the struggle for democracy. This makes the teaching profession a unique and powerful public resource.

Q: *Are schools of education moving toward this thinking?*

Giroux: The short answer is that they are starting to move but very slowly. And I have to say, without naming names, that some of our most progressive schools of education have become disappointingly reactionary. They tend more and more to hire people in the business manager mode and there are few, very few, critical voices to be heard.

Q: *Talk a little about your teaching experience.*

Giroux: It's both very gratifying and very challenging.

Q: *Tell us about the challenging part.*

Giroux: Most of our students are very comfortable with defining themselves as technicians and clerks. For them to be all of a sudden exposed to a line of critical thinking that both calls their own experience into question and at the same time raises fundamental questions about what teaching should be and what social purposes it might serve is very hard for them. They don't have a frame of reference or a vocabulary with which to articulate the centrality of what they do. They are caught up in market logic and bureaucratic jargon. We can't defend what we do that way. We can't make our best case. We always wind up on the defensive and appear to others as second rate and marginal. If, on the other hand, we make the case for critical democracy we can at the same time make the case for the centrality of the teaching profession. Of one thing I am sure, the older paradigm is dying not only in terms of its effectiveness but in terms of its legitimacy as well.

Q: *That's usually referred to as positivism and it has been stated more than once that positivism is dead. Yet it seems to be a very lively corpse.*

Giroux: Oh, it's not dead. I am not saying that at all. What you call positivisim I would want to call technocratic rationality or scientism which identifies the idea of progress with an idea of efficiency which in turn defines itself by abstracting from questions of power and politics and values. What I am saying is: that paradigm is breaking down, not dead. Look at the urban school systems. They are falling apart all over the country.

Q: *Do you find some teaching techniques more effective than others?*

Giroux: My courses are all seminars. I prescribe the materials I think are important but the students have to write papers and defend their positions. This is the basis of a 15-week working-through process. I don't care what positions the students take. I want them to be able to justify whatever position they do take so they come out with a clearer sense of what they believe in and what effects that might have. I think what I really do is politicize the process of education in the minds of the students. As soon as you say people can be agents in the act of learning you politicize the issue of schooling. It becomes political in the best sense of the word, which is to say that students have to become self-conscious about the kinds of social relationships that undergird the learning process. That's a political issue. Another thing I take very seriously in my teaching is illustrating principles with a sense of voice, with somebody's story. There are experiences out there that illuminate larger questions of educational philosophy. We can, for example, talk about the hidden curriculum of racism, about what black kids have to give up to become academically successful and we can do this through their own voices. Or we can talk about people who have no community of memories. We can talk about people who are defined by such a nonbelief in the common good that they can't even imagine an alternative vision according to anything other than highly individualistic and egotistical norms. Those stories are important. That is one of the reasons I have a lot of trouble with liberal and procedural morality. It eliminates the stories in favor of abstract rules. Of course, we need to understand that these stories by themselves do not always speak for themselves. But they can become the basis for analyzing a whole range of considerations that are often hidden in the stories. Experience never simply speaks for itself. The language that we bring to it determines its meaning.

Q: *Speak further to the point about student voices. How do you deal with the objection that students are virtual* tabula rasas *who don't have much to bring to the table?*

Giroux: Let me say what student experience is not. It is not a romantic celebration of adolescence as it sometimes was in the '60s. It is something very different. I am arguing that the notion of experience has to be situated within a theory of learning, within a pedagogy. You can't deny that students have experiences and you can't deny that these experiences are relevant to the learning process even though you might say that these experiences are limited, raw, unfruitful, or whatever. Students have memories, families, religions, feelings, languages, and cultures that give them a distinctive voice. We can critically engage that experience and we can move beyond it. But we can't deny it.

Q: *What about the white, middle-class voice?*

Giroux: That's a voice too.

Q: *But isn't it more than a voice? Isn't it the model we set? Doesn't it encapsulate the best experiences we want to emulate? To be blunt, isn't the best voice an urban minority student can adopt that of the white middle class?*

Giroux: In an instrumental sense that is true. But it is a truth that conceals dangers. The problem with that position is that it makes it hard for people to realize how important the question of voice is. We become unquestioning and fail to realize the symbolic violence the dominant voice can exercise. And I will say this: even for the white middle-class majority education often, most often, functions to silence rather than empower them.

Q: *A telling point. You make teaching sound like very hard work.*

Giroux: It is very hard work. That is why teachers need to be intellectuals, to realize that teaching is a form of mediation between different persons and different groups of persons and we can't be good mediators unless we are aware of what the referents of the mediation we engage in are. Teaching is complex, much more complex than mastering a body of knowledge and implementing curriculums. The thing about teaching is that the specificity of the context is always central. We can't get away with invoking rules and procedures that cut across contexts.

Q: *Your view of education seems to make tradition irrelevant.*

Giroux: As I mentioned before, the nature of our educational problems is new and unprecedented. In that sense there is no tradition to appeal to. But there are elements of a critical pedagogy in all traditions. The radical educator deals with tradition like anything else. It must be engaged and not simply received. Traditions are important. They contain great insights, both for understanding what we want to be and what we don't want to be. The question is: In what context do we want to judge tradition? Around what sense of purpose? We need a referent to do that. If we don't have a referent then we have no context to make sense of tradition. It doesn't supply its own referent.

Q: *Your referent is probably clear by now but could you state it briefly again?*

Giroux: My referent is how do we make this country a real critical democracy.

Q: *Where do you stand on liberal arts education?*

Giroux: A lot of people think everyone should have a liberal arts education. I disagree with that vehemently. Schooling has its own context. Often that context generates methods of inquiry that aren't likely to surface in the liberal arts disciplines.

Q: *You have a new book coming out. What is that about?*

Giroux: It's called *Schooling and the Struggle for Public Life: Critical Pedagogy in the Modern Age.* It will be published by the University of Minnesota Press in the Fall of 1988. It is different from my other books in a number of ways. I attempt to redefine the relationship between schooling and democracy and I look at particular traditions to contextualize this effort. I look at the social reconstructionists of the 1930s, I look at certain traditions in the feminist movement, and I look at some liberation theologians and their sense of struggle and hope. Hope is very important. We have to be able to dream. I also spend a lot of time developing a radical provisional ethic, which is to say an ethic that steers a course between a transcendent, ahistorical referent and a relativity which does not permit an ethic to defend its own presuppositions. Radical educators in this country are capable of a lot of moral indignation but really don't know how to define and justify in an ethical language what they want to do—the particular forms of authority they might want to exercise, the particular programmatic innovations they want to bring about, or, to take on the largest ethical issue of all, what is the nature of the good life we want to defend and how do we do that in ethical terms. We can't always operate in the logic of resistance. We must be able to speak the language of possibility as well. I chart out the theoretical basis of such an ethic in this book. Another thing I do is talk a lot about student voices. I think the primacy of student experience is crucial. But I have already talked about that.

Q: *Can you, as the clock winds down, summarize your educational philosophy?*

Giroux: Probably not, but I'll try. I find myself frequently falling back on a distinction John Dewey made over forty years ago between "education as a function of society" and "society as a function of education." In other words, are schools to uncritically serve and reproduce the existing society or challenge the social order to develop and advance its democratic imperatives? Obviously, I opt for the latter. I believe schools are the major institutions for educating students for public life. More specifically, I believe that schools should function to provide students with the knowledge, character, and moral vision that build civic courage.

Q: *The expression "civic courage" has a nice ring to it.*
Giroux: We are going to need a lot of it.
Q: *We'll talk again sometime.*
Giroux: I hope we do.

Note

*This is a slightly edited version of an interview that appeared in the *Civic Arts Review,* Volume 1, Number 1 (Summer 1988) and is reprinted by permission.

Schools and Families:
A Feminist Perspective

Madeleine Arnot

In this article I will examine, from a feminist perspective, the approach to education developed by left sociologists in the 1970s in Britain and the United States. It is now accepted by many that the mainstream left discourse on the sociology of education was constructed primarily by male academics who have continued to focus almost entirely on boys' educational experiences. This bias, fortunately, has been partially remedied by new feminist research on girls' experience in school and their transition into waged and domestic work. However, while this research is a necessary first step, it does not solve the full range of problems created by the mainstream left discourse. The standard theories are also deficient in the way they pose the relationship of the family to mass schooling and, more specifically, the relationship between class and gender in both the family and the school.

The problem has not been a lack of theorizing about the relationship between class and gender, but the nature of the theories that have become entrenched. The relationship has been formulated in such a way that the separation of family and work—and with it the division of the male public world and the female domestic sphere—has been legitimated. As a result, I will argue, the family has been located outside the economy. It has been portrayed as being insignificant as a social determinant of schooling, and therefore its internal dynamics have not been thought worthy of study. I will also argue that the ideology of *familism,* unlike that of vocationalism, has been inadequately treated as an aspect of social class differentiation. What I will then discuss is the new research on family and school relations which, in my view, has opened the door to a more sensitive and less biased political economy of education and a better grasp of the complexities of class and gender relations.

Although I will be critical of the existing political economy perspective, I think it is essential to remember the main premises of that theory. Within capitalist societies, economic, political, and cultural power is distributed unequally since such societies are based upon the extraction of surplus value. Social class relations represent the relations of exploitation and oppression within such societies. It is not surprising, therefore, that social class has been found to be statistically the most significant indicator of the length and type of an individual's education. It affects the shape of educational careers, the nature of schooling and training received, and the possibility of a higher education after compulsory schooling. It does this for both men and women, for all ethnic groups, and for individuals in all geographic regions within that society. Reid (1981) finds that in Britain, "successful completion of some form of higher education is almost exclusively associated with membership of the non-manual or middle classes, consequently the lack of it with membership of the manual or working classes" (p. 207). Class identity is also the basis from which individuals, albeit often unconsciously, derive their social identities, their occupational aspirations and life styles, their forms of consciousness, and their political interests and activities. Westergaard and Resler (1974) argued that in a capitalist society neither gender, age, region, nor skin color "has the force, the sweeping repercussions of class inequality":

> None of them in itself produces the communality of condition which marks class position in the economic order: a common complex of life circumstances shared by the victims; a contrasting set of life circumstances held in common by the privileged; broadly common ambiguities of condition among those who are neither clearly victims nor clearly privileged. (p. 352)

They argue that to recognize the effects of social class inequality and raise it to higher explanatory status than other social cleavages, such as gender and race, is not necessarily to dismiss the latter as "unreal or unimportant." Rather we are encouraged to recognize the *total nature of social inequality and the effect of social class divisions upon these other social divisions.* As Westergaard and Resler point out, "the economic divisions of class . . . in turn give variations of character and shape to the manifestations of inequality by sex or age, region or color, at different levels of the class structure" (p. 352). It is this "structuring power" of class relations which I believe provides us with the focus for a revised political economy of education. It opens up a whole range of new questions. For example, how has male power (or hegemony) been affected by the power relations of the class structure? How have the two processes of domination—class and male hegemony—come together to shape the educational system and the ideology and practice of its pupils, students, teachers, and administrators? How do individuals form their class and gender identities in sets of social relationships which are often contradictory and ambiguous? How do individuals make sense of the presence of a double division of the world, with antagonistic social classes and two antagonistic sexes?

Maintaining a political economy perspective is also important theoretically, since without an analysis of the material basis of education we can easily fall into the trap of taking for granted the official and liberal versions of the school's neutrality and its ability to act as an independent agent of social reform. It is in this context that I have criticized what I called the *cultural theory of gender,* which is the dominant paradigm in the sociology of women's education (Arnot 1981, 1982). At the level of description, this research is at its strongest. It gives insights to teachers, parents, and pupils and to educational planners into what and where the educational problems are for girls in a school system that tends, particularly in this century, to hide its own gender bias. The research analyzes the internal processes of schools which discriminate against girls, which discourage them from taking high-status school subjects (e.g., science), from attending university, and from entering the male world of political and economic power. Such research focuses on *how* girls come to "underachieve" at school, why they fail to compete equally with boys for entry into high-status professions and careers, and so forth. The prescriptions for social reform which such cultural theory suggests, however, are reduced in their potency precisely because of the lack of understanding of the conditions under which female education has developed. Cultural theory fails to analyze the power basis which has kept alive the arbitrary construction of gender differences, the transmission of an ideology of natural sex differences, and the maintenance of gender inequalities in education either through segregation or through differential treatment. Thus, girls' underachievement appears to be strictly an *educational problem* with an *educational solution*—that of changing individual attitudes. This approach does not identify the structural basis of women's oppression and exploitation in the home and in the waged labor process, which shapes those sex role ideologies and the sexual division of labor. This is precisely the critical cutting edge that political economy offered.

Despite these problems, research with a cultural perspective is valuable for feminists for its focus upon the actual experiences of girls and its very real sense of the injustices involved in the relationship between men and women. Feminists concerned with the oppression and exploitation of women are far more likely to be drawn to such cultural theory than to the male-dominated and -developed paradigm of political economy. Up until recently, nearly all discussion of the sexism of teachers, of sexual harassment of girls and female teachers, of the sexism of school material has been located within such cultural models of education rather than in the Marxist or critical sociology of education. Only too often, the political economy of education has identified the structural basis of women's oppression in capitalism and then has neglected or ignored the concrete reality of that oppression in the relationships between men and women, boys and girls. This can be seen, for example, in the ways in which three major sets of social relations have been defined and discussed: the relationship between schools and the economy, the relationship between school and work, and the relationship between school and the family. In each of these areas, the mainstream left approach has avoided questions that might have been asked and which might have allowed the investigation of women and their particular conditions of living to enter the radical sociological discourse.

Schools and the Economy

The political economy perspective has debated forcefully the degree of dependence and autonomy that schools enjoy within the capitalist economy. Such analyses describe the capitalist economy by the social relations of the waged labor process, particularly in the factory and occasionally in the office. Assumptions are made that economic work means paid work, that efficiency refers to productivity in the waged labor force and that there is essentially only one labor force. However, as we now realize, the family and its labor force cannot be excluded from an analysis of capitalism. The separation of work and family life (the division of production and consumption) was shaped historically by the changing demands of a capitalist system of production, to the benefit of the capital-owning bourgeoisie. This separation of work and family, reinforced through ideologies of the family and "the home," has marginalized and "privatized" the family to the extent that it no longer appears to have a central role in economic life. Domestic work is not defined as 'real' work and *de facto* housewives appear to be outside the 'real' world of economic life.

Sociologists of education, by defining the economic mode of production as that based on the exploitation of waged workers only, have contributed their own ideological support to this process of separation. The family, no longer defined as part of the economy, is not seen as playing any major role in the formation of school life. Because of this, crucial aspects of the relationship between families and schooling cannot be adequately explained or accounted for. These include the transfer of control over "schooling" from the family to the state, how this transfer has shaped the custodial functions of schools, and how the state has been constituted *in loco parentis* (Shaw, 1981).

The search for the social origins of education in just the "industrial" sector produces a one-sided and simplified account of schooling. This account has the effect of ignoring the family–education couple (c.f. Althusser, 1971). David (1978) has argued that this results in a marginalization of women's educational role as mothers and teachers (particularly in early schooling). The content of their pedagogic work has been defined as part of gender reproduction but not class reproduction, as it involves "expressive" and emotional training and the development of the child's personality—characteristics unrelated, apparently, to the formation of class identity. Zaretsky (1976), on the other hand, alerted us to the centrality of such "affective" development in the maintenance of the capitalist social formation. Chamboredon and Prevot (1975) recognized that the division between "spontaneous" forms of pedagogy (which typify the work of mothers in childcare and teachers in primary schools) and the more "instrumental" pedagogic styles (found in secondary schools) is one which reproduces not only the sexual division of labor but also bourgeois *class culture.*

The analysis of mass schooling which limited discussion to the requirements of capital for a skilled workforce or a literate electorate also could not account for the rise of girls' schooling—especially, as Davin (1979) has pointed out, since women were not in skilled jobs and did not have the vote. The rationale for providing girls with education in the 19th century was to transmit the bourgeois family form through schooling. Given this, it is clear that in Marxist accounts of schooling the historical difference between working-class boys' and girls' education could not be understood.

Schooling and Work

The relationship between pupils' education and their future employment has concerned diverse educational theorists from government planners to human capital theorists and left sociologists. For human capital theorists, seeking to estimate the cost-effectiveness of education, the problem has been that women have tended to enter the labor force spasmodically and to receive less benefit (defined as income) than men for their comparable educational qualifications. The solution was that since women could not be included in *manpower* estimates and *manpower* planning, they were excluded from the analysis (Woodhall, 1973). For government educationalists, the issue of a pupil's destination after school was solved in the case of girls since it was assumed they would all marry and have children and that paid work was only a secondary concern for them.

Without putting it so baldly, left sociologists of education have really been making the same assumption. For them, as for the other theorists, the "problem" of social class mobility and the reproduction of social classes has been the question of *boys'* education. This paradigm marked the work of, among others, Bowles and Gintis (1976), Willis (1977), and Corrigan (1979). The relationship between girls' education and their occupational destinies was not studied as a class issue, nor was the nature and extent of their social mobility examined. The other side of the coin was that boys were only perceived as having one destination—waged work—so that schools were not investigated in terms of how far they contributed to the formation of fathers and husbands. Did schools prepare boys, through the ideology of the male breadwinner, for their roles as head of the household and patriarchal authority? Instead of investigating the *relationship* between the family and the waged labor process and how boys and girls are prepared by schools for *both* destinations in different ways, such radical analyses legitimated the artificial separation of the two spheres.

The concern with the outcomes of schooling as defined by paid employment (or unemployment) led many sociologists to concentrate their efforts on understanding the last years of secondary schooling. It is at this point in their school lives that boys are most likely to become truants, to develop their own subcultures, to acquire or not acquire certificates, and to plan their entry into an occupation. If there is any similarity between schools and "the long shadow of work," then it would be found in these last years of secondary schooling. The fact that gender theorists had urged the significance of the early years of schooling for the formation of children's identities appeared to be largely irrelevant to the majority of radical sociologists. (Apple & King, 1977, and Sharp & Green, 1975, are interesting exceptions to this pattern.) By the end of the 1970s, the educational system had been portrayed largely by a snapshot of the final years of secondary school life, with little account taken of the earlier (or later) years of schooling. If, however, the family had been taken as a destination for boys and girls alike, then surely the theorists would have had to deal with the ways in which schooling—from the very start—affects the formation of class and gender identity.

Family and School

The interest of critical sociologists of education in the relationship between the family and the school has been intermittent. In the 1960s and 1970s, a concern for working-class underachievement in schools led to theories of cultural deprivation which outlined the importance of family culture. Such theories recognized that schools transmit the culture, the educational criteria, and the social expectations of the bourgeoisie. What was important for the child, therefore, was the distance between his or her family class culture and that of the school. Such theories emphasized the central role the family played in mediating a class-determined education. However, in criticizing the thesis that working-class families were in some way "culturally deprived" and faulty, radical sociologists turned away from the family toward more "economic" explanations of school failure. The central focus was on how schools reinforce the privilege of the bourgeoisie and the exploitation of the working class, through preparation for paid work.

In these new accounts of schooling, pupils were portrayed as "negotiating" the messages of their teachers, while in the home, learning appeared to take place via a process of "assimilation." The family was seen as a depository of class culture, derived from the fathers' experiences as waged workers. All of the fathers' dependents were assumed to have acquired his class consciousness. There was an assumption that class culture and its forms of consciousness were *donated* rather than being learned in any active sense. The dynamics of family life and the conditions under which children acquire their class identities were not investigated. Rather, culture was seen as a form of *capital*, owned primarily by the bourgeoisie and *inherited* by its children, a form of property which was "non-negotiable," but could be exchanged for educational qualifications and eventually social privilege. The result was that there was no concept of struggle within families, especially since the study of youth cultures rejected the generation gap. The emphasis upon social class forced genera-tional studies (and gender relations) out of mainstream sociology of education. Family culture tended to be represented as an "input" into schooling, through the apparently unproblematic construction of working-class or middle-class identities. Yet generational conflict between mothers and daughters and fathers and sons over appropriate definitions of gender are also part of the process of acquiring a class identity.

Most people know from their own experience of family life that there is conflict within families, especially over the notions of femininity and masculinity. But this insight has generally been neglected by sociologists of education. While McRobbie (1978) and Thomas (1980) show that teenage girls believe they have close friendships with their mothers, there has been no investigation of how these friendships reflect a female alliance against males and in particular against the father's authority and behavior in the home (Newsom, Richardson, & Scaife, 1978). Similarly, we do not know how the sex alliance between fathers and sons can be used in family struggles.

Codes of behavior for both girls and boys are constructed out of the ideological materials available to them, from the sets of age, gender, and class relations. Contradiction characterizes their experiences. Hebdige (1979) has argued (in the case of black male youth) that contradictions of location and ideology can produce a new youth "style" which "is not *necessarily* in touch, in any immediate sense, with [their] material position in the capitalist system" (p. 81). In other words, there is no automatic transference from male working-class culture to that of male youth subculture. Wilson's (1978) research shows that teenage working-class girls face a major contradiction between "promiscuity which appears to be advocated by the 'permissive society' and the ideal of virginity advocated by official agencies, and to a large degree, the families" (p. 68). The working-class girls in Wilson's study constructed their own *sexual code* which determined whom to have sex with and under what circumstances. Their self-classification distinguished between "virgins," "one-man girls," and "easy lays." Girls negotiated the form of femininity prescribed by their parents and the alternative versions offered, for example, by the mass media. The new sexual code therefore did not just grow out of their class position.

The resistance of girls to their parental culture is very often dismissed as being a marginal phenomenon. It is explained as a demonstration that the girl wishes to be "just like a boy" (an apparently perfectly natural thing) rather than resisting the pressures to be a traditional girl. Yet, in her study of female juvenile delinquents, Shacklady-Smith (1978) shows that these girls positively reject male supremacy and family definitions of femininity. She shows how these girls develop self-conceptions of being "tough, dominant and tomboyish" by fighting, getting drunk, having sexual intercourse, and being aggressive. What they were involved in was a "double rejection" of legal norms and the traditional stereotyped conceptions of femininity, perceived by the girls as too constraining. Here again, we find a negotiation rather than an assimilation of family culture.

The school and the family can have a range of different types of relationships, which cannot be easily described either by the physical notion of distance or by the use of a dichotomy of working-class and middle-class cultures. Schools can "add to," by reinforcing, family culture. They can also act "against" family and thus cause contradictions and conflict for the child. Finally, they can be a progressive force—for example, setting up new models of gender relations which are liberating for girls. It is especially this third aspect of family-school relations which has been lost in Marxist accounts of school life. Yet schools do offer some working-class girls access to higher status and "cleaner" occupations (such as nursing and teaching) than their mothers' manual work. Schools may provide a means of breaking down gender stereotypes of women's inferiority by giving them a means to improve their relative standing vis-a-vis men. This was certainly the case in Fuller's (1980) study of West Indian girls in British school. These girls were in favor of school and of obtaining academic qualifications since these would allow them to challenge the double stereotypes of "blackness" and femininity. Similarly, we can view the increase in the numbers of middle-class girls who enter higher education as not just the increasing hold of the bourgeoisie over the university sector, but also a victory for women over their ascribed status in society. The fight for education has played a significant role in the quest for equality between the sexes, and it is a role that has been largely ignored in critical histories of education.

Family Cultures

I would now like to turn to work which does focus upon family-school relations. This area contains, in my view, some of the most interesting new developments in the analysis of class and gender. What characterizes this research is an interest in the consistency or inconsistency faced by members of different social classes and sexes in the messages they receive in these different contexts. As a result,

I feel that the complex dynamics of the lived experience of class and gender relations are beginning to be glimpsed and that the ambiguities which mark a system such as patriarchal capitalism are being brought into focus for the first time.

Ve Henricksen (1981) offers an initial foray into the consistencies and contradictions experienced by different social classes and the two sexes. She points out the similarity of training offered to working-class and middle-class girls—a training for family life. This training encompasses the notion of *familism,* which she defines as an "exaggerated identification with the myth that the family is the only place where a woman may experience self-fulfillment." Girls are taught at an early age that their future means becoming mothers and housewives, and they are expected to plan their futures in accordance with this fact. Boys of whatever class are, on the other hand, pushed toward a belief in individual achievement, self-interest, and material success—what Ve Henricksen calls *individuation* (or in other words, the capitalist ethic). Class differences may, however, have an important effect on the strength of an individual's belief in such ideologies. For example, Gaskell's (1977–78) research in British Columbian schools showed that working-class girls were even more conservative than middle-class girls in emphasizing sex roles in the home, male power, femininity, and the stability of sex roles. From a class perspective Ve Henricksen argues that whereas the middle-class children are socialized into the ideologies of social mobility and achievement in work, the working class's own culture stresses solidarity and collectivity in work, consciousness, and culture. These class cultures cause dilemmas for middle-class girls who have to juggle the dual expectations of being a wife and having a full-time job at the same time. They also cause dilemmas for working-class boys who are expected to be individually successful and to participate in the meritocratic rat race while conforming to the working-class ideals of collective action. The middle-class boy, with the dual identities of individuation and social mobility, experiences a certain consistency of demands made on him; so do working-class girls, who can find a certain compatibility in the dual demands of family life and collective working-class solidarity.

While Ve Henricksen's theory is sensitive to the contradictions which can occur within the family, she neglects to discuss the conflict which can occur *between* family and school class cultures. She ignores the imposition of bourgeois values upon working-class children through the development of state schooling, arguing that the key reference groups for each generation are only "family, friends and school teachers." There is no analysis of the differences between parental attitudes, the class-based assumptions of schools and school teachers, and the particular forms of peer-group cultures developed by pupils. The contradictions between these are critical aspects of the lived experiences of boys and girls of all social classes. It is these contradictions which form the basis of the research by Australian sociologists Connell, Ashenden, Kessler, and Dowsett (1982). These authors reject the view that families are self-contained and closed units, "havens from a heartless world." They also reject the view that families and schools are separate spheres, pointing out that pupils are not in transition from one institution to another but actually live in families while they attend school. The issue for them is the link between family circumstance and schooling. By taking into account the organization of work, the location and type of home, and the relations between the sexes within each family, the authors conclude that families are places "where larger structures meet and interact." As they put their view:

> We do not mean to suggest that families are simply the pawns of outside forces any more than schools are. In both cases, class and gender relations create dilemmas (some insoluble), provide resources (or deny them), and suggest solutions (some of which don't work), to which the family or school must respond in its collective practice. (p. 73)

A family is, in their definition, a closely knit group which has an intense inner life and a reasonably stable organization. Further, this group of individuals makes choices and takes certain paths through the variety of situations it has to confront—marriage, work, having children, the schooling of their children, unemployment, and so forth. In terms of socialization, therefore, Connell and his colleagues argue that a family does not form a child's character and then deliver it prepackaged on the doorstep of the school. Rather, "the family is what its members do, a constantly continuing and changing practice, and, as children go to and through school, that practice is reorganized around their schooling" (p. 78). According to these sociologists, *families produce people,* rather than reproduce social relations or class cultures in the abstract, and they produce them under often "terrible constraints," including the constraints imposed by existing class and gender relations in society. The result is not predictable in every case. But what they see as vital is for sociologists to follow the consequences of such processes of production. In the schools, the consequences can be found in the variety of strategies adopted by pupils from different family circumstances. These strategies—such as compliance, pragmatism and resistance—can all be adopted by a pupil and used with different teachers. The impact of such different strategies, nevertheless, is not one which is likely to destroy the processes of social class reproduction.

The Reproduction of Female Class Relations

I would now like to turn briefly to the new feminist historical work on the development of mass schooling. Here a new awareness is being developed as to the particular ways in which class and gender relations come together for *girls*. What does seem to be the case historically is that girls' education went across class lines in that both middle-class and working-class girls were prepared for their domestic futures by an educational ideology that stresses service to their menfolk rather than to themselves. But the precise notions of femininity presented to middle-class and working-class girls were not the same. Middle-class girls were offered the bourgeois ideal of the "perfect wife and mother"—an ideal which encompassed the notion of the Christian virtues of self-denial, patience, and silent suffering as well as the aristocratic values of ladylike behavior (which meant refusing any paid or manual employment) and ladylike etiquette. What the working-class girls received was a diluted and modified vision of the 'good woman'—an image of the 'good woman,' wife, mother and housekeeper who had no pretension of becoming a lady and aspiring above her station. Such an ideal envisaged working-class family caretakers who would prevent their families from slipping into crime, political ferment, disease, and immorality—and who in many cases would be reliable domestic servants for their middle-class counterparts (Purvis, 1980, 1981).

This dilution of the dominant gender definition can most probably be found today in the courses for the "least able" girls. These girls are taught the practical skills of cooking and domestic science as preparation for female roles in the family. In contrast, middle-class girls are most likely to be learning the arts and languages, social sciences and history—subjects more suitable for their role as educated mothers and domestic hostesses. It is difficult to know what differences there are between the notions of femininity expected of working-class and middle-class girls in schools today since so much of the research neglects class differences in favor of showing how girls as a group are treated differently than boys. What research there is, such as that by Douglas (1964) and Hartley (1978), suggests that teachers label working-class and middle-class girls differently in the classroom. The higher the social class the better behaved the pupil was seen to be. Working-class girls were seen as much rougher and noisier, much less tidy, and much less able to concentrate.

Connell and his colleagues, in this context, talk about the school's role in producing rather than reproducing masculinity and femininity, through what they call *masculinizing* and *feminizing* practices. These practices are different for each social class. They argue that schools create a hierarchy of different kinds of masculinity and femininity. Rather than reproduce sex stereotypes, they establish *sets of relations* between male and female pupils which will differ by social class. Private schools, therefore, are likely to set up a different set of relations between male and female pupils than state schools. Okeley's (1978) analysis of her own educational experiences in a private English boarding school reinforces this view. What these schools reproduced, through their particular work in creating "ladies" and "gentlemen," was the sexual division of the bourgeoisie. When we talk about different types of school, however, we have to remember that the reproduction of *female class relations* through education takes a different shape from that of boys. For boys the reproduction of social differences, particularly in Britain, is often described as a matter of the division between private and state schools. The type of school attended is often as good an indicator of social-class origins as father's occupation (since only the privileged minority of boys from professional and managerial classes, along with the sons of landed aristocracy and capitalists can afford to attend private schools). These boys will go on to take advantage of the entry that such schools offer into higher education, the high-status professions, the government, and more recently industry. The dominance of those educated privately in positions of economic and political power has, of course, been a major political issue since the Second World War.

The development of private education for girls has had a very different pattern, especially marked by its shorter history. The division between private and state schools has been differently constituted for boys and for girls. Class differences were weaker for girls for a variety of reasons. According to the Public Schools Commission (1968), the founders of private girls' schools fought for state education for *all* girls. Their political ambitions stretched across the class divide in their search for equality of opportunity for all girls and the freedom of all women to enter the professions of law, medicine, teaching, and public service. Secondly, female teachers in private schools moved freely between different types of schools; they did not accept the view that private and state schools were mutually exclusive sectors. The Association of Headmistresses, unlike that of Head-masters, represented all girls' schools whether private or state, and drew girls in from all different social origins (especially because of the lower fees). As a result, the Public Schools Commission concluded:

> These schools are not as divisive as the boys' schools. Their pupils are few in number and they do not later wear an old school tie—literally or metaphorically. The tie would be of no use to them in their future careers. No magic doors to careers are opened at the mention of any school's name, however socially distinguished the school may be. The academically distinguished schools obviously help their pupils to a place in the universities but so do those in the maintained or direct grant sectors. (p. 67)

Educational privilege was not, therefore, a class privilege of daughters of the bourgeoisie, compared with the men of that social class. The low-level education which girls often received in both private and state schools made them uncompetitive in the labor market. The small proportion who went into higher education was a problem faced by all girls' schools, or by all schools with girls in them (Public Schools Commission, p. 69).

Despite the fact that the division between state and private schools is not a major discriminator between girls of different social classes when their occupational destinies are taken into account, the type of education offered to middle-class girls does differ greatly from that offered to working-class girls. In fact the class gap between girls has been found to be *greater* than between boys, when university entrance is taken into account. According to King (1971), "middle class boys are the most advantaged and working class girls the most disadvantaged, the former having 21 times more chance of taking a full-time university degree than the other" (p. 140). Westergaard and Little (1965) pointed out that the failure of working-class girls to reach higher education is due to the fact that the resources (cultural, economic and psychological) necessary for a working-class child to overcome the obstacles on the way are very rarely extended on behalf of a girl (p. 222).

This brief history suggests that the reproduction of female class positions in Britain is based more firmly upon the transmission of cultural values (such as familism) than upon the vocational preparation of women for a stratified work force. The transmission of bourgeois conceptions of femininity and their dilution for girls in the working classes may even be a more effective means of differentiating girls than the ideology of vocationalism for boys, since such processes of class discrimination are so well hidden.

Gender and School Experience

According to Connell and his colleagues, class and gender relations are best thought of as *structuring processes* rather than "systems." As such, they are to be found within the dynamics of family, school, and industrial life simultaneously, even if their effects differ in the different spheres. Class and gender relations have their own histories which may merge or may be independent of each other. What is important for the child is the *relationship between such processes*. For the working-class boy, for example, the construction of his masculinity would be in the context either of economic insecurity or "hard won and cherished security":

> It means that his father's masculinity and authority is diminished by being at the bottom of the heap in his workplace, and being exploited without being able to control it; and that his mother has to handle the tensions, and sometimes the violence, that result. It means that his own entry into work and the class relations of production is conditioned by the gender relations that direct him to male jobs, and construct for him an imagined future as breadwinner for a new family. And so on. (p. 181)

In this extract one can see how the simplified versions of the transition from school to work have been changed by a sensitivity to not just the presence of gender relations but also the role of family life in determining the shape of an individual's identity and occupational choice.

When discussing pupils' experience of schools, Connell et al. talk about the *hegemonizing* influences of the school in a way which has much in common with the notions of male hegemony and the dominant gender code which I discussed in an earlier paper (Arnot, 1982). In that paper I used the concept of gender code to refer to the social organization of family and school life where the attempt is made to "win over" each new generation to particular definitions of masculinity and femininity and to accept as natural the hierarchy of male over female. This attempt to win the consent of boys and girls to particular definitions of gender is limited by the strategies and responses adopted by pupils to the social and ideological structures of school life. Often pupils collectively will develop their own culture, creatively and actively transforming the very material of school and family life, and reshaping their meaning in ways that have more relevance and interest for them. These youth cultures may not in themselves challenge the structuring processes of gender and class relations but they do make the outcome of schooling unpredictable.

Empirical research on these youth cultures unfortunately rarely investigates the meaning masculinity has for boys. Willis's work on working-class lads stands out in this respect and reveals, furthermore, not just the essential nature of masculine identity for manual workers but also the sexism involved in that construct. Their anti-school culture is based on the celebration of sexuality—in this case an aggressive, physical machismo—which gives working-class boys a weapon to fight a class-determined education. Far more work is needed, however, before we can say we understand the ways in which class and gender relations relate together for boys from different social classes.

Thomas's work (1980) is a particularly interesting study since it is a comparison between working-class and middle-class girls. Middle-class girls, she found, developed an *anti-academic* counter-culture in which they celebrated a femininity which was based upon notions of beauty, fashion, and the requirements of female glamour occupations such as top secretary and receptionist. By individually negotiating the school's approval of traditional notions of femininity and their encouragement of girls to find jobs for themselves, these girls worked their school lives into line with their interests, asking for special courses in secretarial work, deportment, fashion, and the like. They exaggerated the importance of prettiness, docility, and poise. In contrast, working-class girls responded collectively rather than individually to the pressures of the school and developed an *anti-school* counter-culture. These girls stressed female sexuality to the extent that they were quickly labeled as sexually deviant. They stressed the value not of glamour jobs but of love, romance, and motherhood. What such working-class girls resisted was not just the imposition of certain notions of femininity in the school but also the set of class relations which left them with very dismal occupational futures. Thomas (whose findings paralleled those of McRobbie (1968) in her study of British working-class girls) concluded that:

While they may share ultimately domestic occupational destinies, and may have their personal identities similarly molded by a common 'culture of femininity' girls from different social class backgrounds nevertheless experience appreciably different social, material and cultural conditions which mediate their lives and are reflected in differential class responses to notions of femininity, romance, domesticity and motherhood. In their response to school and work, too, girls draw on the specific values and traditions of their 'parent' class cultures, and these values are mirrored in their differential rates of participation and achievement in the formal educational system. (p. 136)

Conclusions: Reintegrating Family and Work

Developing a political economy of education which takes the family seriously will not just mean that researchers should interview more parents, or should ask pupils how they feel about their parents as well as about their teachers. What it means above all is that we have to recognize the specificity of the family "site" of class and gender relations and see it as the "location" of individuals while *at school.* Such a location, like that of the school, is not static but is a complex ensemble of practices and relationships. If we want to talk about the "lived experience" of family life, therefore, we must understand the nature of the power relations involved in the family, class culture *in the making,* and the forms of negotiation over gender identity. In the home, just as in classrooms, notions of good behavior and rules of conduct are negotiated by the participants. Each set of social relations is important, but as Connell and his colleagues argue, so too is the *relationship between these sets of social relations.* The family and the school are interwoven spheres of activity simultaneously responding to each other. What is critical for the individual child is how to maintain a relationship between the two spheres on a day-to-day basis. Coping with the formal and informal relations between school personnel and parents, how parents remember their own educational histories and how pupils then carry "the burden" of parental aspirations or feelings of failure, how teachers make assumptions about different types of families and how they respond to parental involvement. The child from this perspective, is the *mediator,* the *go-between,* carrying the class-cultural messages of the home and the school through the school gates each day, influencing each in turn by his or her own practices and responses. In contrast with the relations between school and work, there is no transition from the family to the school; there is only perpetual motion. It is this motion that needs to be captured in the accounts of schooling under capitalism.

From a feminist perspective what is obviously of major concern is the contradictions and the dilemmas faced by boys and girls in trying to sort out gender messages. The researcher should ask, for example, how an adolescent girl makes sense of her experiences of sexual harassment by boys in the playground and classroom in relation to her experience as a protected daughter in the family home. Alternatively, how does she reconcile the demand that she take adult responsibility for certain domestic arrangements with being a school "child" who is forbidden the use of such adult symbols of femininity as jewelry, fashionable clothes, and make-up? How does a boy cope with being beaten academically by a girl at school and yet told by teachers and parents that he will eventually be held responsible for the family income and a dependent and subordinate wife? Such realities may seem trivial but they are the stuff that school and family life is made of. The tension for girls and boys is not how to "obtain" or "acquire" abstract notions of gender but how to use particular concepts of femininity and masculinity which work *in practice* in the context of social class membership. The cultures of different social classes, manifested in different types of family life, offer only certain choices and restrict the possibilities in certain directions for the expression of gender. This does not mean that each individual of the same social class will have an identical notion of what it is to be masculine and feminine but that all members of the same social class are more likely (than any member of another social class) to be confronted with similar situations to respond to.

The experience of family life with all its contradictions and complexity is one of experiencing sets of power relations (e.g. between men and women, parents and children, male and female siblings). That experience will be manifested in a a set of *gendered practices*; i.e., *the forms of expression* of particular sets of social relations. Such gendered practices will be adapted, modified and "translated" ("recontextualized") in the setting of school corridors and classrooms. As Anyon (1983) has argued, such practices will involve a complex web of private and public forms of accommodation and resistance. The challenge for sociologists is to unravel the web, uncovering the class specificity and identifying the gendered practices.

Finally, a revised political economy of education needs to reformulate the issue of a pupil's destination after schooling. The current extent of youth unemployment has obviously meant that any simple theory of the transition from school to waged work is no longer viable, but even today we can find research on youth unemployment which does not investigate the issue as one affecting the conditions of family life or gender relations. Unemployed school leavers mostly remain living at home, with increased financial dependence upon the parents rather than the state. This has meant extra work and financial worry for the parents, more domestic work for the female members of the household, and different sets of relationships between members of the family. In the case of girls the issue of unemployment after school is a very different political issue from that of boys' unemployment. As I have argued in the paper, girls have been assumed to be "destined," if not actively prepared by schools and families, for eventual marriage and motherhood. The experience of female unemployment, therefore, is not treated as such a serious problem as the unemployment of male school leavers who are expecting to find waged work in order to fulfill themselves. The dichotomy of family and work and its ideological underpinning in concepts of gender difference has not yet been shifted in the rhetoric of either state educational planners or radical sociologists. What is needed is to see in what ways families and schools construct a particular relationship between future work and family life and how this relationship is mediated by youth today. The reality of unemployment facing school leavers, the changing shape of family life, the pressure by women to enter waged work and male jobs—all these influence the expected relationship between domestic and waged work. What must now enter the radical discourse is a concern to assess the impact of these changes upon girls' and boys' schooling and self-perceptions. It is only by reintegrating the family and the waged labor process in our analyses of schooling that we can hope to provide an adequate and a radical critique of current class and gender relations in education.

If the family is analyzed in these ways by critical sociologists, then the potential is there for an integration of femininst and political economy perspectives. An awareness among feminists studying education of the need to provide a materialistic analysis of gender relations will be complemented by a concern among critical sociologists to involve themselves in issues which directly affect women and which grow out of the family–school–work relations. For example, the concern for the age of entry of children into state schools, the concern for after-school-hours daycare, school meals service, school transport, the role of the social services in treating children from "broken" homes and single-parent families, the treatment of school absenteeism—these are all matters which affect women especially. In my view they are matters which can no longer remain outside the mainstream of radical discourse and practice.

Note

*This paper is a revised and shortened version of a paper presented at the Political Economy of Gender Relations in Education Conference, Ontario Institute for Studies in Education, Toronto, Canada. I am grateful to Alison Griffith and Paul Olson for comments on the earlier draft and for their permission to publish this version. I am also grateful to the editors of the *Journal of Education* for their very helpful advice.

References

Althusser, L. (1971). Ideology and ideological state apparatuses. In L. Althusser, *Lenin and philosophy and other essays*. London: New Left Books.

Apple, M. W., & King, N. (1977). What do schools teach? *Curriculum Inquiry, 6* (4), 341–358.

Anyon, J. (1983). Intersections of gender and class: Accommodation and resistance by working-class and affluent females to contadictory sex role ideologies. In S. Walker & L. Barton (Eds.) (1983). *Gender, Class and Education*. Sussex: Falmer.

Arnot, M. (1981). Culture and political economy: Dual perspectives in the sociology of women's education. *Educational Analysis, 3* (1), 97–116.

Arnot, M. (1982). Male hegemony, social class and women's education. *Journal of Education, 164* (1), 64–89.

Bowles, S. & Gintis, H. (1976). *Schooling in capitalist America*. London: Routledge and Kegan Paul.

Chamboredon, J. C., & Prevot, J. (1975). Change in the social definition of early childhood and the new forms of symbolic violence. *Theory and Society, 2* (3), 331–350.

Connell, R. W., Ashenden, D. J., Kessler, S., & Dowsett, G. W. (1982). *Making the difference: Schools, families and social division*. Sydney: Allen & Unwin.

Corrigan, P. (1979). *Schooling the Smash Street kids*. London: MacMillan.

David, M. E. (1978). The family education couple: Towards an analysis of the William Tyndale dispute. In G. Littlejohn, et al. (Eds.), *Power and the state*. London: Croom Helm.

Davin, A. (1979). Mind you do as you are told: Reading books for board school girls 1870–1902. *Feminist Review, 3*, 80–98.

Douglas, J. W. B. (1964). *The home and the school.* London: MacGibbon and Kee.

Fuller, M. (1980). Black girls in a London comprehensive school. In R. Deem, (Ed.), *Schooling for women's work.* London: Routledge and Kegan Paul.

Gaskell, J. (1977–78). Sex role ideology and the aspirations of high school girls. *Interchange, 8* (3), 43–53.

Hartley, D. (1978). Sex and social class: A case study of an infant school. *British Educational Research Journal, 4* (2), 75–81.

Hebdige, D. (1979). *Subculture: The meaning of style.* London: Methuen.

King, R. (1971). Unequal access in education—sex and social class. *Social and Economic Administration, 5* (3), 167–175.

McRobbie, A. L. (1978). Working class girls and the culture of femininity. In Women's Studies Group, Centre for Contemporary Cultural Studies, *Women Take Issue.* London: Hutchinson, in association with the CCCS.

Newson, J., Richardson, D., & Scaife, J. (1978). Perspectives in sex role stereotyping. In J. Chetwynd & O. Hartnett (Eds.), *The sex role system.* London: Routledge and Kegan Paul.

Okeley, J. (1978). Privileged, schooled and finished: Boarding education for girls. In S. Ardener, (Ed.)., *Defining females.* London: Croom Helm.

Public Schools Commission (1969). First Report (Vol. 1). London: HMSO.

Purvis, J. (1981). The double burden of class and gender in the schooling of working class girls in nineteenth century Britain. In L. Barton & S. Walker (Eds.), *Schools, teachers and teaching.* Sussex: Falmer.

Purvis, J. (1980). Towards a history of women's education in nineteenth century Britain: A sociological analysis. *Westminster Studies in Education, 4,* 45–79.

Reid, I. (1981). *Social class differences in Britain* (2nd ed.). London: Grant McIntyre.

Shacklady-Smith, L. S. (1978). Sexist assumptions and female delinquency: An empirical investigation. In C. Smart & B. Smart (Eds.), *Women, sexuality and social control.* London: Routledge and Kegan Paul.

Sharp, R., & Green, A. (1975). *Education and social control: A study in progressive primary education.* London: Routledge and Kegan Paul.

Shaw, J. (1981). In loco parentis: A relationship between parent, state and child. In R. Dale, G. Esland, R. Fergusson & M. MacDonald (Eds.), *Education and the state,* Vol. 2: *Politics, patriarchy and practice.* Sussex: Falmer.

Thomas, C. (1980). Girls and counter-school culture. *Melbourne Working Papers,* No. 1. Melbourne: Department of Education, University of Melbourne.

Ve Henricksen, H. (1981). Class and gender: Role model considerations and liberation in advanced capitalism. *Interchange, 12* (2, 3), 151–164.

Westergaard, J., & Little, A. (1965). *Educational opportunity and social selection in England and Wales.* Paris: OECD.

Westergaard, J., & Resler, H. (1974). *Class in a capitalist society.* London: Heinemann Educational Books.

Willis, P. (1977). *Learning to labour.* Farnborough: Saxon House.

Wilson, D. (1978). Sexual codes and conduct: A study of teenage girls. In C. Smart & B. Smart (Eds.), *Women, sexuality and social control.* London: Routledge and Kegan Paul.

Woodhall, M. (1973). Investment in women: A reappraisal of the concept of human capital. *International Review of Education, 19* (1), 9–28.

Zaretsky, E. (1976) *Capitalism, the family and personal life.* New York: Harper Colophon Books.

Sex, Pregnancy, and Schooling: Obstacles to a Critical Teaching of the Body

Laurie McDade

To teach critically as an act of learning and as an engagement with living is to discover, name, and confront the relations of power that occur in schools and communities. These relations may be linked to the ideological, material, historical, and situational conditions found at a school site and in a community. However, the power present in these relations does not lie dormant as a thing occurring separate and apart from who the people are—separate from the meanings they share, separate from the histories they have inherited and lived, or separate from the conduct of the daily life of their work. "Power operates not just on people but through them" (Simon & Dippo, 1986, p. 197), and it is through that collaboration with and elaboration of power that people, as social actors, are participants in creating what is known in their communities. Teachers, then, do not act, react, and enact this enterprise with power and of knowing alone. They do it with others who register their actions, their voices, and their silences.

Everyday moments of teaching at schools in communities, then, are personal, pedagogical, and political acts incorporating the minds and bodies of subjects, as knowers and as learners. When we are at our best as teachers we are capable of speaking to each of these ways of knowing in ourselves and our students. And we may override precedents in the educational project that value the knowing of the mind and deny the knowing of the heart and of the body. Students, the partners in this enterprise of knowing, are whole people with ideas, with emotions, and with sensations. If we, as teachers, "are to arouse passions now and then" (Greene, 1986, p. 441), the project must not be confined to a knowing only of the mind. It must also address and interrogate what we think we know of the heart and of the body.

This paper addresses the question of knowing the body and focuses specifically on how a critical teaching of issues related to the body is or is not facilitated in schools. To do so, I will speak directly to the contemporary dilemma of teenage pregnancy in schools, which teachers have told me is a difficult issue for them in the classroom. An attempt will be made to sketch out what I see as obstacles to a critical teaching of students who are or who will become school-age parents. Since schools are sites that maintain obstacles to addressing these separated identities of students, I will review the ideological, material, historical, and situational conditions of these separations as they are experienced by teenaged women as students and as mothers. To do so, I will draw on my ethnographic research on one community and its dilemma over sex, pregnancy, and schooling (McDade, 1987).

Examining the Ideological Separation of Mind and Body

Teachers who find themselves teaching a pregnant student often mention the "uncomfortableness" that the visibly pregnant student creates for them and their class. Teachers point to the imposition that the pregnant student's presence creates in the conduct of a "normal" lesson, and they point to the difficulty in keeping students on track within the content of their curriculum. Teachers in traditional classrooms find themselves disoriented and perplexed by a pregnant student's attitudes and behavior. Her physical presence transgresses the separation of body and mind in the classroom. As one English high school teacher explained,

> There is no doubt that when Pam began to show I got uncomfortable and even annoyed. How could she? Sure we have a high rate of pregnancy here, but it usually happens in other classes and not in honors. So when she started to show I spoke to her and asked her what she was going to do with the baby and school and what about the father. She got belligerent and told me to mind my own business. Can you believe it? I always thought that she would be one to go on.

Such a statement captures the disturbance that the public presence of teens' sexual and reproductive activity creates in the institutional conduct of the daily life of classrooms for many teachers. Traditionally separated, the merged status of student and parent (or parent-to-be) violates the ideological opposition of mind and body that has been incorporated into the ritual organization of the school, as well as into its curriculum and instruction. The separation of mind and body at the school site, however, is differentially experienced by male and female students since male students are capable of concealing their school-age parenthood from social attention, if desired. Females, on the other hand, who become pregnant, who remain in school, and who maintain their pregnancies which become visible in the organization of school life, are likely to encounter a dissonant array of ideologically repressive manifestations in the daily responses to their newly changed status.

The presence of pregnant students in the daily organization of the school defies the repressive sexual order located at school sites. When physiologically pregnant students become "socially pregnant,"[1] there is a structural dislocation resulting from their presence in the conduct of the everyday life of the school. In many school districts pregnant students may be rescheduled out of traditional classrooms since many state educational codes permit schools to "classify" visibly pregnant students as chronically ill and disabled. These classifications permit schools to qualify for special education funds for pregnant students. Depending upon specific state policies, pregnant students may be placed in special programs or rescheduled for homebound instruction, for attendance at an alternative school, or for transfer to another school site. Such reclassifications not only represent a structural dislocation of visibly pregnant students in the everyday practice of schooling, but also mirror a social dislocation that results from the public knowledge of their sexual and reproductive behaviors.

Students, as well as their teachers, speak about an "uncomfortableness" that pervades their presence in schools. Pregnant teens frequently talk about the heightened scrutiny they receive from other students, as well as from their teachers. Pam, the pregnant student about whom the English teacher described her frustration, angrily maintained,

> It just makes me sick and tired of these teachers with their "tsk-tsk" and pushin' their noses in my business. And them kids are no better. Like the one I told you who wanted to feel my stomach in the lunchroom. I told him, "You touch me, and I'll cut your porker off." I'm just fed up with the whole thing. I'm thinkin' on goin' to the pregnancy school soon now that everyone knows—for some peace of mind. It's too much pressure for me, I don't feel right.

Pam's feelings were shared by many of the pregnant teens who participated in this study. The discussions of their school experiences are vivid examples of the oppressive atmosphere that begins to surround them when their reproductive and obvious heterosexual intercourse become part of their social identities at school. This structural and social dislocation of pregnant students in schools is legitimated by an essentially repressive ideology that the minds of students are to be educated as their bodies are to be controlled.

Such an ideology is apparent in the treatment of pregnant students in schools but also is detectable in the organization of curriculum and instruction about sexuality and reproduction. Partly due to the parochial understanding of nonadult sexuality in local community settings in the U.S. and partly due to the preference of educators for discussing the mind and not the body, what I call "a pedagogy of the body" traditionally has been segregated from the academic disciplines. This segregation in effect tells students that the issues surrounding sex and reproduction are "different" in intellectual and affective content. Thus, the pedagogy of the body has historically been assigned to health and physical education classes where the emphasis traditionally has been on the *functions* of the sexual and reproductive anatomies of the human body. More recently issues of sexuality and reproduction have migrated to sex and family life education classes in U.S. schools as adult concern for the specific sexual and reproductive *problems* of teenage bodies has increased. Regardless of where the curriculum and instruction is presented, however, this pedagogy of the body is most frequently organized in an instructional framework that is theoretically based in orientations to bodily humanness as different and apart from a humanness of the mind. As first theorized by Freud (1930, 1949) and later Marcuse (1955) the control of bodily instincts enables the activities of the mind to flourish. However, the human body as a functional mass of instincts that poses problems for societies diminishes human physiology to a biological determinism that denies the ecological and environmental integratedness of intellectual, affective, and physical domains (Brake, 1982; Fausto-Sterling, 1985). Both functional and problematic depictions of the body target abnormal, antisocial, and pathogenic features of the body with a moralistic probe that denies a human dignity to the sexual and sensual realities of the body.

Consequently, the organization of sexual knowledge as discrete curricular components follows from an orientation of control over sexual behavior which is presented as precipitous to reproduction and to family. Thus, sexual expressions are most frequently couched in a rhetoric of responsibility and duty to family, linking sex to reproduction and to family. "Sex," according to one male student "is like work when teachers talk about it!" Most absent from their presentations "is that sex is a juicy number," according to the same male student who believed that the way schools presented sex information was unrealistic and not the "way it really was in real life." Absent from school dialogues about sex and reproduction, then, are references to the pleasures, satisfactions, or enjoyments of physical, sexual, or emotional intimacies. Present are cautionary and precautionary statements in response to the current national "epidemics" thought to put growing numbers of adolescents "at risk." Consequently, much of the discussion of human sexuality in public school classes emphasizes the vulnerability of the body and negative consequences that physical intimacy initiates. As Joseph Diorio (1985) aptly states,

> Any curriculum field which is tied closely to a set of social problems easily can come under the control of those problems, not just in the sense that study within that field is justified as a source of practical solutions, but in the more fundamental sense that the nature of the field itself comes to be defined in terms of the problems which it is expected to alleviate.

School-based education about sex is largely conceptualized as a curriculum designed to cope with the problems of real or imagined human sexuality. Thus, teachers of health, sex, and family life education programs are most frequently uncritical of the knowledge presented in classrooms. The programs rarely permit equivocations regarding the complexities of real-life decisions, and the discussions of sexual or reproductive decisions frequently take on an "either-or" framework. As one pregnant female teen explained,

> I told my health teacher in class that the pill is not always good for you and that it can hurt you. She didn't believe me and told me that I was listening to too many rumors. I said to her that I had a friend who got sick to her stomach and swelled up, and she told me that it probably wasn't because of the pill. She didn't know what she was talkin' about 'cause it wasn't really a friend it was me. And when I had went to the clinic the doctor changed my prescription 'cause he said it was too strong for me. That's when I said it was too dangerous and stopped takin' them.

Thus, when knowledge about sex is questioned, examined, and challenged in school classrooms, the responses are usually parochial, hard-line rejections of the possibilities for contradictions. Delivered as a corpus of functional and instrumental lessons, students are expected to master sexual information and somehow transfer it to their real lives in order to deter undesirable problems. "The way it really is," as one student maintained, is rarely taken seriously and heard in classrooms. Rather, the sexual education messages in the 1980s are about *problems*.

Examining the Material Coercion of the Pregnant Teenage Body

Sexual politics and reproductive rights, terms first used by 1970s feminists to underscore the connectedness of personal life, bodily self-determination, and political consciousness, are now the terrains upon which the New Right struggles for control over the teenage body. The focus is teenage sexuality and the assault is on the "epidemic" of illegitimate teenage pregnancy. Anchoring the rhetoric is the "epidemic" language that fuels the campaign against the sexual activity of teenagers who are portrayed as having produced soaring rates of illegitimate pregnancies in order to attain welfare dependance.[2]

The connection between a repressive sexual ideology and a coercive economy is clear in the recent changes of federal policy and funding. As of the 1980 presidential election, federal budget allocations were directed to controlling the teenage pregnancy "epidemic." An initial neo-conservative action added the "Adolescent Family Life Demonstration Projects" to the Public Health Service Act in the 1981 budget with the intent "to promote self-discipline and other prudent approaches to the problem of teenage pregnancy" (Section 955, OBRA 97–35). "Prudent approaches" included promoting adoption and emphasizing abstinence programs for unmarried adolescents. The policy makers supporting the bill maintained that teenagers were being taught to "say yes" to "early sex" with government money.

In 1984 another strategy instituted by the Deficit Reduction Act redefined the legal term of "emancipated minor" requiring that teenage mothers be living independently of parents in order to qualify for welfare subsidy. Here, the assumption was that the availability of welfare subsidies encouraged poor young women to become early mothers as a means to supplement their incomes while still living in a dependent status at their parents' residences. This redefinition required teens who lived with parents to solicit financial support from their children's grandparents or move to an independent residence to qualify for independent subsidies.

These economic measures were accompanied by a roster of proposed but unratified bills to control teenage sexual and reproductive behavior in the course of the past seven years of the Reagan Administration. In 1982, for instance, a Department of Health and Human Services revision proposed a parental notification clause, what was referred to as the "squeal law," to family planning counseling of teens. The requirement was to change the confidentiality prerogative of teenagers who sought birth control counseling at the clinics and to make clinic funding contingent on the notification of the teens' parents. In successive years attempts were made to curtail the ability of clinics to make referrals to teenagers requesting abortion counseling by encumbering funding with other stipulations. One proposed stipulation was to require teenagers to produce an affidavit of parental consent. Another was to require that health care professionals inform teenagers of the pain the fetus was to experience during abortion procedures. The most recent has been a stipulation requiring the removal of abortion referrals from the roster of options offered at family planning sites.

In addition to these federal sanctions, state governments have initiated coercive economic measures to "curb teenage pregnancy" as in the state of Wisconsin's 1985 Abortion Prevention and Family Responsibility Act. The state's legislation requires paternal and maternal grandparents to support the grandchildren of their teenagers. The law's intent is to "give parents a financial incentive to counsel their children on appropriate sexual behavior" (Donovan, 1986, p. 266). The Wisconsin representative who sponsored the act contends that "We had to hit parents in the pocketbooks to get their attention. . . and to shift the burden away from the welfare system" (p. 265).

All of this evidence points to the connection between a neo-conservative ideology of sexual repression and a coercive economy directed at the "epidemic of teenage pregnancy." The strategies reveal a shift in sentiments away from *in loco parentis* concern toward preventive coercion. The economic coercion applied to the delivery of teenage public health and birth control services is predicated on the government's right to invade the sexual and reproductive privacy of teenage people. The invasive sexual and reproductive strategies backed by coercive economic policies is an act that threatens the personal integrity of teenage citizens, usually female, in the deep and

intimate terrain of bodily determination. The national themes of
sexual repression and of coercive economy are connected to affect the
behaviors and attitudes of teens in the intimate life of the family.

The coercion, however, is not isolated to the teenage female but,
as demonstrated in these legislative and fiscal actions of the state,
involves adult community members, not only parents but also health
providers, whose interactions with teenagers are altered by changes
in the legal codification of ideological themes and material conditions.
The implications, as well, are not exclusive to those community
members who have been designated as the caretakers of the teenage
body, its sexual and reproductive character. Implications exist for
teachers, as well, who do not conform to the sectarian view of their
roles as pedagogues of minds to the exclusion of bodies. Teachers who
make as their project the education of these "reclassified" socially
pregnant students often find themselves on shifting ideological and
material terrain as the terms of this dichotomy are constantly
renegotiated with each passing twist in national and local themes
of adolescent sexual and reproductive control. Particularly, those
teachers who make their project the education of pregnant students
in alternative settings to the traditional school find themselves
vulnerable to coercive acts occurring in the local practice of schooling.
The next section of this paper will focus on one community situation
which illustrates how teachers may become the subjects of ideological
and economic coercion at local sites during contestations for power
and control in dilemmas of sex, pregnancy, and schooling.

Examining a Historical and Situational Moment of Teenage Pregnancy in Schools

The community situation that is the subject of this examination
occurred in 1984 in New Town, a pseudonym for a northeastern city
of 40,000 people.[3] In 1984 New Town shared an ideological and
economic history characteristic of many northeastern cities. It had
survived what had been labeled the results of "urban decay" and
"benign neglect." In the 1960s and 1970s white and middle-income
families had fled integration of residential neighborhoods and of
public schools by moving to the suburbs or by establishing enclaves
in wealthier wards. Successive plant closings in New Town and its
periphery eliminated wage labor employment for unskilled and semi-
skilled workers, leaving a core of jobless and poor families in the
center of New Town. By the mid-1970s approximately 41.9% of New
Town's minority population were under- or unemployed in districts

where 44.2% were black and Puerto Rican residents living below the poverty line. However, New Town by the 1980s was in the process of "revitalization," which at other locales might be understood in terms of "redevelopment" or "urban renewal." New Town's "revitalization" was both an ideological and an economic program cosponsored by public and private funding. The program had both a public relations and a physical development component.

In 1975 representatives of a research development corporation were contracted by a remaining multinational health products corporation to study the status of New Town. The research assessment outlined a strategy for a "revitalization" campaign that was to be a "joint venture between the private and public sectors of the city." The "revitalization" plan proposed the establishment of a private development corporation, New Town Development Corporation (NT DevCo), to "plan, direct, construct, market, and manage the physical development of New Town." At the same time a public relations corporation, New Town Tomorrow (NTT) was to "formulate community goals, create a believable and desirable image, and identify and evaluate priorities in the revitalization program." This strategy introduced a language, sentiment, and economy into the heart of the city that would last for more than a decade.

By 1984 both public and private investments in the physical development of the city totaled more than 269 million dollars of committed and allocated funds. In addition to economic and physical development, NTT addressed the tensions among residents with regard to the "problem people" who were reported to have moved into New Town when it was on its downward decline. The arena in which this tension was most visible was public education. NTT reported

> lack of parental interest in schools; lower achievement levels and standards; new behavior patterns in schools that are so "different" as to be disturbing to teachers and other children; different moral values and differences in environmental circumstances.

To address this educational dilemma of "difference," NTT spawned the New Town Education Task Force, which created a "theme of excellence" for New Town schooling. In spite of the de facto segregation between public and private schools and the 40% dropout rate characteristic of black and Puerto Rican students at the public high school, the Task Force promoted a picture of schooling excellence in a brochure that was distributed citywide to every New Town household and business in 1984. The same month that this brochure was distributed, the New Town School Board passed a 1984–1985 budget that deleted the alternative high school for pregnant and parenting teens, the Family Life Center, from its list of schools. This deletion became the center of a controversy that mirrored the New Town struggle over revitalization.

This decision to close the alternative high school for pregnant and parenting teens had both an ideological and an economic component. At the juncture when physical revitalization was increasingly being promoted in public relations messages to produce an upbeat "New-New Town," the alternative school brought attention to some of "the problems" in the city. For those who supported the closing of the 15-year-old program, the time had come to recognize that the school "cost the taxpayer money and rewarded girls for their bad behavior," according to one New Town school administrator. Thus, in the spring of 1984 the controversy regarding the elimination and closing of the Family Life Center moved to center stage as portions of minority, poor, and progressive middle-class citizens challenged the defunding of the alternative school.

A Struggle for Hearts and Minds: The Family Life Center

The elimination of the Family Life Center, the FLC as teachers and students called it, was understood by its advocates to be one of many political and economic acts of disenfranchisement of New Town's poor by pro-revitalizers of the city. Following the February 1984 announcement of the FLC's closing, the spring was a time of struggle over the fate of the school program and the commitment of the school administration to its pregnant and parenting students.

Although the controversy in New Town essentially could be described in terms of two competing factions, pro- and anti-FLC, the most vocal representatives on both sides were discerned by their institutional affiliation and professional status. The FLC supporters were most visibly led by the professional network of social caseworkers and grassroots community workers who managed social service programs for pregnant and parenting teenagers in New Town. According to social service records New Town ranked sixth in its state for teenage fertility, and it was believed by social service and health care workers that teenage pregnancy was an "epidemic" in New Town. FLC supporters understood the closing of the FLC to be "another strike against poor folks in New Town," according to one social caseworker. The anti-FLC position was most visibly represented by New Town's school board, school administrators, and other city officials. According to the anti-FLC constituents, the time had come to end a program "that was about teaching teens to say 'yes' " to sex and pregnancy.

Throughout the spring of 1984 position papers and news articles indexed a list of rationales that were offered for the elimination of the FLC program. By the end of that spring official explanations for the school closing had moved from depicting pregnant and parenting teens as economic burdens of the city to representing them as victims caught up in a deceptive educational program that sealed their fate as underachievers and future welfare dependents. Official statements by the superintendent pointed to the FLC teachers as underqualified and incompetent classroom teachers who were intent upon promoting the nurturing and mothering aspects of the school to the detriment of the students' and the district's academic excellence. In some cases the superintendent underscored the provisional certification held by some teachers at the FLC, maintaining their underqualification for their positions.

In spite of the number of reasons proffered by the superintendent for closing the FLC, the FLC supporters firmly believed that the real reason for which the school program was being dismantled was a political one. They believed that the revitalization program promoting the "New-New Town" planned for a "cover-up of the problems of the city," of which teenage pregnancy was one, and for the eventual removal of those who had been labeled "problem people." They saw the FLC closing as a political act, an assault against the ideologically and economically disenfranchised portion of the city's population.

The public debate around the FLC closing occurred primarily between two male contenders: the superintendent of schools who represented the anti-FLC group and the director of the grassroots community daycare center who became the spokesperson for the pro-FLC constituents. The personalities of the two contenders frequently became the focal point in much of the controversy. The superintendent was depicted by FLC supporters as the mayor's henchman for revitalization while the daycare center director was attacked by the anti-FLC group as a self-interested and power-hungry leader of the minority community who was out to advance his own organization. Throughout the spring of 1984 the newspaper coverage of the FLC closing featured these two contenders' altercations as letters to the editor increasingly became more vitriolic. By mid-spring of that year the superintendent sought to negotiate with the FLC supporters to quell the heightened animosities within the city.

During the meetings between the anti-FLC school administration and the pro-FLC social service groups, two community themes
became manifest. For pro-FLC constituents "a concern for the girls"
was primary in the language used to make sense of the controversy.
According to FLC supporters, the school board and its administration
were prioritizing "money ahead of people." They argued for "a concern
for the girls" and for a concern for the poor people of New Town and
not "just for those in positions of power and wealth." Anti-FLC
constituents responded to "a concern for the girls" with "a concern
for the city and its schools." Their argument was that the economy
of the city affected the well-being of its population and, essentially,
what was good for the image and economy of the city would eventually
be good for its poor people in terms of jobs and security. In addition,
the anti-FLC constituents depicted the alternative school as
antithetical to the quest for academic excellence in New Town's public
educational system. Using the new state high school regents exam
as a focus, the New Town school administration argued that the FLC
hurt the ratings of the school district and consequently its agenda
for "excellence" and "revitalization."

The anti-FLC constituents saw the school's supporters as
"bleeding hearts" who put ideals ahead of reason and who were self-
interested lobbyists really campaigning for a program that made their
jobs easier at an expense to the city's taxpayers. In one meeting, when
the director of the New Town daycare center accused the superintendent of "playing politics with kids' lives" and of "not really being
concerned about the girls," the superintendent responded with
accusations that the daycare director should "wake-up and
understand that there's more to running a city or a school than well-
intentioned programs that don't deliver."

Social Actors in Oppressive Relations: Teachers and Students

The controversial situation of the FLC closing was a violent
disruption in the lives of teachers and students. Teachers at the FLC
believed that portents of the school's elimination had appeared in the
mid-1970s with the advent of revitalization. At that time the part-
time teachers' benefits were cut, maintenance work on the trailer that
housed the school decreased, and requests for supplies were delayed
until expenditures could be justified by the FLC director to the
district's business office. The FLC director maintained that in 1984
things had "gotten so involved" that she spent most of her time
"filling out forms rather than being with the girls."

As a collective, the FLC teachers argued strongly that their school reduced the dropout rate among pregnant teenagers when students enrolled in the school. Without the program, they maintained, "the girls will drop out, they won't want to go to a school that makes it a handicap to be pregnant." The most vocal FLC teacher, who chose the name Betty Ames for these research reports, believed that the FLC provided pregnant students with the mothering and support necessary to keep them from dropping out of school. In the spring of 1984 she said,

> There are people in New Town that think the kids are getting a free ride here. You know, everything is coming easy with them and it's not. They have to work hard here and they have to produce. It's just that they are all pregnant and if they are sick, you know, we make the work for them. It's easier for us to make the work for them because you have two, three or four in a class and if that person is out, you just go back and review that person. They can't do this at the high school. But they think we're just making it too easy for them. It's like they want to punish the kids because they're pregnant. None of these girls want to be pregnant, none of them. They want to have sex but they don't want to get pregnant, so they're being punished enough.
>
> I think the administration is very short sighted. They're not seeing the problems they are bringing on the taxpayers later. . . . You know, if you don't educate the parent, how are you going to educate the children? . . . I don't see why they can't see this. They like to say it's changing but it's like breeding ignorance on top of ignorance. It seems as if the system is designed to keep these people ignorant and I mean, if you start off keeping them ignorant in the school system then you can control it. Keep them ignorant and you can control them. You know, education can be a dangerous thing. It can backfire on you, so you keep them ignorant.

Betty Ames, like the other FLC teachers, strongly believed that the FLC closing was a political act caught in the web of power relations between the rich and poor and the black and white groups of New Town. Her conviction that the closing of the FLC represented an attack on the poor, black, and uneducated was shared by most teachers at the school, who were black and white women living in New Town or its immediate surroundings. They believed that it was difficult for the poor residents in New Town neighborhoods to "get behind" the school because the parents of teens and their friends were too disaffected and too afraid of having to deal with high school personnel. Though parents and "friends of the school" frequently dropped by the FLC that spring to talk with the staff about the closing, New Town's minority residents and parents of the FLC students were not prominent advocates with the administration for maintaining the school.

FLC teachers, as well, were not vocal public advocates for their school. Although the FLC teachers analyzed the political contours of New Town life and assessed the ideological and economic conditions that jeopardized the alternative school's potential for survival, they did so privately during daily lunch breaks and after hours during telephone conversations with one another. Teachers' reticence to take vocal, public stands was explained by one FLC employee as "you don't make waves in public 'cause you never know how they might black ball you." The FLC teachers feared retaliation by New Town's school administration and did not hold faith in their labor union as a trustworthy advocate for "special teachers." Most were provisional or part-time employees and had been so for many years with the school system. As heads of their households because of a husband's death or because of divorce, they had sought employment close to their homes, many of which were in the neighborhoods close to the school. Teachers felt themselves to be keenly vulnerable to the loss of a "good reputation," and one teacher maintained, "It's one thing to be let go 'cause they close the school, it's totally another to be fired and lose a good reputation for a chance at other jobs."

Betty Ames, the most outspoken FLC teacher, insisted that the superintendent had "terrorized them [the teachers] during a meeting" at which he explained his reasons for closing the alternative school. Betty claimed that the superintendent was "manipulatin' the facts" about the FLC to "make us look bad." She argued that it was only herself who spoke up for the school because she "could afford to be vocal" about the closing. At the meeting Betty challenged the superintendent's figures on dropouts from the FLC and on learning conditions at the school. She explained that she did this because she was less vulnerable than the other FLC teachers: she had recently moved out of New Town, she was still married, and her husband had just received a promotion in the winter of that year. She believed that if she were to be "punished for speaking out for the school," she would not "have to worry about where the next pay check would come from."

Thus, the quiet and constrained critical voices of the FLC teachers could be heard at only the most private times of the school day when teachers met behind closed doors for lunch or planning periods. The tension and despondency of the teachers' talks at these times reflected their fear of what might occur to them if they were to break their public silence. The threat of job termination, of the administration's retaliation on future letters of recommendation, and of the public humiliation they believed they suffered when New Town's administration challenged their teaching abilities, all served to constrain the public voices of the FLC teachers. Although their muffled and muted critiques could be heard outside the door of the classroom in which teachers lunched, rarely did teachers share their interpretations with the FLC students. Even as the pressures and tensions escalated throughout the spring and the teachers' voices were raised in anger behind closed doors, teachers did not provide to students their perspectives on the FLC controversy.

Frequently, students congregated around the closed door to the teachers' lunchroom or walked ever so slowly past the door in order to eavesdrop. When students could hear pieces of the conversations, they would return to the other FLC students with "the rap" and would attempt to make sense of the new developments they could derive from the teachers' talk, the word on the street, the radio, and the local newspaper. With this information, the FLC students assessed whether they would finish the year at the school before it "was shut down, and we were kicked out."

The teachers of the FLC maintained this cloak of privacy around their teacher talk because they believed that they needed to protect the pregnant students from the stress of the controversy that spring. Many of the teachers were aware of the difficulties the FLC students experienced at home and "at this hard time in their lives." According to one FLC teacher, "It wouldn't be fair to pile this trouble with the school on top of everything else they have to deal with." Thus, the FLC teachers did not include in their informal or formal lessons with students an understanding of the political context of New Town relations or the difficulty which they, as teachers, were to experience because of the closing of the school. Rather, they continued to concentrate on their shared philosophy of "educated motherhood," stressing that education and a high school diploma would benefit a woman *and* her child. As one veteran FLC teacher frequently was heard telling her students, "If you're not gonna' do it for ya'self, then do it for your child, girl. Lord knows, the little one is gonna' need a mother who can think." This statement was believed by its speaker to eventually work a "seriousness" for the FLC students who she believed could be convinced to work harder at their studies. She also believed that if the FLC students knew what was "really happenin'" about their school, "they might not be as serious about it."

For the students at the FLC who believed that their babies were going to be a hopeful promise of better things to come, teachers' beliefs persuaded them that their education had a role to play in "bein' a better mother by knowing more and bein' smarter." The teens believed that their high school diploma would benefit their children and, thus, "be a good thing to get, so my child knows she can do it, too," according to Diane, a teenage student parent of four-month-old Yadianna. Diane stayed at the FLC after her baby's birth because she believed it would help her to negotiate the stress of school and new motherhood. Though the choice accentuated the social and structural dislocation she experienced from her peers, she believed it was in her own and her child's best interest to attend the FLC. Diane, like most of the FLC students, believed the school helped her complete her high school education.

Diane was respected by the FLC students because she had birthed her baby and was staying in school to get her diploma. At a lunch time session one spring afternoon, Diane became a spokesperson for the FLC students when we talked about what was happening at their school. She had hurriedly sat down at the table with eight other students and myself and inadvertently spilled her milk on the table, which angered the other FLC students. As an explanation to them for her clumsiness, she said in Spanish and quickly translated to English that she had just overheard Mrs. A say that the school would be definitely closing by the following year. Diane also said,

Now I think of the school closing, and I get upset. People don't understand us. They don't understand this is 1984. You just don't wait now, that's the older days. Girls have sex, they get pregnant. The government doesn't know how to handle the situation. They should fund the FLC. They should get more daycare funding, more places for pregnant teens, more staff, and not spend money on parking lots and new condos. The teachers here are not get-overs, Mrs. A is tight on attendance. We girls don't need to be pressured, our peer pressure is enough. A lot of us would drop-out but the FLC lets us continue. I'm not ashamed I'm a student and a parent. It's just incredible, they decided to close the school. Just the fact that this school helps us be parents and students. This thing—the closing—is doing a lot of damage. It won't prevent pregnancies. We don't plan our pregnancies, it just happens. People look at me and say I'm so smart, intelligent, you know? It's like I'm so peculiar, I'm supposed to be stupid to get pregnant.

Diane gave voice to the air of student dispossession that characterized much of the dialogue that spring among the FLC students. Diane's assessment of the situation articulated the connection of several themes that occurred daily in the FLC students' conversations without their teachers. She expressed the general sentiment that existed among the "FLC girls," as she called them, that there was little understanding of their lives by the nebulous entity she labeled "the government." The FLC had become for them a place of their own. It enabled them to continue that part of their lives wrapped up in school and the desire for getting a high school diploma. The pregnant and parenting students at the FLC found other black and Puerto Rican teens to whom they could talk about the problems they were having with their boyfriends and their parents.

Thus, the closing of the FLC invaded the students', as well as the teachers', commitment to an educated motherhood and the notion that being pregnant (and a parent) and being a student were not separable in their lives. Students believed that the FLC "helped pregnant students stay in school" but the controversy and the air of dispossession that enveloped the school during the spring of 1984 was alienating for students. By June 1984 only four students remained at the school; a few had transferred to the traditional high school because "the FLC atmosphere was too depressing," while other students gradually became truant or dropped officially from the rolls.

For teachers, too, the closing was an invasion into their daily lives. White along with black FLC teachers withstood the stormy events of the spring months which resulted in a deep sense of loss and emotional turmoil. By summer three white teachers found jobs elsewhere, and the director adopted a handicapped child of a pregnant teenager who had attended the FLC and decided to stay at home the following year. Black teachers, however, had not found other jobs and experienced both physical and emotional debilitation by the school year's end. Betty Ames, the most outspoken teacher-critic of the closing, had been "pink slipped" a month before the term ended. Essa, the oldest veteran of the FLC who constantly chided the teens to be a "mother who could think," was taken to a hospital emergency ward with "a dizziness and tingling sensation" in her hands. Shalima, the youngest black teacher at the FLC, lost her job and had separated

from her husband by the end of the 1984 school year. She believed
the tension of the FLC closing escalated the tension in her marriage.
By the summer of that year she was supporting herself and her two
children by selling hand-made jewelry and etched Islamic prayers in
a New Town storefront. Thus, the closing of the FLC when registered
in immediate personal outcomes for the school's teachers was
disproportionately negative for black women whose total resources
and options were considerably less than those of white women
working at the school.

Resolving Conflict and Realizing Oppressive Power Relations

> Once a situation of violence and oppression has been established,
> it engenders an entire way of life and behavior for those caught
> up it—oppressor and oppressed alike. (Freire, 1970, p. 44)

Considering this evidence, it is hardly an overstatemcnt to assert
that both teachers and students of the FLC experienced a "violence"
in the elimination of the program they believed to fulfill the social
contract of teaching and learning in a way important to pregnant
students. Certainly, the sociocultural world of the FLC was invaded,
disrupted, and dislocated leaving all participants at the site feeling
dehumanized and emotionally dependent upon an oppressive city
government and school administration. However, to depict the New
Town controversy as a simple contestation between oppressor and
oppressed does not capture the complexity of the situation as it
occurred historically and situationally in the community. To fully
investigate the oppressive relationships of power in the FLC
controversy of New Town, it is vital to focus on a critical contradiction
in its evolution, the resolution of the public conflict. To do so, it will
be necessary to leave the school site and move back to the New Town
community as a locus of action in the historical and social drama of
the FLC closing.

In the spring of 1984, essentially, all pro-FLC discussions about
the fate of the school occurred among professional social work
community members who were not directly involved in the conduct
of the alternative school but who ostensibly were in positions of power
impacting upon the lives of FLC participants. Through pro-FLC
lobbying for the school, the superintendent capitulated by the end
of spring 1984 on the first plan to close the alternative school.
Although by May 1984 the administration still planned to defund the
school, the language used to describe the fate of the FLC had been

revised. In its place was a strategy to "move" the FLC program to the high school and, then, to close the trailer in which the FLC was housed. Thus, during the series of meetings throughout the spring of 1984 the proposed closing of the FLC was transformed into a strategy to "move" or "relocate" the FLC program to the high school, and a committee of social service and community workers was called upon to "work with" the school administration "during the difficult transition period." In a public statement to New Town parents in June of 1984 the superintendent maintained that the move to the high school was "for the good of the girls"; he said, "the nurturing and support will still be there."

The shift in the New Town school administration's position marked an appeasement to public pressure. The organized opposition to the closing was quelled through negotiation with the daycare director and social service workers whose selected agencies would provide supplementary services to the new "Family Life Program" (FLP) at the traditional high school. Agencies providing the services would receive specially set aside money from a county grant for this purpose. The superintendent had supported the daycare center as the key agency in distributing the funds, and the daycare center director supported the move of the FLC to the high school. In doing so, the anti-FLC school superintendent had proven his commitment to "a concern for the girls" and the pro-FLC daycare director had legitimated his "concern for the city."

On December 17, 1984 a New Town social service meeting was held to provide the daycare center director the chance to report on the FLP project to his colleagues. The director announced that the agency had not received its money from the county and "I wonder," he said, "if they ever really meant for us to get through all the red tape." According to the daycare director the program was a miserable failure. The other social service workers exchanged reports on the "failure" of the program with many agreeing that "by last count most of the girls were gone"—were on homebound instruction, were truant, or were officially dropped from the rolls.

The Meaning of the Struggle for the Family Life Center

The community controversy in New Town over the continuation of the FLC alternative school for pregnant teens represents how one event may be enfolded into the meanings of oppressive actions residual in a community's relations of race, class, and gender domination. The revitalization of New Town clearly favored white and middle-class residents, and the Family Life Center was a structural site that marked for New Towners the contradictions of ideological and economic shifts in the everyday struggle of living in New Town. The FLC not only underscored the presence of the "problems" of New Town—the problems of race, class, and gender— but also mirrored the national fervor over the ideology and economy of controlling female adolescent sexuality and pregnancy.

The closing of the FLC was a violent invasion of the subject-ivities of the teachers, students, and parents. For 15 years New Town had maintained the structural separation of pregnant teens in the FLC with the assumption that the program would encourage high school completion. The students who were separated "for their own good" were overwhelmingly minority, poor, and female. As a schooling practice, then, the FLC had implications for the race, class, and gender of its participants, and its closing potentially jeopardized the ability of poor, black, and Puerto Rican teenage females to remain in school while becoming mothers. In 1984 teens were to be reinte-grated into the traditional high school once again "for their own good," which more precisely represented the changing situational features of local ideology and economy. Teens and their parents were not included in the discussions of the fate of the FLC. Rather, they were informed of the results of negotiations.

Noticeably absent, as well, from the discussions were the FLC teachers—all women—whose fate was decided principally by two leading male brokers of power, one representing the school administration and the other representing the administration of social services in New Town. As the two leaders resolved their differences on the public stage of reconciliation and "cordial relations" (Giroux, 1985), the school's fate and those of its teachers and students were apparent. The resolution was presented in a linguistic coding "for the good of the girls" that beneath the surface indicated a camouflaged invasion. As noted by Freire, "All domination involves invasion—at times physical and overt, at times camouflaged, with the invader assuming the role of a helping friend" (1970, p. 150).

The non-involvement of teachers, as well, was a deceptive and distorting act of submission and omission. Yet their non-involvement was a perplexing dilemma only partially explainable by the FLC teachers' fear of losing their jobs and denial, perhaps, of the inevitable result of the closing of the FLC. By December 1984 one of the seven teachers had survived to remain teaching in New Town but would be asked to retire the following year when the FLP program was disbanded at the high school by a new principal. The new principal, who advocated "teaching students to say no to early sex," had redirected social service energies toward promoting abstinence and sexual responsibility and toward preventing pregnancy—all very prominent national themes.

FLC teachers at New Town clearly felt constrained in their abilities to advocate for the students and themselves. Their attitudes of maternal protectionism toward students and stoic professionalism toward their community led to a silent complicity in the demise of the school. As well, the FLC closing controversy was clearly preceeded by a number of indications as to the school's questionable standing in the district for a number of years. By their physical separation from the main site of the high school and by their status as "special teachers to pregnant students," they were vulnerable as are all teachers of special programs and alternative schools set up to "meet the needs of special students." Once designated as a special or alternative program, district commitment or what is bureaucratically called "institutionalization of a program" is clearly dependent on solid administrative support or a groundswell of politically astute enthusiasm for its promotion. The FLC was one of many "special programs" at all levels of governmental sponsorship which have come and gone their respective ways as the nation has moved right from the liberal intentions of the 1960s.

The Critical Teaching of Sex and Pregnancy in the Schools

At this moment of ideological and economic conservatism both at the national and local levels, issues of sex and pregnancy for U.S. schools will continue to pose contradictory dilemmas revealing acts of domination in educational practices. What, then, for critical teaching at schools like the FLC or in districts like New Town? More specifically, what then for a teaching agenda that addresses highly charged political issues of sexuality and/or reproduction, issues which I suggest are incorporated into the repressive ideology of a pedagogy of the body?

First, it is vital to recognize that the pedagogies of sex and the body have been presented to students with great absences and silences. Such absences and silences make lessons seem "unreal" to students as if teachers like parents were concealing "juicy" information behind closed doors. Such concealment often slides over to issues of sexual politics as in the case of the FLC. As evident in the pedagogy of the FLC, teaching with a protectionism designed to shield students from stress or harsh realities may be acts engendered by kindness but certainly are those which result in promoting misinformation or disinformation to students. Such acts of paternalism or maternalism are self-deceptive at best and at worst collusive in depriving students of a critical vision of the world in which they live. The result is a depressive lethargy of powerlessness which became evident in students' slow withdrawal from the FLC through its last spring. As seen, the protectionism was unsuccessful, and students as knowers and observers in their own right often made rather astute appraisals about the powerful and powerless in New Town, as did Diane. What is of paramount importance, then, between teachers and students is an immediate engagement in the act of knowing and interrogating reality as it occurs in the daily life of people and communities. Questions regarding teacher and student under-standings of their world must be voiced, and both need to engage in creating a discourse of examination before explanation may be approached. Such a strategy is suggested by Freire's pedagogy of the question that permits teachers to have no right answers but, rather, to be capable of posing good questions (Macedo, 1985). I can only wonder, for instance, what might have happened at the FLC if teachers had posed questions to students regarding the events in New Town. And, what might have happened had both teachers and students "taken apart" the controversial events in New Town, and then had been "a part" of those events?

Second, teachers in programs like the FLC need to examine their relationships with administrators and school boards and see them-selves as potential subjects of domination. With an identity of professionalism there often comes a glaze of integrity and "fair play" that is both naive and self-deceptive. Frequently telling themselves that they will be acceptable if they do a good job, workers—including professionals—chastise themselves with the internalization of a rhetoric of impotence and vulnerability that tells little about their abilities and more about the social and material conditions of the institutions in which they work. Certainly dependence upon district administrators for future referrals was a very real element of FLC teachers' concerns, and the firing of one teacher like Betty Ames was an act of symbolic terrorism on the potential fate of each FLC teacher. Thus, the "disempowerment"[4] that teacher-workers anticipated over their own lives in the act of being fired from their FLC jobs rather than "let go," was abusive and violent. Equally violent was the stressful reactions the women experienced under the daily threat of occupational and economic insecurity. As FLC teachers experienced the results of stress-related ailments, it became evident that their collective silence had not been without detriment to themselves and that this detriment was disproportionately experienced by black women teachers.

Finally, what the FLC controversy says to us about critical teaching is that a vision much larger than one focused on a classroom or a school is required of teachers who are vulnerable to invasive forms of disempowerment. Teachers must be reflective about their worlds which extend beyond the sphere of their particular classrooms, their departments, or their schools. All are situated historically and are embedded in a web of complex relations inextricably connected to the ideological, material, and social conditions of schools and communities. The relations are about power as a form of control—the keeping of it, the exercise of it, and the reproduction of it. The language we choose to use to describe these relations also is about the power of language to both actively and passively conceal and distort those relations. However, once those relations are discovered they must not be denied or silenced, they must be named and confronted. Old struggles must be connected to new struggles, and teachers must apply their voices and critical visions to showing these connections to their students, to their colleagues, and to members of their communities. In New Town the FLC teachers were not critical readers of the historical moment—of the ideological and material components of a revitalization agenda that did not endorse a school like the FLC. And teachers, for the most part, were apolitical in the process of the closing. They, as well as compliant social work negotiators, were deceived by a cooption of their own "caring" rhetoric, "a concern for the girls." Most importantly, then, FLC teachers were not wary of the shifting ideological terrain upon which "a concern for the girls" might be claimed in 1984. They had not "read the world" (Freire & Macedo, 1987) outside the FLC or considered the changing mood of their community.

So, too, should this changing mood suggest to us a larger caution of national rhetoric embedded in concerns for sexual and reproductive epidemics of the young. We must be vigilant in questioning all assaults on sexual and reproductive rights, realizing full well the political nature of conservative agendas purporting to be for "a student's own good."

Notes

1. Social pregnancy, as distinguished from physiological pregnancy, is that point when a woman and her social group recognize her as pregnant.

See Miller (1978) for a fully detailed explanation of this distinction. For teenage females the effect of social pregnancy bears witness to her sexual activity and, therefore, introduces her into the symbolic realm as sexually and reproductively active, behaviors held as dissonant for adolescent women.

2. Not only have teenage fertility rates declined through the 1970s and 1980s from the highest teen pregnancy rates of the 1950s, but also the connection between illegitimate teenage births and welfare subsidy has been challenged by a number of authors, as well. See David Ellwood and Mary Jo Bane who examine this connection (1983).

3. A more detailed version of this community situation can found in McDade (1987).

4. The term "disempowerment" is deliberately used here to connote the opposite of "empowerment." I use disempowerment to depict the active, willful and commissive acts of violent expressions of power *over* people—teachers, students, and parents—that result in further and continued denial of their abilities to realize "empowerment."

References

Brake, M. (1982). *Human sexual relations: Towards a redefinition of sexual politics.* New York: Pantheon Books.

Diorio, J. (1985). Contraception, copulation, domination, and the theoretical barrenness of sex education literature. *Educational Theory, 35*(3), 239–254.

Donovan, P. (1986). Will grandparent liability help curb teenage pregnancy? *Family Planning Perspectives, 18*(6), 264–268.

Ellwood, D., & Bane, M.J. (1983). Slipping into and out of poverty: The dynamics of spells. Cambridge: National Bureau of Educational Research, No. 1199.

Fausto-Sterling, A. (1985). *Myths of gender.* New York: Basic Books.

Freire, P. (1970). *Pedagogy of the oppressed.* New York: Continuum Publishing.

Freire, P., & Macedo, D. (1987). *Literacy: Reading the word and the world.* South Hadley, MA: Bergin & Garvey.

Freud, S. (1949). *Three essays on sexuality.* London: Hogarth Press.

Freud, S. (1930). *Civilization and its discontents.* London: Hogarth Press.

Giroux, H. (1985). Critical pedagogy, cultural politics, and the discourse of experience. *Journal of Education, 167*(2), 22–41.

Greene, M. (1986). In search of a critical pedagogy. *Harvard Educational Review, 56*(4), 427–441.

Macedo, D. (1985). Toward a pedagogy of the question: A conversation with Paulo Freire. *Journal of Education, 167*(2), 7–21.

Marcuse, H. (1955). *Eros and civilization.* Boston: Beacon Press.

McDade, L. (1987). Community responses to teenage pregnancy and parenting: An ethnography of a social problem. (Doctoral dissertation, Rutgers University.) *Dissertation Abstracts International, 87:* 8714514.

Miller, R. (1978). The social construction of physiological events: Acquiring the pregnancy identity. *Studies in symbolic interaction.* Volume I. Norman K. Denzin (pp. 181–204). Connecticut: JAI Press.

Simon, R., & Dippo, D. (1986). On critical ethnographic work. *Anthropology and Education Quarterly, 17,* 195–202.

Presence of Mind in the
Absence of Body

Linda Brodkey and Michelle Fine

We commonly tell stories about what happens to us and what
we make of our experience. In a sense, then, the stories documenting
our lives tell what we find worth remembering and contemplating
and sharing with others. It is of course the "others" who complicate
the telling of stories, for stories are not usually told to ourselves alone,
but to those we hope will understand our construction of events. The
stories included in this essay concern the sexual harassment of
students by professors. We have tried to reconstruct the historical
and institutional circumstances of telling along with the stories told
because the transformative potential of the narratives cannot be
understood apart from the context in which they were written and
read.[1]

The sexual harassment narratives were written by undergraduate and graduate women at the University of Pennsylvania in
response to an open-ended question on the Penn Harassment Survey.[2]
These students are of the generation of women for many of whom,
as Annette Kolodny recently put it, "feminism is either outdated—
because of the naive belief that 'there aren't any problems any
more'—or a distorted melange of media images and Reagan-era
backlash" (p. 461). For some of them, Kolodny adds, "feminism is both
personal and problematic" because their mothers "tried to reject
traditional family roles in a society that offered their offspring no
compensating structures and amid a movement too new to prepare
us all for the consequences of such radical change" (p. 461). Yet the
women who wrote these narratives know what sexual harassment
is. Their narratives confirm the findings of survey research on college
and university campuses: women students are routinely harassed;
post-secondary institutions have been egregiously hesitant to address
harassment (much less write, publish, and enforce sexual harassment

policies); and remedies for reporting and grieving sexual harassment favor, if not harassers, their institutions (Robertson, Dyer, & Campbell, 1988). After reading and reflecting on these narratives, we have come to believe that the future of academic feminism is activism and that activism begins in pedagogy.

The narratives clarify the findings of the Penn survey, namely, that women are reluctant to report sexual harassment and reticent when they do tell because they suspect that institutional indifference will lead to reprisals of one sort or another. We think their fears are justified and in turn warrant feminist curriculum intervention. What we have learned from women's narratives of their experiences of harassment, however, suggests that we will need to encourage all students and women in particular to explore not so much the fact but the complexities of harassment. After all, harassment sits at the nexus of gender, power, and sexuality in the academy—as it does in all institutions. Exploring it will take the students and us far outside the boundaries of legal definitions and institutional remedies. It will even take us outside of current feminist analyses of gender and sexuality, for most women students judge sexual harassment to be beyond the reach of law and feminism.

To teach this new generation is to try to understand that they encounter sexual harassment as women whose civil rights have been guaranteed since birth, and hence as women who had believed themselves to be protected by those laws—and have only recently found that they are not. And to work with them is also to realize that even as their narratives reveal the partiality of their visions of gender and sexuality, they critique the partiality of our more seasoned feminist analyses of gender inequity and sexual violence. We are arguing for feminist pedagogies to accompany what Donna Haraway calls "situated and embodied knowledges," the partiality and plurality of which contest "various forms of unlocatable, and so irresponsible, knowledge claims" (1988, p. 583). Partial perspectives exert a sobering influence on feminist pedagogies, privileging self-conscious acts of critical vision and imagination that are openly hostile to the already established vantage points of either relativism or totalization, which Haraway sees as "promising vision from everywhere and nowhere" (p. 584). Yet she is also suspicious of all "innocent" positions, including what can be seen from the vantage points of subjugation, and offers positioning as a responsible political and epistemological feminist practice for continuing the conversation on gender already in progress in the academy. The pedagogical and political project then is to interrogate the ways in which the sexual harassment narratives undermine the transformative potential of narration by effectively withdrawing their narrators from the conversation we had hoped they would enter.

Telling It Like It Is/Was and Like It Isn't/Wasn't

Given that the Penn Harassment Survey focused primarily on sexual harassment, and given the demographics of students at Penn, the narratives written by undergraduate and graduate women raise almost exclusively the concerns of white women from the middle and upper social classes. Yet their narratives confirm the findings of other campus surveys and hence frustrate any hopes we may have had that knowledge of civil rights defends women against their harassers. Of particular concern here are the narratives written in response to Question 21:

> It would be helpful to us if you would describe this experience in detail. Please do so omitting any incriminating information (e.g., names, courses, etc.). You may include a separate piece of paper if necessary.

Ignoring for the moment the likelihood that the proviso to omit incriminating information may have also discouraged many women students from including details of any kind and the fact that the quarter-inch allotted for response was inadequate, we offer the narrative below as typical, inasmuch as the woman provides a markedly attenuated description of the event itself relative to the elaborate explanation of both her professor's behavior and her decision not to report him.

> When the incident happened, his attention lasted about one month. It did not occur to me that it was "sexual harassment" per se because I don't tend to think in terms of deviant behavior.
>
> I perceived a troubled man experiencing a mid-life crisis— and more important—a colleague with whom I genuinely shared intellectual commitments and interests. Unfortunately, he saw a young, bright cutsie who could help him with his work and who could potentially serve as an escape route from his unsatisfactory marriage. Basically, all I had to do was make my "No" repetitive and very clear, but the situation was so muddled and in many ways, not so cut and dried as "sexual harassment."

Things occurred on a very subtle level and are not reported for this reason. All professors have to say is "She's unstable, paranoid, imagining things or lying, etc." Graduate women don't have a leg to stand on. (File 403-31)

Many statements in this account warrant commentary. She refers to "the incident" but never describes what her professor actually did. We're not then certain if she considers the "attentions that lasted about one month" sexual harassment and hence "deviant behavior" or if, as she later asserts, "the situation was so muddled and in many ways, not so cut and dried as 'sexual harassment'." She contrasts her complex view of him ("I perceived a troubled man experiencing a mid-life crisis—and more important—a colleague with whom I genuinely shared intellectual commitments and interests") with his simple view of her ("Unfortunately, he saw a young, bright cutsie who could help him with his work"). Here lies her conflict. And it matters because she has located the danger in his gendering of her, that is, in being turned into a woman. For she goes on to explain that his professional abuse is but a preface to an attempt to transform her into a woman whose body "could potentially serve as an escape route from his unsatisfactory marriage." She tells us that she dealt with her harasser as one might a perverse child—"Basically, all I had to do was make my 'No' repetitive and very clear"—and then explains that she and all the others have no other recourse, since "all professors have to say is 'She's unstable, paranoid, imagining things or lying, etc.'" And her last words, "Graduate women don't have a leg to stand on," summarize both her own situation and her position on the gendering of women by their male professors.

Leaving Your Body to Science

We have a good deal of sympathy for this graduate woman's rendering of the academic world she inhabits, where her experience of gender has been reduced to slut and madwoman. While we delight in her refusal to take her professor's extracurricular forced-choice exam, we are, nonetheless, troubled by the argument that she and other women students use to represent their strategies for resisting harassers, for it certainly looks as if their practice is to transcend their bodies and deny that women students are women. We say this because of the stunning regularity with which women students position themselves in their narratives as disinterested bystanders who have witnessed rather than experienced sexual harassment and who have been asked not to describe what happened to them, but to explain why professors harass their women students.

> This behavior increases when his wife leaves town, if we are in a situation involving liquor or if we are in the presence of other individuals who find this behavior entertaining. (File 947-31)

> Male faculty in a department in which I conduct research make suggestive comments, joke and tease most of the time. There are no female faculty members of the department and my assumption has always been that they were simply ignorant of how their behavior was affecting the females who are associated in this department. (File 431-61)

> He was drunk which I'm sure contributed to the problem. (File 344-51)

What troubles us about the women's explanations of the extenuating circumstances surrounding acts of harassment is the extent to which each has positioned herself as a narrator who, because she has personally transcended the experience, is "free" to evaluate her harasser's behavior from the vantage point of an expert witness. She does this by assuming a clinical posture with respect to sexual harassment, treating the event as a mere symptom of a disease she must diagnose. Instead of a personal narrative recounting her own anger, sorrow, pain, or even pleasure, she impersonally catalogues his motives: he drinks; his wife is out of town; his colleagues egg him on; he's socially maladroit; he's old; he doesn't know any better. She's taking good care of him. That wouldn't concern us all that much except that the narrative positions women assign themselves suggest that they understand their own survival to depend on the ability to cleave their minds from their bodies. This mind/body split reproduces in each of them the very cultural ideology that has historically been used to distinguish men from women and justify gender oppression. By severing mind from body and then privileging the "mind's" dispassionate, even clinical explanation of events, each woman materially reproduces in her narrative the very discursive dichotomies that have historically been used to define a seemingly endless string of culturally positive terms (male/mind/reason/culture) in contrast to a negative string (female/body/intuition/nature) (see, e.g., Caplan, 1986).

We take such representations of self as mind by women students as pleas to be seen by professors as *not women*. In poststructural terms, the women attempt to achieve unity and coherence as writers in an academic discourse, often called science, that has in recent history offered a few privileged white males the comforting belief that they and they alone legislate reality. These men reside in a world in which "mind over matter" means that what counts is what each individual man can know, understand, and represent as empirical. While poststructural theories argue convincingly that the unity afforded our divided sense of ourselves as discursive subjects is an illusion (e.g., Belsey, 1980; Brodkey, 1989), we are presumably most attracted to discourses that promise to represent us to ourselves and others as empowered subjects—as the agents who speak the discourse rather than the objectified subjects of which it speaks. For many faculty and students scientific discourse regulates academic speech and writing. And we think the women students are trying to reproduce a version of scientific discourse by positioning themselves as narrators who, having transcended their bodies, are then entitled to use their dispassionate observations as the bases of their clinical explanations of men's motives and cynical speculations on institutional reprisals. What happened to their bodies (sexual harassment) is not problematic and hence plays little part in the narratives; why it happened (his motives) and what would happen (reprisals), however, remain problematic long after the event and hence the narratives tell the story of a torturous struggle to represent themselves as genderless.

We see each woman student as offering to pay an exorbitant, not to mention impossible, price for the coherent self represented in her narrative. In exchange for her "mind," she leaves her body to science. Such a strategy for resisting harassment, however, uncritically accepts the illusory coherence of scientific discourse and presumes that human subjectivity is essentially rather than multiply determined (overdetermined) in democratic societies. Yet there is overwhelming evidence in theory, research, and practice that mind, body, gender, sexuality are not facts we must live with but social constructions we have learned to live by.

Learning to Stand Together

Our goal in this essay is to discern the potential for a liberatory pedagogy of political analysis in the sexual harassment narratives. We understand such inquiry to be transformative, that is, intellectual work in which students and teachers think in terms of both epistemology (ways of knowing the world) and activism (ways of acting in the world). To this end, we have found it useful to review the narratives first in light of feminist standpoint theory (e.g., Hartsock, 1985), and then in light of critical pedagogy (e.g., Giroux, 1988) calling for educational projects of possibility that pose teachers and students as intellectual and political agents.

In *Money, Sex, and Power,* Nancy Hartsock argues that because women experience themselves as continuous with the world and men experience themselves as discontinuous with the world, they stand in materially different relationships with themselves, other people, and the world of objects. Thus, women and men view the world from entirely different and indeed opposing standpoints. Hartsock traces the construction of these opposing and gendered epistemologies to early childhood experiences of body and boundary as described in the work of Nancy Chodorow (1978), reasoning that girls, "because of female parenting, are less differentiated from others than boys, more continuous with and related to the external object world" (p. 238). Such a division of labor in parenting, argues Hartsock, means that "girls can identify with a concrete example present in daily life" while "boys must identify with an abstract set of maxims only occasionally present in the form of the father" (p. 238). Relationality is particularly useful in explaining how women reason from experience. And it is plausible to conclude, as Hartsock has, that designating women as the primary caretakers of children results in gender-differentiated epistemologies, in which even harassed women would tend to see, create, and value relationality.

While Hartsock's notions inform us about what women might have been trying to do in their narratives, the idea that a single feminist standpoint could account for all women is not plausible. It obscures the complexity and diminishes the importance of differences, such as race and class, in women's lives. Further, the theory does not address the extent to which personal development through "object relations" is confounded by the cultural hegemony that affects the way women think about, talk about, and organize against harassment in the academy. In other words, the struggle toward standpoint cannot be abstracted from the struggle against the distractions and attractions of dominant ideology (Gramsci, 1971). It is, after all, inside an academic hierarchy of asymmetrical relations between students and teachers that women students answered question 21 like "good" students, thereby representing their personal experience of sexual harassment in the same disinterested terminology used in the survey.

Saturating standpoint theory with the understanding that cultural hegemony is also determining, we are better able to under-stand how women students might have independently arrived at similar political stances in their narratives of sexual harassment. Instead of *describing* what happened, their narratives try to *explain* what happened by imagining what might have motivated their harassers and what might have happened had they reported the harassment. A standpoint of relationality may account for the formal structure of the narratives, but the contents spell hegemony. The transcendent narrator is a standpoint from which a writer can relate the concerns of harasser and harassed alike. But the motives and reprisals women name come out of that dreary stockpile of conclusions/premises/arguments that individualism and proceduralism commonly use to explain why "you can't fight city hall" and why men can't be held accountable for harassment.

The political potential of the standpoint of relationality as an activist epistemology is severely tested by the content of the sexual harassment narratives, inasmuch as it becomes clear that when women link the incident to men's motives and institutional reprisals, they are left standing alone and wishing they were not women. Their analysis of motives and reprisals leads them to believe that since men harass women for untold reasons, women who report harassment will be subjected to more of the same arbitrary treatment from the institution. The dispassionate language in which graduate women speculate on institutional reprisals is academic and this strikes us as all the more eerie not only because it reproduces the mind/body split, but because their fears are far from academic. Consider, for instance, the way in which this student juxtaposes form and content in the following passage:

> I *think* female graduate students *probably* bear the brunt of sexual harassment at the University. *Most* of the guys who harass you or *just make life difficult* are your teachers and dissertation committee members. Graduate students here have no power. We're dependent on our departments for financial aid, and are afraid that these professors *could* black-ball us in our future careers. (File 344-51; emphases ours)

Because sexual harassment is woven into the very fabric of faculty-student relations, women do not as a matter of course appeal to legal remedies; institutional procedures only further jeopardize their professional lives. Student complaints about sexual harassment are not likely to be taken as seriously by the institution as allegations of capricious grading or irregular office hours. While the modulated phrasing may mean that women students are confronting irrational behavior from their professors by responding rationally, and relationally, this very act of using their heads effectively preempts these women's taking an activist stance.

Harstock understands the epistemology of standpoint as liberatory:

> Because of its achieved character and its liberatory potential, I use the term "feminist" rather than "women's standpoint." Like the experiences of the proletariat, women's experience and activity as a dominated group contains both negative and positive aspects. A feminist standpoint picks out and amplifies the liberatory possibilities contained in that experience (p. 232).

We do not see relationality in the sexual harassment narratives as liberatory or even potentially so, and think it could only become so if feminist educators were willing to work with students to imagine liberatory possibilities not raised when analysis fetishizes individual men's motives and institutional reprisals. In other words, we see relationality as an epistemology that helps to explain the reasoning of women students who experience inequity, bypass their outrage, and rationalize that the way it is is all there is.

A subjugated standpoint does not necessarily facilitate collective activism on behalf of women who, in the absence of support, have individually devised ad hoc strategies for deflecting harassment. With such strategies, a particular woman may be able to prevent or protect herself against individual acts of harassment. Such strategies, however, neither interrupt nor disrupt the material and ideological gender asymmetries organizing the academy. Such strategies do not call public attention to sexual harassment as simply the most overt and explicit of those practices reminding women that we are not card-carrying members (pun intended) of the academic club (and again).

What we've learned from reading these narratives is that if the women appear not to have said "what really happened," that was because we were only listening for the legal categories that "count" as sexual harassment: that is, evidence of social transgressions that are specified by the EEOC guidelines and that can be documented empirically in terms that the court understands. The voices of women students in the sexual harassment narratives speak of a pervasive, routinized, and institutionalized sexual intimidation calling for a far more radical institutional project than heretofore suggested by either adversarial law or positioned feminism.

The violent behaviors that feminism and law bracket as sexual harassment and that institutions then treat as exceptional practices do not begin to capture the sense of danger lurking in the women's narratives. The unspoken oppression strikes us as all the more brutal when, as in the example below, difficulties with language suggest she may also be a foreign student:

> I went to private office to visit this person. He greeted me at the door, closed the door and locked it. He leaned over me, standing very close and started unbuttoning my overcoat. I fumbled with coat buttons trying to make light of/ignore his behavior, and trying to dissipate his sexual attention. He helped me remove my hat, coat, scarf and hang them up. He took my hand and led me over to couch in office. We had often sat in that part of the office before to chat, with him on couch (often lounging) and me on chair facing him. He sat down on couch and pulled me by my hand to sit next to him. I pulled to try to sit in chair as per usual; he would not let go. He lay down on couch and pulled me down to sit next to him on edge of couch, near his hip level. He released my hand and I moved back to far end of couch. There were no chairs nearby. I could not move to sit elsewhere without drawing tremendous attention to my action: 1) I would be overtly rejecting him if he was seriously pursuing me sexually; 2) I would be quite rude if he then decided to pretend he had no sexual intentions. My first thought was not to provoke him since the door was locked and the office quite soundproof. He kept urging me to sit closer to him and I declined. He finally took my hand and pulled me, I resisted but moved closer as a last resort before an outright struggle and possible scream. He kept holding my hand. He then tried to pull me down on top of him, coaxing me verbally. I refused. I stayed upright and using as much strength as necessary and shook my head no, looking him straight in the eye. Luckily, he wanted to seduce me, not assault me violently. (File 1974-31)

Her narrative reminds us that even though legal categories account for his behavior, she appeals not to law but popular psychology to explain her professor's motives: "I felt that this incident was due more to an ego-attack of older man (mid-60s) rather than the machinations of a sexual psychopath." If a stranger had attacked her on the street, no doubt she could have seen it as an assault. But she casts her professor's "strange" behavior in the most benign light possible—by comparing him to a psychopath—presumably so that she can imagine completing her studies:

> We have resumed our usual interactions. In this case, there was enough of a personal friendship to use as a basis to deal with the incident on a person-to-person way. Had that not been the case, however, I would have risked losing the support of an internationally renowned scholar with impressive professional contacts and influence. That's quite a bit of leverage to have over someone, isn't it? (File 1974-31)

This narrative is unusual because its extensive analysis is grounded in a description of the event itself. To be sure, she offers the usual explanations of motives, but she elaborates the harassing incident in tandem with her many modes of resistance before stating her ambivalence about the institutional vulnerability of graduate student women.

When oppression is normalized, privatized, and rooted in a powerful and pervasive institutional ambivalence toward the oppressed, a woman student is more likely to pose and resolve the conflict in her narrative by glossing the incident and concentrating on explanations:

> A mutual sexual attraction grew between myself and a professor. It was in part physical—in many settings and to people at large, the professor projects his sexuality—but was also based upon the discovery of shared values. This bond struck a chord with me, as I felt very lonely and isolated, for the usual—and institutionalized—reasons that graduate students feel this way. (File 1851-31)

Her seeming calm is soon belied, however, by a catalogue of fears iterated in many of the narratives: "I shortly grew alarmed both at the power of my own feelings and the increasing power of the professor's feelings"; "Although I did not feel physically threatened—that seemed unlikely—I became afraid that he would begin to manipulate me by using the power of my own feelings and my need for him"; "This fear arose as I learned how he was irrationally competitive with us [graduate students]"; "I felt that I had lost both his respect and his important professional support"; "I knew if needed he would not 'go to bat' for me in the personally influential ways that professors have to work for their students" (File 1851-31). In a later, more sustained passage, she explains why the fears that simmer internally are not to be expressed formally:

It seemed impossible to resolve the situation by talking it over with him—the relationship always had an unspoken nature about it, and he very likely would have stonewalled me, making me feel totally responsible for what had happened. I did not feel that it would be helpful to speak to any other faculty members given my own involvement and the provocative and controversial nature of a sexual and political relationship which is not even supposed to exist. I also feared discrediting myself and I felt that the faculty's personal loyalties rested with this professor. (File 1851-31)

The women who wrote the narratives know they've been treated unfairly by their professors. And while they do not blame themselves, their reluctance to insist that professors are responsible leaves women students recognizing harassment but transfixed rather than transformed by their knowledge of oppression (see Fine, 1986). The fact that personal knowledge does not necessarily become grounds for political action is clear not only from the narratives, but from the survey. Even though 45% of graduate and professional women students reported some sexual harassment over the past five years, over 80% handled it "by ignoring or going along with it or by avoiding contact with the offender." And, indeed, only between 0% and 6% of graduate students (depending on the type of harassment) report filing a formal grievance in response to an incident of harassment (de Cani, Fine, Sagi, & Stern, 1985, p. viii).

Feminist interpretation means reading these stories as true but partial accounts of sexual harassment. But feminist pedagogy strives to recover the intellectual and creative energy dispersed when women try to transcend their bodies and find themselves standing alone against their harassers. This is a pedagogy that would transform that wasted individual energy into a collective desire to identify and examine the institutional practices that succor sexual harassment and begin to institute counterpractices that do not. The possibilities for pedagogy in the next section arise out of our analysis of the narratives and pose a feminist project in terms of transforming the scene of institutional harassment so that women in the academy are free to study and teach—with our bodies and minds intact.

Learning How to Speak in the Academy

In this section we set out to amplify in pedagogy some political projects that we now think may have been attenuated in the sexual harassment narratives. We do this realizing that the survey itself may have encouraged harassed women to resolve prematurely the tensions and complexities their narratives posed. The designers of the survey had hoped that open-ended questions would offer women students an opportunity for both critique and empowerment. Instead, women respondents commonly took this opportunity to consolidate experiences about which they were seemingly quite ambivalent and effectively returned all responsibility for advocacy to the committee. At least this is how we have come to understand the lengths some women went to in thanking the committee:

> Thanks for your concern over this issue. I realize that I was less than responsible to my fellow students for not pursuing a formal "complaint" but I'm glad to help with the survey. (File 1799-11)

> I do appreciate being able to tell someone about this who will take this information seriously. (File 1851-31)

> I thank you for conducting this questionnaire. I hope you publish the results and information on the procedure for reporting situations. (File 1486-11)

> Thanks for listening! (File 1418-31)

We take seriously Giroux's reminder that "oppositional political projects. . . should be the object of constant debate and analysis" (p. 69). We recommend basing the curriculum on a *negative critique* of these and/or other individualistic and futile attempts to interrogate or interrupt forms of institutional oppression organized around gender, race, and social class. Central to this project is the demystification of institutional policies and practices that cloak social inequities. We need to engage young women and men in exploring how our analyses of the causes and consequences of social inequities construct not only our understandings of the present, but our images of what is possible in the near or far future. Unable to imagine institutional change, the women who wrote the sexual harassment narratives default to reworking relationships with faculty, or, even more consequentially, to reworking or denying their bodies.

Feminist pedagogy begins by animating the policies and procedures that contribute to harassment. The faceless image of authority sustains the illusion that institutions are immutable and hence oppression inevitable. This is the illusion feminists must first seek to dispel if we hope to enable young women and men to see oppression as mutable through critical and collective reflection and action. A pedagogy intentionally remote from political activism incidentally fosters the very alienation, individualism, and cynicism we confronted in these narratives. We were heartened to find young women who grew up in the wake of civil rights legislation and witnessed the victories and losses of movement feminism in the courts and state legislatures struggling against harassment. Their collective narrative, however, is a story of despair, for each woman encounters the lechery of professors alone, with little hope that law can, or that the institution will, intercede on her behalf. And so she tries to rise above the scene of harassment in narratives reminding us that the halls of academe are littered with the bodies women students leave hostage in their flight from professorial treachery.

We could set an intellectual and political process in motion by asking students to imagine how a series of university representatives might respond to the narratives. What would the university counsel, the lawyer whose job it is to subvert grievances and suits against the institution, make of a narrative about the institutional threat of violence rather than an actual act of violence? How might the director of the Women's Center respond? Or a feminist professor? A non-feminist professor? A faculty member who has been or thinks he may be named in a sexual harassment suit? The editor of the student newspaper or the alumni magazine? And what about the dean of the school? The man or woman chairing the department? The president of the university? The president of student government or the faculty senate? The counseling staff? What changes if we know that the narrator is white, black, straight, gay? The harasser white, black, straight, gay? While the list is far from complete, it points out that since institutions speak not one but several "languages," students need to apprise themselves of the range of "dialects" representing their university.

At any given moment in its history, the representatives of a university will be unevenly committed to preserving the status quo, which means that the possibilities for political change are always contingent on revealing heterogeneity within what only appears to be a single voice to outsiders. While it is nearly always the case that the university lawyer will not hear such a narrative, the other representatives are not nearly so predictable in their responses. The related narrative task suggested by the first is, of course, revision.

Having imagined what university representatives might do with the narrative as written, how might a particular narrative be rewritten to secure a hearing from each of the representatives? We are not suggesting an *exercise* in writing for audiences, but recommending that students do this kind of imaginative work before they meet and interview representatives concerning their jobs and their positions on harassment of women and minority constituencies on campus. This collaborative work requires students to take careful notes, report back to peers and faculty, and compare findings and impressions; they should do this before making any decisions about who and what to write, and before making plans for more sustained collective action. We see what can be learned from representatives of the institution as a first lesson in understanding how power is or is not dispersed locally and as a first step toward interrupting the illusion that institutional authority is literally anonymous.

What happens next is of course contingent on what students and teachers are willing to deem appropriate under the circumstances. Students might go on to write a white paper on the status of women students on their campus, a series of articles for the student or a city newspaper, a pamphlet for entering students and their parents, a broadside for students, faculty, and staff. Or they might decide that their preliminary research warrants additional studies of the institution and its relations with students on a number of issues that include but are not bounded by sexual harassment. The point is that it would be pedagogically irresponsible to set up an intellectual exploration such as we are suggesting and assume that students will have succeeded only if they reproduce familiar feminist analyses, that is, execute what we have already conceptualized. There is no feminist standpoint they must find. There is instead a feminist project, struggling to find the crevices in the institutional facade that glosses over oppression of students, staff, and faculty across lines of race, class, and gender.

The unevenness of institutional commitment to the status quo does not mean that any particular strategy meant to engage university representatives in a conversation will result in desired/ desirable political change. We have only to review the recent political successes of the New Right in the academy and elsewhere to realize that heterogeneity is itself no guarantee that discussions will move administrations to more progressive policies. While speaking is certainly a form of action, institutional representatives often understand talk as a way of appeasing and defusing student, faculty, and staff activists. Students as well as educators need to bear in mind that talking and writing to representatives may not be enough unless they are also willing to enlist support from institutions that are (or have representatives who are) interested in their university. Included among the possibilities are: the press, professional organizations, legislators, community activists committed to gender and race equity, alumni, well known political "radicals" willing to visit campus and speak out for students, and parents who thought that education would support, not undermine, their children. While political networking is as difficult to learn as to maintain, such a network is critical both as a lever for starting conversation inside the institution and as an alternative if, or once, a conversation breaks down. Outside the boundaries arbitrarily set by the academy, moreover, young women and men are sometimes better positioned to notice and interrupt the institution's version of reality and protectionism, and so better positioned to represent themselves as informed and critical agents of change.

Learning What to Do When Talk Is Just Talk

Women have been known to contemplate and even commit outrageous acts when conversation fails. The most dramatic example we know of happened at the University of Pennsylvania in the early 1980s. Once a week, with great regularity, the campus was secretly decorated with photographs of prominent male faculty, whose pictures were captioned "WANTED FOR CRIMES AGAINST WOMEN" and signed by "The Women's Army." Along with others, we presumed this to be the work of a small group of undergraduate women who, distressed that conversation with the provost, university government, and individual faculty failed to draw sufficient attention to problems of sexual harassment, resorted to extraordinary methods for naming the problem.

University officials and many faculty were alarmed that the "Women's Army" was irresponsibly accusing men. Which it was. Yet we also read these actions as evidence of the women's despair over adamant institutional refusal to listen and act. At the time, Penn had an elaborate set of mechanisms for voicing student dissent, but "listening" was revealed as a way to appropriate such dissent, that is, to appease "angry young women." We have heard that at some other institutions, young women on campus welcome parents on Parents Day with the gruesome statistics of the likelihood that their daughter will be harassed and/or raped during her four years at college.

We are not recommending these strategies. They are not attempts to alter the conditions of women's lives. They are the voices of despair that institutional indifference provokes. People have been known, however, to throw caution to the wind when institutions refuse to talk, or when they intentionally set out to confound by offering talk in lieu of policy. Women are particularly vulnerable once engaged in conversation, since the willingness to talk is considered the most important evidence of growing trust and cooperation. And most of us, needless to say, find it excruciatingly difficult to break frame and "go public," even when it becomes evident that the official conversation is fruitless.

While the work of the "Women's Army" and their sisters elsewhere does not provide models of political projects aimed toward transformation, the outrageous is nonetheless of untold pedagogical value. Worst-case scenarios stretch the sense of possibility even as they terrorize the imagination. Images of the "irrational strategies" we may want to avoid help us to imagine how to insist that institutions take seriously their conversations with women.

Feminist Archives for Intellectual Activism

The analysis suggests the need for an archive of feminist intellectual activism to chronicle the varied ways of identifying, analyzing, interrupting, and, under exceptionally perverse circumstances, disrupting gender-based power asymmetries in the academy. Feminist activism must reposition itself inside a larger politics of solidarity with "other self-conscious political projects" (Harding, 1988, p. 163), which at the very least would also include struggles around race/ethnicity, class, disability, and sexual orientation. Such an archive could already be stocked with: reports of the re-emergence of women's consciousness raising groups on campus; core curricula which mainstream feminist, African-American, and Third World scholarship (and organized efforts to marginalize or eliminate them); charters for establishing women's centers; arguments for developing gay men's and lesbian women's studies programs; policies of professional organizations that monitor the use of sexist language in presentations and publications (Conference on College Composition and Communication) or the presence of African-American studies and women's studies courses within accredited programs (American Psychological Association).

As impressive as we find this list, the narratives caution us that far more is needed. This new generation of women is equipped with a striking sense of entitlement and yet beset by fears that their female bodies are liabilities, their minds male, their professors likely to corrupt their intellectual relationships, and their legal rights hollow. We can't anticipate what they will contribute to either the archive or the struggle, but social history assures us that it will not be precisely what we added. After all, they inherited rather than advocated for the gains of the 1970s, yet they share the threat of stunning disappointments in the 1980s and 1990s.

Perhaps the lesson we most need to learn is that it is as important for students as it is for teachers to become researchers— students as well as teachers are intellectuals and need to see themselves as informed political agents. We have learned that teachers and students need to collaborate critically across generations, histories, life circumstances, and politics to create curricula and pedagogies that seek to transform institutions not by reproducing or resisting the practices of oppression, but by confronting the institution on intellectual grounds. Only thus can we imagine a context in which every woman's story could realize its full liberatory potential, and no woman would decline to tell her story because "Any information would be incriminating" (File 2174–C31).

Notes

1. We take this opportunity to thank the Quad Women's Group, the undergraduate women at Penn who in the four years we met with them weekly surprised and delighted us with stories of their lives as students, daughters, lovers, and friends. This essay is infused with dreams, desires, and fears that materialized in those sessions and emerge here in our own academic dream of a story in which women stand together in their struggle to reclaim the bodies that accompany their minds.

2. The Penn Harassment Survey was sent to students, faculty, and staff in March of 1985, and the Report of the Committee to Survey Harassment at the University of Pennsylvania was published the following Fall in the *Almanac,* the weekly university publication for staff and faculty (de Cani, Fine, Sagi, & Stern, 1985). The committee reported that 1,065 of the 2,251 usable questionnaires included answers to open-ended questions. Concerning undergraduate and graduate women's responses to the open-ended question asking them to describe an experience of harassment, 37 of the 66 undergraduate responses reported harassment by either professors or teaching assistants and 44 of the 68 graduate responses concerned professors. While we did not include their narratives in this essay, readers will be interested to learn that of the 36 untenured women faculty at Penn who wrote about

harassment, 17 reported being harassed by faculty (13 of whom were senior) and 1 by her dean; that 12 of 20 responses from tenured women faculty definitely concerned another faculty member (including 2 department chairs); and that 18 of the 32 women staff who responded reported being harassed by either their supervisors or faculty (pp. IX-X). That any woman at Penn is potentially subject to harassment, regardless of status, reminds us that some men violate women's civil rights as a matter of course and that they do so with relative impunity inside the academy.

References

Belsey, C. (1980). *Critical practice.* New York: Methuen.

Brodkey, L. (1989). On the subjects of class and gender in *The literacy letters. College English, 51*(2), 125–141.

Caplan, C. (1986). *Sea changes: Essays on culture and feminism.* London: Verso.

Chodorow, N. (1978). *The reproduction of mothering: Psychoanalysis and the sociology of gender.* Berkeley: University of California Press.

de Cani, J., Fine, M., Sagi, P., & Stern, M. (1985). Report of the committee to survey harassment at the University of Pennsylvania. *Almanac, 32* (September 24), II-XII.

Fine, M. (1986). Contextualizing the study of social injustice. In M. Saxe & L. Saxe (Eds.), *Advances in applied social psychology* (Vol. 3). New Jersey: Lawrence Erlbaum.

Giroux, H. (1988). *Schooling and the struggle for public life: Critical pedagogy in the modern age.* Minneapolis: University of Minnesota Press.

Gramsci, A. (1971). *Selections from the prison notebooks.* New York: International Publishers.

Haraway, D. (1988). Situated knowledges: The science question in feminism and the privilege of partial perspective. *Feminist Studies, 14,* 575–599.

Harding, S. (1988). *The science question in feminism.* Ithaca: Cornell University Press.

Hartsock, N. (1985). *Money, sex, and power.* Boston: Northeastern University Press.

Kolodny, A. (1988). Dancing between left and right: Feminism and the academic minefield in the 1980s. *Feminist Studies, 14,* 453–466.

Penn Harassment Survey. (1985). Philadelphia: Office of the Vice-Provost for Research, University of Pennsylvania.

Robertson, C., Dwyer, C. E., & Campbell, D. (1988). Campus harassment: Sexual harassment policies and procedures at institutions of higher learning. *Signs, 13,* 792–812.

Knowledge, Power, and Discourse in Social Studies Education[1]

Cleo Cherryholmes

Social studies education has to do with teaching about our knowledge and understanding of society. Discourse about social studies education ranges across a wide variety of topics, from what we know and think we understand about society to methods of classroom instruction. A recent body of literature has begun to develop that considers how social phenomena influence social studies education and discourse about it. Anyon (1981) has demonstrated the constraint of social class stratification on classroom practice; Cherryholmes (1980), the pervasiveness and control of objectified, positivist treatments of social structures and processes; Giroux (1982b), ways in which existing social relations are reproduced through social studies education; and Popkewitz (1979), the impact of ideology on our research and practice. The purpose of this essay is to contribute along these lines, to illuminate further how what is said about social studies education is a function and product of the materiality of other social practices and discourses.

To begin, consider the nature of discourse and discursive practices. What is discourse? Benveniste (1971) gives this characterization:

> Discourse must be understood in its widest sense: every utterance assuming a speaker and a hearer, and in the speaker, the intention of influencing the other in some way. . . . But discourse is written as well as spoken. In practice one passes from one to the other instantaneously. (p. 209)

The utterances that constitute a discourse are not randomly put together. A discourse does not admit linguistic anarchy. A discursive practice structures a discourse. In order to figure out where knowledge and power fit in social studies education it is necessary to gain insight into its discursive practice. A discursive practice, Foucault writes, "is a body of anonymous, historical rules, always determined in the time and space that have definced a given period, and for a given social, economic, geographical, or linguistic area, the conditions of the enunciative formation." (1972a, p. 117)

Discourse, whether it concerns fields Foucault has studied such as the development of modern penal institutions, grammar, or sexuality, or is about social studies education, occurs within a system of rules. The anonymous, historically conditioned rules that constitute a discursive practice nominate those who can speak with authority, create the possibility for what can be said and—just as important— dictate what remains unsaid. However, Foucault's description of these rules as anonymous needs to be qualified. In social studies education, for example, some of the rules by which discourse proceeds may be legal, such as those that determine procedures whereby social studies textbooks are approved by a state selection committee. Or the rules may be administrative directives, such as those adopted by a local school board or curriculum committee. Or the rules may represent professional norms and commitments such as those found in social studies methods textbooks and professional journals. In the broadest sense knowing the rules of a discourse, whether one is able to state them or not, is knowing who may contribute to it and what is an appropriate contribution.

In social studies discourse there are people who speak to hearers about what they know and think they understand about society and how to teach about it according to some set of rules. The relationship between the subjects and objects of social studies discourse is presented, when it is explicitly considered at all, as unidirectional: subjects speak about objects. Social scientists speak about voting, constitutions, land forms, past wars and revolutions, natural resources, and so on. Social studies educators speak about teaching methods, testing procedures, and the like. Discourse about social studies education has often been among individuals (subjects) talking about and acting on the social structures of society and the school (objects). At best, this is only half the picture. The question posed here is how the social structures of practices and discourses shape, both through constraint and through the creation of opportunity, state- ments about social studies education. This may be thought of in terms of Giddens's (1979) theory of structuration, which can be applied to help us understand how in social studies discourse social structure and human action produce and reproduce each other anew. Giddens argues that "the structural properties of social systems are both the medium and the outcome of the practices that constitute those systems" (p. 69).

Two lines of thought from quite different traditions will be brought together: speech act theory from the work of English analytic philosophers will be combined with some ideas that have been advanced in Michel Foucault's work on the history of systems of ideas. Speech act theory focuses on acts performed when statements are uttered. Foucault's thought is more concerned with macro-level social structures within which discourses are conducted. It will be shown that these different ways of looking at the uses of language are complementary and together offer important insights into contemporary discourse about social studies education.

The Philosophy of Language and Michel Foucault

The view of language that speech act theory brings to the analysis of discourse is that when one makes an utterance one is performing an act. What one is doing in making a statement is grounded in previously existing conventions, institutions, and social practices. Speech act theory underscores the materiality of discourse. Austin (1968) and Searle (1969) made important contributions to the philosophy of language with the notions, respectively, of performative utterances and speech act theory. Before Austin's work speaking was often thought of as making utterances about something external to language. Language was transparent or neutral. In the positivist view statements were analytic, synthetic, or nonsense (Ayer, 1946). Austin showed that under appropriate conditions saying something was doing something. Searle (1971) later demonstrated that this was true of all utterances and not—as Austin had first thought—solely those that were first person singular, present indicative, and active.

When someone says, "I think social studies education should concentrate on American history and values," they are *advocating* an educational goal. Another person might argue that "Students cannot analyze complex social problems before the eighth grade," and be *describing* the results of a selected piece of child development research and/or *prescribing* a course of action. Austin originally contended that speech acts were successful when a given set of conditions were met: an accepted conventional procedure was present, the circumstances were appropriate, the procedure was executed correctly and completely, the individual was sincere, and the speaker so conducted herself/himself (1968, pp. 14–15). Under this construction speech acts took place in the context of integrated and well-defined social institutions.

When Searle expanded the argument to include all utterances, an additional problem was raised. In the most straightforward case a speech act acquires its meaning and force from background conventions, circumstances, and procedures. When the institutional backdrop is less clear the speech act and its meaning are likewise less clear. There may be no definite institution to give an utterance its meaning or there may be conflicting background institutions that produce confusion or ambiguity for the hearer. In some cases the speech act is not problematic; in other cases the act being performed must be ferreted out as its meaning is negotiated and clarified.

Speech act theorists have attended more to speech acts and less to the institutional rule-giving context of speech acts. Foucault, on the other hand, focuses on the structural characteristics of discourse. Said (1975) sees a connection between these two types of discourse analysis, based on grouping Foucault with the French structuralists:

> Thus the main group of French structuralists sees the world as a closed set of what J. L. Austin calls "performative statements." Closed not because its limits can be grasped as a totality, but because its first and beginning functional principles are a finite set of rules. (p. 331)

Habermas (1979) draws the connection between speech acts and institutional context a bit differently:

> The acceptability of a speech act depends on (among other things)...the existence of speech-act-typically restricted contexts....The illocutionary force of a speech act consists in its capacity to move a hearer to act under the premise that the engagement signalled by the speaker is seriously meant: in the case of institutionally bound speech acts, the speaker can borrow this force from the binding force of existing norms. (p. 65)

Foucault's rules for a discursive practice go a long way toward constituting the background conditions that give meaning and force to a speech act.[2]

Discourse is constituted by utterances. What we claim to know and what we claim as true are linguistic. An adequate account of discourse, therefore, will also account in some way for truth and knowledge. Foucault (1980) develops this view of truth:

Truth is a thing of this world: it is produced only by virtue of multiple forms of constraint. And it induces regular effects of power. Each society has its regime of truth, its "general politics" of truth: that is, the types of discourse which it accepts and makes function as true; the mechanisms and instances which enable one to distinguish true and false statements, the means by which each is sanctioned; the techniques and procedures accorded value in the acquisition of truth; the status of those who are charged with saying what counts as true. (p. 131)

The rules of a discursive practice emanate from underlying power relations. Rules and power relations constrain what can be said and designate those who can speak. "Power," as used here, refers to social, political, and/or material asymmetries by which people are differentially rewarded and indulged for performing certain acts and sanctioned and deprived for performing other acts. The rules by which discourse is conducted are not just guidelines to linguistic usages; they represent material and social conditions. Putnam (1975) makes a point about meaning along the same line. The meaning of a word is determined in part by a sociolinguistic division of labor that represents an underlying material division of labor.

Knowledge claims and power relations interpenetrate. This is readily comprehended when it is considered that knowledge claims are products of discourse and discourse is structured by rules and power relations. Furthermore, what we claim to know is often used in attempts to legitimize or contest existing power relationships. Power as the social, political, and material substructure of discourse operates to create opportunities for what can be said as well as suppress what remains unspoken:

What makes power hold good, what makes it accepted, is simply the fact that it doesn't only weigh on us as a force that says no, but that it traverses and produces things, it induces pleasure, forms knowledge, produces discourse. *It needs to be considered as a productive network* which runs through the whole social body, much more than as a negative instance whose function is repression. (Foucault, 1980, p. 199, emphasis added)

In the case of social studies education, power resides in the state and its textbook adoption procedures and is invested in those who serve on textbook adoption committees. Through their deliberations and decisions, state textbook adoption committees enunciate rules that define what can be written in social studies textbooks. These rules also prescribe topics on which authors must remain silent. In the case of teacher education programs, power is held by social studies methods teachers; they are privileged to say what counts as knowledge in the field.

There is yet another side to discursive practices. People make commitments to the discourses in which they participate. They believe in the validity and rightness of how to proceed. This is an ideological dimension of discourse. Bernstein (1976) views ideology as a "set of moral, social, or political beliefs and attitudes that informs and shapes an individual's (or a class's) interpretation of the world and his behavior. . . . Ideologies are based upon beliefs and interpretations which purport to be true or valid" (pp. 107–108). Here ideology has an ideal but not material side. It has both normative and empirical content in commitments and understandings about the way the world is and should be. Giroux (1982b) connects these beliefs and interpretations to the materiality of social relations: "The character of ideology is mental, but its effectivity is both psychological and behavioral; its effects are rooted not only in human action but also inscribed in material culture" (p. 31). Power relations are rationalized in terms of ideological commitments and beliefs. There is a widespread commitment among social studies educators to social scientific research as a method of determining the effectiveness of instructional techniques and curriculum materials. Authority to speak on these matters resides with those who are skilled researchers. Ideological commitments are grounded in such social arrangements and beliefs.

Power relations and the normative commitments they represent shape a discursive practice and determine what can be said and not said. But these factors have been largely excluded from discussions about social studies education. Much has been said about how things are and should be. Little has been said about how the way things are determine what is said and can be said. Utterances are acts; they are material. If it is never considered how our utterances are products of social processes and power relations, then we cannot claim to be deeply reflective about or in control of what we do. Shapiro's comment on Foucault is particularly insightful: "It would be appropriate within his [Foucault's] view, to reverse the familiar notion that persons make statements, and say that statements make persons" (1981, p. 141). Power, as it were, puts words in our mouths. Discursive practices antedate speakers; they outlast speakers.

At this point, it is useful to go back to speech act theory because it provides a thoughtful perspective for some of the claims just made.

If Searle is correct that all speech is performative it is also the case that what is being done is much clearer in some instances than in others. The first performative utterances identified by Austin were straightforward: "I promise," "I do" (as in a wedding ceremony), and "I bet." But it is less clear what is being done with other utterances, such as "Should social studies education concentrate on developing democratic values or teaching historical and geographical facts?" A question is being asked, but what does the question mean? Are any conventions other than a linguistic request for a judgment or opinion being invoked? To answer this in any detailed way would require information about the circumstances and situation. For example, was this question posed by a parent at a school board meeting or by a social studies methods teacher to a class of prospective teachers? In either situation one might ask why other goals were not mentioned, such as the promotion of social justice or global understanding. The statement is a linguistic *product* whereby intentions and meanings are negotiated, modified, and created.

It is an exaggeration, I think, to claim that all utterances are entirely determined by the discursive practice in which they occur. There are several reasons for backing away from such a determinate position. First, not all discursive practices are equally well integrated. As one moves from informal to formal discourse, say from classroom conversation to a judicial hearing, the statements that are admissable, who may speak, who has authority, and so on are much less open to question. Second, priorities must be determined at the boundaries of a discursive practice when it comes in contact with other discursive practices or material arrangements. For example, when the issue is one of determining what goals should be promoted in public education there is likely to be a wider variation in suggestions if parents and members of the business community are involved than if educators are the sole participants. Third, for whatever reason, say because of incomplete socialization, an individual may challenge and violate the "anonymous, historical rules" that govern the discourse. (For example, someone may inject into the conversation mentioned above that schools should not train students simply for jobs in the economy since that would serve to reproduce the existing economic system along with its inequities. Someone else might argue that schools should facilitate an individual's personal growth and psychological fulfillment.) Fourth, the different institutions that embody and enforce "anonymous, historical rules" will not police all utterances with equal and unvarying vigilance. Just as incomplete or erratic socialization of an individual contributes to variance in what is said, different settings and conditions admit utterances of a wider range. Across discursive practices there is variation in utterances that are offered and there is variation in utterances that will be indulged, tolerated, and taken seriously.

At the general level of social discourse Foucault's analysis undoubtedly is on target in many important ways. But speech act theory at the level of specific utterances points to some discursive looseness and slack. What is being suggested is that the lack of social and linguistic integration provides an opportunity to break out of ongoing discursive practices. More needs to be said, however, about how one can gain control of discourse.

Following Foucault's argument (1973, pp. ix-xiv), one can identify three elements in a disciplinary discourse such as that about social studies education. There are principles of *formation* that order how objects, concepts, theories, and so on are organized and identify what the discourse is about. There are principles of *transformation* that govern how progress is made and what counts as progress in the field, such as the role of opinion vs. valid research findings. There are *correlations* between the field and its several environments. For example, social studies education has relationships with quantitative research, public policy analysis, child development research, the social sciences, and ethical and normative theory to name a few. Said (1975) expressed Foucault's handling of these three factors very well: "The originality of Foucault's criteria is the effect of their use *together*....Putting them together...robs any one of them of a privilege over the others: thus the potentially exclusive inwardness of 'formation' is corrected by an exterior 'correlation'" (p. 309). Discourse about social studies education often takes the fragmented tack that Foucault argues against. It is easy to slip into a style of analysis that lets one focus on the academic structure of social studies education or discuss its history without considering external influences and constraints. Said (1975) offers penetrating insight into Foucault's thought:

> In emphasizing the detailed complications of these criteria, Foucault shows them to be—from the standpoint of a historian—demonstrably effective in separating words from things, in making it clear once and for all that words operate according to laws of their own. (p. 310)

Depending upon the criterion one chooses, whether it is formation, transformation, or correlation, one can construct coherent, plausible, and *separate* accounts of social studies education. Even though each discursive account is constructed on its own terms, the events are the same. But in order to understand fully each account, one must lay bare and make explicit the discursive practice and social structure from which it developed. If one were to provide an analysis of social studies education internal to the endeavor or if one demonstrated how things historically got the way they are, without relating either to external practices, one would be left primarily with discursive artifacts. These artifacts might tell us how certain objects and events fit and are organized within a discursive practice, but they would not give us control over that practice.

Foucault (1972b) does not focus just on overdetermination and control. He is also interested in a progressive politics that moves beyond determination. A necessary condition for progressive politics is that the "anonymous and historically conditioned" rules that structure discourse and politics be made explicit:

A progressive politics is one which recognizes the historic conditions and the specified rules of a practice. . . . A progressive politics is one which defines in a practice the possibilities of transformations and the play of dependencies between these transformations. . . . A progressive politics does not make of man. . . the universal operator . . . it defines the levels and the different functions which the subjects can occupy in a domain which has its rules of formation. . . . A progressive politics. . . consider[s] that the discourses. . . form a practice which is articulated upon. . . other practices. . . . A progressive politics, with respect to the scientific discourse, does not find itself in a position of "perpetual demand" or of "sovereign criticism," but it must know the manner in which the diverse scientific discourses, in their positivity. . . are part of a system of correlations with other practices. (pp. 246–247)

A progressive politics is one that is concerned with illuminating the structure within which the politics of everyday life is conducted. By focusing on the structural elements of what we are discussing and doing, the goal is to gain insight into why we claim to know what we do and why we do what we do. This brings us back to our original question: What counts as knowledge in social studies education and what power relations and ideological commitments structure this view of things? Knowledge and power not only interpenetrate; they are mutually constitutive. Knowledge is related to power in social studies education not only by making assertions about power as a subject matter. Knowledge is also related to power because it is the product of power. What counts as knowledge in social studies education is constrained by power relations that are internal as well as external to the discipline and profession. Now we will consider how the dependencies among discursive formation, transformation, and correlation play out in some areas of discourse about social studies education.

Three Traditions in Social Studies Education

Barr, Barth, and Shermis (1977) identify three orientations to social studies education: citizenship transmission, the social science disciplines, and reflective inquiry. For analytic purposes the operative assumption here is that these are coherent, noncontradictory schools of thought.

"The purpose of Citizenship Transmission is that a particular conception of citizenship shall be both learned and believed" (Barr, Barth, & Shermis, 1977, p. 59). If there is a discursive practice in social studies education that promotes citizenship transmission, where is it to be found? Barr, Barth, and Shermis give us hints of what to look for and where to look: "Citizenship Transmission teachers begin with a set of oughts and givens—that is, knowledge, assumptions, and beliefs which are treated as self-evident truths which need to be accepted at face value" (p. 60). They continue by suggesting that this content finds its way into texts, syllabi, and state-mandated guidelines.

Consider the discursive contributions of social studies textbooks. Elementary social studies textbooks follow rather closely the expanding "communities of man" orientation advocated by Hanna (1963). This is found in almost all such series that are currently on the market. The point that Barr, Barth, and Shermis make about treating knowledge as "self-evident truths which need to be accepted at face value" is evident in these materials. The text materials are heavily laden with geographical and historical knowledge claims; controversy is avoided. Knowledge claims about evolution, social justice, political beliefs, social class, equality, and political power are, for the most part, absent.

Some of the ideological commitments and supporting or contesting power relations behind citizenship transmission are obvious, others less so. The major underlying commitment is to social institutions and processes as they are presently arranged. The status quo is implicitly, when not explicitly, supported and positively valued. Because of the largely implicit nature of this evaluation the discussion of social knowledge and issues is hardly open to interpretation, let alone criticism. The ideological commitment is to the reproduction of society as it is. Loyalty to the government and obedience to the law encourages a view of society that focuses on cooperation and consensus and avoids controversy and conflict (Apple, 1971).

When one asks what underlying power relations support this discursive practice it is clear that *the market situation* within which textbooks are produced and sold supports citizenship transmission. Textbook publishers make large financial investments in order to produce books that are well written, stylishly produced, and visually appealing. A kindergarten through grade six elementary textbook series may involve a capital outlay of $2,500,000 to $3,000,000; a single secondary school text may often cost more than $400,000. In many states there is strong competition among publishers to win inclusion on state-approved lists. Most of these "closed" states are in more conservative areas of the country. Therefore, a rational strategy for textbook publishers to follow, assuming they have a goal of profit maximization, is to develop a product designed not to offend persons with a conservative social orientation. Companies vie for advantage in terms of format, maps, style, teacher editions, tests, and so on, but they do so within a fairly standard approach to social studies. The market situation is such that vocal conservative textbook critics are often perceived as having a veto over textbook selection. The extent to which they actually can exercise a veto obviously varies from one locale to another, but it is rational for a publisher to adopt a conservative production and marketing strategy. A minimax regret decision rule seems to be operative, where one acts in such a way as to minimize one's maximum regret. In this case the regret to be minimized is lost textbook sales.

Textbook content is largely anonymous in Foucault's sense. Advertisements for textbooks underscore their anonymity. Ads that run in *Social Education,* for example, almost never list authors. Ad copy stresses "increased content coverage," "more skills development," "added statistical data," "redesigned maps," and so on. One might hypothesize that as the power relations that shape a discourse become stronger the discourse itself becomes more anonymous. It becomes more anonymous because fewer degrees of freedom exist for variation. Although textbook authors may like to think they are writing innovative materials and breaking "new ground," in fact the discourse is structured by powerful, external forces. Normative commitments embedded in textbook discourse are submerged in the commonality of what is being said and what is left unsaid.

A second major orientation to social studies education identified by Barr, Barth, and Shermis is grounded in the content and methods of the social sciences. The normative commitment left implicit is to a society composed of rational, calculating citizens who go about solving their own and society's problems. There is little room for value analysis because mainstream social science purports to be value-free. A goal of the disciplines is to describe and explain things by generating and testing theories. (See Bernstein, 1976, chapter 1 for a detailed account of this view of the social sciences.).

This discourse differs from citizenship transmission in that its rules for inclusion and exclusion are not found in the market. The rules are derivative from social science methodology and activities. This is a fundamentally conservative position because social and political structures are accepted as given. The social scientist according to positivist or neo-positivist interpretations has no role in changing society, only in analyzing and understanding it. There are other inter-pretations of social science, such as those found in phenomenology (Schutz, 1963) or critical theory (Habermas, 1971), but these have had little impact as yet on social science research conducted in the United States.

Social scientists determine what counts as knowledge. They decide what can be talked about and what is left unsaid. If the subject is politics, for example, topics of discussion may include political party affiliation, voting turnout, party platforms, and political structures, while discussion of socio-economic inequality and injustice are excluded.

The neo-positivist influence on mainstream social science contains an epistemological orientation that is conservative in its acceptance of social structures as they are. (See Cherryholmes, 1980, for a detailed account of this in social studies education.) The power relations that support this discursive practice are centered in the social science disciplines and operate in terms of what is allowed to count as knowledge. What counts as knowledge is still largely influenced by the positivist view of cognitive significance that statements are only meaningful if their truth or falsity can be determined (Carnap, 1966).

The deference that educators pay to social scientists and their norms reinforces the authority of the scholars. It is important to note that the views of human nature and of society espoused by the citizenship transmission and social science traditions are fundamentally reinforcing. Their normative commitments ostensibly are to different outcomes: citizenship transmission to tradition and things as they are, and social science disciplines to social scientific knowledge and rational, social calculation. The supporting sets of power relations are also quite different. But the consequences are reinforcing. Things are to be apprehended as they appear, and fundamental questions about the nature of society and social processes are not to be posed. The two discourses function to include and exclude many of the same topics.

Barr, Barth, and Shermis identify reflective inquiry as yet a third approach to citizenship education. "The purpose of Reflective Inquiry is citizenship defined primarily as decision making in a socio-political context" (p. 64). This is decision making broadly construed. Advocates of reflective inquiry do not distinguish between "method" and "content" as do social science advocates. Instead the method of identifying and solving problems is assumed to interact explicitly with the content that defines the problem and its solution. The foremost treatment in the social studies literature can be found in Hunt and Metcalf (1968), a distinguished and well-known social studies methods text. The focus of reflective inquiry is not just on a rational, calculating citizenry as in the social science traditions but also involves a questioning of personal values. Barr, Barth, and Shermis argue: "The Reflective Inquiry problem is a two-pronged affair: it points outward to objective, empirical phenomena, and it points inward to perceived feelings and values and private outlooks. It is both a social and a personal problem" (p. 66). Reflective inquiry conceives of the citizen as contemplative and active. But the structures within which action is taken are sometimes taken for granted. Hunt and Metcalf probed the closed areas of society and raised questions about social structure even though they did not take the argument concerning social inquiry as far as other writers have recently (Giroux, 1982b; Anyon, 1981).

Cherryholmes (1980) contrasts assumptions in social studies education that are based on the work of Karl Popper to those based on the ideas of Jurgen Habermas, showing that classroom inquiry as outlined in Hunt and Metcalf represents only one view of social science and social studies inquiry. Giroux (1982a) provides a detailed and informative introduction to critical theory as an alternative view of social studies education.

The power relationships that support this view of social studies education are weak indeed when compared with citizenship transmission or even social science education. The force of the reflective inquiry position derives from the relatively specialized academic base of philosophical pragmatism. One source of its power resides in the authority of educational philosophers and social studies methods teachers who adopt this perspective. But reflective inquiry, per se, with a few exceptions that came from the "new social studies" movement of the 1960s, is not to be found in social studies textbooks. Reflective inquiry poses questions that run counter to the powerful interests that support citizenship transmission and the lesser interests behind social science education. A disjuncture in social studies discourse arises because the underlying power relationships of this alternative orientation admit topics for consideration that are excluded by the two positions previously discussed.

Research Journals in Social Studies Education

The *Journal of Social Studies Research* is published by the Department of Social Science Education at the University of Georgia. It is in its seventh volume. The selected objects of social studies discourse have included classroom interaction and teacher expectations (Jeter & Davis, 1982), social studies content knowledge in pre-service elementary education majors (Diem, 1982), evaluation of peer micro-teaching and field experience (Napier & Vansickle, 1981), student ratings and teacher behavior (Land & Smith, 1981), the development of instruments to measure citizenship knowledge and skills (Hepburn & Strickland, 1979), and sex differences in student interests in discipline areas (McTeer, 1979), among others.

Discourse from educational psychology and social science research methodology strongly influences these research studies in social studies education. An implicit assumption in much of this research is that this form of quantitative knowledge is useful in controlling social studies education as process and product. If one shares this assumption, that only knowledge in the model of logical positivism or empiricism counts as knowledge, it follows that there will be a tendency to focus on objects that lend themselves to quantitative research. Those who are authorized to speak in such a discourse, therefore, are those who have the technical skills demanded by behavioral social science research.

Normative commitments of positive behavioral research assume that in social studies education there are utility functions to be maximized. (See Fay, 1977, for a more general argument on this point.) In the present case these may be thought of in terms of achievement scores or attitudinal changes. Furthermore, the knowledge produced by empirical research will equip curriculum developers, teachers, and administrators to produce higher achievement scores. The discourse, then, centers on managing instruction and on providing students with the appropriate organization and experiences that will facilitate their higher achievement. The power relations that support these activities, again, originate in the academic disciplines and in the popular press. Quantitative educational research is authoritative. Only statistically established relationships among validly measured constructs count as knowledge. Excluded are topics such as ideology, social structure, equality, justice, and social conflict. Those who speak with authority invoke topics and arguments from experimental design, statistical modeling, measurement theory, and so forth. Compared to the market relations supporting textbook production these are relatively weak, but they serve to support the same conservative, uncritical view of social education. Those who possess quantitative research skills have power in this discursive arena. The discursive practice of positive educational research joins with discursive practices outside social studies education to avoid criticism and conflict.

Theory and Research in Social Education is a quarterly in its tenth volume that has published articles dealing with the following topics: the reappraisal of theoretical goals of research in social education (Shaver, 1982), culture and rationality from Frankfurt school thought (Giroux, 1982a), models of theorizing and curriculum theorizing (Wilson, 1982), limitations of an educational-psychological paradigm in social studies education (Clements, 1981), relationships between moral thought and moral action (Fraenkel, 1981), the limits of moral education (Leming, 1981), and the reconstruction of social education (Stanley, 1981), among others. Articles reporting quantitative empirical research are not absent but they do not dominate the intellectual tone of the journal.

The eclecticism of the articles signifies a variety of discourses from neo-positivist, phenomenological, and critical perspectives. Intradiscursive debates dealing with issues that are almost wholly contained within the field of social studies education (e.g., Shermis, 1982; Hurst, Weiss, & Kinney, 1980; Barth & Shermis, 1980) as well as those that are inter-discursive between different fields of discourse (e.g., Giroux, 1982a; van Manen, 1975) are also found here. This forum displays a disjunction of several discursive practices. There does not seem to be a uniform ideological commitment in its articles. The power base of this discursive arena is weak; it is found in the persuasiveness of ideas that are advanced and the power relations that support each of them. When compared to the power relations that surround textbook adoption it is weak indeed. But at least the discourse about social studies education itself is up for consideration. As one moves from the correlations between the economic marketplace and social studies discourse to contentions about internal transformations, and as one moves from a well-defined social-scientific discourse about social studies education to discourse about the nature of social studies education, the power of the discourse in terms of influencing classroom practice erodes.

Conclusion

This brief sampling of discourses about social studies education suggests a number of preliminary inferences about the field. First, no single discourse with a coherent set of objects or themes identifies the field of social studies education. Instead, a variety of discursive practices have been found that range from a commitment to traditional values to social scientific research findings to critical approaches to social action.

Second, relationships with other discursive areas are important in shaping the field of social studies. The correlation between the marketplace and social studies supports a strong commitment to citizenship transmission through an emphasis on noncontroversial treatments of historical and geographical facts. A strong influence from the social sciences is found in quantitative research as well as in a view of social studies as the study of the social sciences. Third, the ideological commitments of these alternative discursive practices are different. Some discursive practices attend mainly to supporting current social arrangements and institutions, excluding controversy and social conflict, whereas others look at individual autonomy and still others the interaction between social-structural constraints and individual autonomy and freedom.

Fourth, the power relationships that support these alternative discourses about the field vary substantially in scope and potency. The power relationships that dominate the field support social and political conservatism. Those who question existing social arrangements are least powerful. One should not expect this situation to change quickly.

Fifth, noting what is *absent* in these discourses tells as much about the field as what is asserted. The most powerful and widespread discursive practices omit references to social injustice, inequality, social and political oppression, and social conflict. Textbooks attend to the presentation of women and minorities in a much more balanced way than heretofore, but explicit treatments of the issues of sexism and racism are still rare.

Sixth, it would seem that teacher education programs offer an important opportunity to explore alternative approaches to social studies education. The nature of textbooks is controlled by the forces of the market. Teacher educators in methods classes and social studies teachers in their own classes are subject to fewer constraints; these are relatively open settings. It was mentioned earlier that looseness and slack in a discursive practice may be attributable in part to variation in what may be said and the fact that all institutional settings do not police utterances with the same diligence. To varying degrees, teachers have autonomy if they choose to exercise it. But without a self-conscious understanding of the determination and control of existing discursive practices the opportunities of this openness may be missed. The anonymous rules of the discourse may remain operative even in situations that are potentially free.

In bringing this essay to an end it is useful to return to Foucault's argument. Discursive practices create places for speakers. This depends upon an underlying distinction between language and speech. Under one construction language is constituted by a combination of words and the rules by which they may be combined. This provides for the possibility of an infinite number of expressions. Speech refers to those expressions that are uttered. For a variety of reasons people speak only a small portion of what can be said. A discursive practice, say about social studies education, structures what is said. It legislates for some utterances and against others. What we claim to know and what we believe is true are also part of such discourses. For example, some discourses about social studies education admit statements about statistical tests in determining whether students learn more facts while playing a simulation game than when listening to a lecture. This discourse, however, may not admit statements challenging the importance of learning one set of facts compared to another. In this way people, when they participate in a discourse such as that about social studies education, may be thought of as anonymous because when they speak they select from words and statements that are admissible for that discursive practice.

Part of Foucault's project and a goal of this essay, quite simply, is to help people *get control* over the constraints and power relations of their discursive practices: in the present case, the discursive practices that constitute social studies education:

> The essential political problem...is not to criticize the ideological contents supposedly linked to science, or to ensure that his own scientific practice is accompanied by a correct

ideology, but that of ascertaining the possibility of constituting a new politics of truth. The problem is not changing people's consciousnesses—or what's in their heads—but the political, economic, institutional regime of the production of truth. (Foucault, 1980, p. 133)

Analysis combined with political action is required. In social studies education if choices among discursive practices are to be illuminated and clarified then it is necessary to make explicit the political structure of those discursive practiccs. Otherwise, political commitments of discursive practices will remain largely invisible and our utterances beyond our control. Discourse about research design, educational objectives, curricular sequence, and so on are not simply about knowledge, but also about power.

Notes

1. I am grateful to Susan Florio and Gail McCutcheon for comments on an earlier version of this paper.

2. Because Foucault's rules come from a different intellectual tradition and school of thought than Austin's appropriacy conditions or Habermas's speech-act-typically restricted contexts they are not technically equivalent. It may be accurate to say that we do not know if they mean quite the same thing because neither literature has been systematically developed in the direction of the other. They are certainly complementary in important ways.

References

Anyon, J. (1981). Social class and school knowledge. *Curriculum Inquiry,* (Spring) *11,* 3–42.

Apple, M. (1971). The hidden curriculum and the nature of conflict. *Interchange, 2,* 27–40.

Austin, J. L. (1968). *How to do things with words.* New York: Oxford University Press.

Ayer, A. J. (1946). *Language, truth and logic.* New York: Dover.

Bernstein, R. J. (1976). *The restructuring of social and political theory.* New York: Harcourt Brace Jovanovich.

Barr, R. D., Barth, J., & Shermis, S. S. (1977). *Defining the social studies.* Washington, D.C.: National Council for the Social Studies.

Barth, J. L., & Shermis, S. (1980). Response to Hurst, Weiss, and Kinney. *Theory and Research in Social Education,* (Winter) *8,* 57–59.

Benveniste, E. (1971). *Problems in general linguistics.* Coral Gables, Florida: University of Miami Press.

Carnap, R. (1966). *Philosophical foundations of physics.* New York: Basic Books.

Cherryholmes, C. H. (1980). Social knowledge and citizenship education: Two views of truth and criticism. *Curriculum Inquiry, 10,* 115–142.

Clements, M. (1981). A social paradigm: An ethical perspective. *Theory and Research in Social Education,* (Fall) *9,* 1–24.

Diem, R. A. (1982). Measurements of social studies content knowledge in preservice elementary education majors. *Journal of Social Studies Research,* (Winter) *6,* 8–12.

Fay, B. (1977). *Social theory and political practice.* London: Allen Unwin.

Foucault, M. (1972). *The archaeology of knowledge.* New York: Harper Colophon Books.

Foucault, M. (1972). History, discourse, and discontinuity. *Salmagundi,* Summer-Fall *20,* 225–248.

Foucault, M. (1973). *The order of things.* New York: Vintage Books.

Foucault, M. (1982). Power/knowledge. New York: Pantheon Books.

Fraenkel, J. R. (1981). The relationship between moral thought and moral action: Implications for social studies action. *Theory and Research in Social Studies Education,* (Summer) *9,* 39–54.

Giddens, A. (1979). *Central problems in social theory.* Berkeley: University of California Press.

Giroux, H. (1982). Culture and rationality in Frankfurt school thought: Ideological foundations for a theory of social education. *Theory and Research in Social Education,* (Winter) *9,* 17–56. (a)

Giroux, H. (1982). Ideology, culture and schooling. Unpublished paper, Boston University. (b)

Habermas, J. (1971). *Knowledge and human interests.* Boston: Beacon Press.

Habermas, J. (1979). *Communication and the evolution of society.* Boston: Beacon Press.

Hanna, P. (1963). Revising the social studies: What is needed? *Social Education*, (27 April) *27*, 190–196.

Hepburn, M. A., & Strickland, J. B. (1979). The development of instruments to measure students' citizenship knowledge and skills. *Journal of Social Studies Research*, (Summer) *3*, 50–57.

Hunt, M. P. & Metcalf, L. E. (1968). *Teaching high school social studies*. New York: Harper and Row.

Hurst, J., Weiss, S., & Kinney, M. (1980). A step beyond defining social problems: A response to Shermis and Barth. *Theory and Research in Social Education*, (Winter) *8*, 45–55.

Jeter, J. T., & Davis, O. L. (1982). Differential classroom interaction in social studies as a function of differential expectations of pupil achievements. *Journal of Social Studies Research*, (Winter) *6*, 1–7.

Land, M. L., & Smith, L. R. (1981). College student ratings and teacher behavior: An experimental study. *Journal of Social Studies Research*, (Winter) *5*, 19–22.

Leming, J. S. (1981). On the limits of rational moral education. *Theory and Research in Social Education*, (Spring) *9*, 7–34.

McTeer, H. J. (1979). Sex differences in students' interest in certain discipline areas of the social studies. *Journal of Social Studies Research*, (Summer) *3*, 58–64.

Napier, J. D., & Vansickle, R. L. (1981). Evaluation of a peer microteaching and field experience component in a secondary level social studies preservice teacher education program. *Journal of Social Studies Research*, (Winter) *5*, 1–8.

Putnam, H. (1975). The meaning of "meaning." In H. Putnam, (Ed.), *Mind, language and reality*. New York: Cambridge University Press.

Said, E. W. (1975). *Beginnings: Intention and method*. New York: Basic Books.

Searle, J. (1969). *Speech acts*. Cambridge, U.K.: Cambridge University Press.

Searle, J. (1971). Austin on locutionary and illocutionary acts. In J. Rosenberg & C. Travis (Eds.), *Readings in the philosophy of language*. Englewood Cliffs, New Jersey: Prentice-Hall.

Schutz, A. (1963). Common-sense and scientific interpretation of human action. In M. Natanson, *Philosophy of the social sciences: A reader*. New York: Random House.

Shapiro, M. (1981). *Language and political understanding*. New Haven: Yale University Press.

Shaver, J. P. (1982). Reappraising the theoretical goals of research in social education. *Theory and Research in Social Education,* (Winter) *9,* 1–16.

Shermis, S. S. (1982). A response to our critics: Reflective inquiry is not the same as social science. *Theory and Research in Social Education,* (Summer) *10,* 45–50.

Stanley, W. B. (1981). Toward a reconstruction of social education. *Theory and Research in Social Education,* (Spring) *9,* 67–89.

van Manen, M. (1975). An exploration of alternative research orientations in social education. *Theory and Research in Social Education,* (December) *3,* 1–28.

Wilson, A. H. (1982). Probing the connection between modes of language and curriculum theorizing in social studies. *Theory and Research in Social Education,* (Winter) *9,* 91–104.

Multicultural Education: Minority Identities, Textbooks, and the Challenge of Curricular Reform

Cameron McCarthy

Our country is a branch of European civilization. . . . 'Eurocentricity' is right, in American curricula and consciousness, because it accords with the facts of our history, and we—and Europe—are fortunate for that. The political and moral legacy of Europe has made the most happy and admirable of nations. Saying that may be indelicate, but it has the merit of being true and the truth should be the core of any curriculum. (Will, *Baton Rouge Morning Advocate,* December 18, 1989, p. 3)

Those who claim the superiority of Western culture are entitled to that claim only when Western civilization is measured thoroughly against other civilizations and not found wanting, and when Western civilization owns up to to its own sources in the cultures that preceded it. (Morrison, 1989, p. 2)

Spurred forward by pressure from African-Americans, Latinos, Asian-Americans, and other marginalized groups for fundamental race-relations reforms in education and society, and by the efforts of mainstream educators to provide practical solutions to the problem of racial inequality in the United States, multicultural education emerged in the late 1960s as a powerful challenge to the Eurocentric foundations of the American school curriculum (McCarthy & Apple, 1988). Multiculturalism is, therefore, a product of a particular historical conjuncture of relations among the state, contending racial minority/majority groups, educators, and policy intellectuals in the United States at a time when the discourse over schools became increasingly racialized. From the first, African-Americans and other minority groups emphasized a variety of transformative themes, insisting that curriculum and education policy address the vital questions of the distribution of power and representation in schools and the status of minority cultural identities.

In the past two decades, however, these transformative themes in the multicultural movement have been steadily "sucked back into the system" (Swartz, 1990). As departments of education, textbook publishers, and intellectual entrepreneurs have pushed for more normative themes of cultural understanding and sensitivity training, the actual implementation of an emancipatory multiculturalism in the school curriculum and in pedagogical and teacher education practices in the university has been effectively deferred. ("Emancipatory multiculturalism" is defined here as the critical redefinition of school knowledge from the heterogeneous perspectives and identities of racially disadvantaged groups—a process that goes beyond the language of 'inclusivity' and emphasizes relationality and multivocality as the central intellectual forces in the production of knowledge [McCarthy, 1990].) Indeed, in the past few years there has been a virulent reaffirmation of Eurocentrism and western culture in debates over the school curriculum and educational reform (Bloom, 1987; Hirsch, 1987; Ravitch, 1990). In this essay, I will situate the topic of multicultural education in the context of current debates over Eurocentrism and 'Western-ness' and the way these discourses are consolidated in the social studies textbooks used in American schools. I will conclude by offering some suggestions for curriculum and educational reform that can help to facilitate emancipatory multi-cultural education and the fostering of minority cultural identities in the classroom.

Westernness and the American Identity

Although developments have taken place in contemporary popular culture toward a certain radical eclecticism (a postmodern sensibility in the areas of art, architecture, music, and literature that in some ways brazenly absorbs third-world and ethnic images) the school system, particularly the school curriculum, remains steadfastly monological. For example, while popular artists such as David Byrne and Paul Simon directly incorporate Afro-Brazilian and South African styles into their music (albums such as *Rei Momo* and *Graceland* are good examples), and while minority artists like Spike Lee, Euzanne Palcy, and the Afro-Asian Black Arts movement in England have begun to influence new ethnic themes in television and film culture, American educators have responded with a decided lack of enthusiasm for cultural diversity and at times with a sense of moral panic with respect to demands for a ventilation of the school curriculum (O'Connor, 1990). The dominant school curriculum therefore exists as a powerful symbol of the contemporary American educator's willful retreat from the social and cultural heterogeneity that now surrounds the school in every urban center in this country.

Indeed, educators and textbook publishers have over the years directly participated in the trotting out of a particularly cruel fantasy about the story of civilization and this society—one in which the only knowledge worth knowing and the only stories worth telling are associated with the handiworks of the bards of Greece and Rome. Within this frame of reference, art, architecture, music, science, and democracy are portrayed as the fertile products of Europeans and their Caucasian counterparts in the United States. It is, as Aime Cesaire (1983) would say, "a funny little tale to tell." But this is in fact the essence of our school knowledge. Through the school curriculum and its centerpiece, the textbook, American schoolchildren come to know the world as a world made by European ancestors and white people in general. The world in which schoolchildren actually live is, on the other hand, a world, populated by minorities and third-world people. This world, according to conservative critics like Allan Bloom (1987), has been brought to ruination by these peoples of other lands. Contemporary conservative writers have sought to reinvigorate these myths. Bloom, for example, maintains in *The Closing of the American Mind* (1987) that the protests of African-American students and women in the 1960s brought this country's university system and its curriculum to the present nadir. Others maintain that we are doing so poorly in comparison with the Japanese because we let the underprepared masses into the schools and the universities in the 1960s (*Education Week,* May 14, 1986). Others such as Diane Ravitch (1990) contend that, though the American populace is diverse, the primary cultural and institutional coherence that currently exists in our society is unequivocally European in origin. It is the durability of these European values of order, democracy, and tolerance, Ravitch maintains, that has protected us from the cultural chaos that afflicts countries in Eastern Europe, the Middle East, Africa, and Asia. ("The political and economic institutions of the United States were deeply influenced by European ideas. Europe's legacy to us is the set of moral and political values that we Americans subsequently refined and reshaped to enable us, in all our diversity, to live together in freedom and peace" [Ravitch, 1990, p. 20].)

But these kinds of remonstrations get us nowhere beyond nostalgia and its obverse, cynicism. Here we can find no real solace—no new ground to help guide us through the events and challenges of the present era. This rather philistine reassertion of Eurocentrism and Western-ness is itself a wish to run away from the labor of coming to terms with the fundamental historical currents that have shaped this country—a wish to run away from the fundamentally 'plural,' immigrant, and Afro–New World character that defines historical and current relations among minority/majority groups in the United States (Jordan, 1985, 1988). To claim a pristine, unambiguous Western-ness as the basis of curriculum organization (as Bloom, Hirsh, Ravitch, and others suggest) is to repress to the dimmest parts of the unconscious a fundamental anxiety concerning the question of African-American and minority identities and 'cultural presence' in what is distinctive about American life. The point I want to make here is similar to the argument that Toni Morrison (1990) makes about Western literature in a recent essay: that there is nothing intrinsically superior or even desirable about the list of cultural items and figures celebrated by traditionalists such as Hirsh and Bloom. At the end of the last century, English cultural critic Matthew Arnold did not find it fit to include in "the best that has been thought and said" (Arnold, 1888, 1971; Czitrom, 1982) any American writer. This is a powerful reminder that 'Western' is not synonymous with 'American,' no matter what some people think. It also reminds us that the notion of Western-ness is a powerful ideological construct—one thoroughly infused with ongoing social struggle over meaning and values. What is Western is therefore highly problematic, as Jordan (1985) has argued. For example, do we want to say that Ernest Hemingway is in and Alice Walker is out? Where is the line denoting what is Western to be drawn within the school curriculum? Where does Western-ness end and where does American-ness begin?

No wonder that schools, like universities, have existed as hostile institutions with respect to the cultural identities of students of African-American, Asian, and Latino backgrounds. No wonder we are experiencing what observers call a resurgence of racism and intolerance in educational institutions all over this country (Viadero, 1989). The fact is, the school system still effectively marginalizes minority youth with respect to access to instructional opportunity, access to an academic core curriculum, and so on. Our educational institutions are not genuinely multicultural or integrated even at those formally desegregated institutions. Linda Grant (1984, 1985), in her ethnographic studies of desegregated schools, has shown that there is de facto segregation at these schools with respect to such variables as access to teacher time and to the general material resources made available to minorities in the school setting. Grant (1984) argues that the organization of the curriculum at the desegregated school concentrates African-American and Latino students in dead-end, non-acadenic tracks, which not only contributes to minority failure but structurally facilitates the disorganization of minority identities by selecting and labeling these students as 'underachievers' and 'at-risk.'

The Textbook

Nowhere is this marginalization and suppression of minority cultural identities more evident than in the textbook industry—both in terms of the absence of minority history in schooltexts, and in terms of the exclusion of emancipatory indigenous scholarship from informing the process of textbook production altogether. But (as I will argue) change in textbook content is only one aspect of what is necessary for meaningful reform toward the goal of genuinely multicultural curriculum and school experiences for all students. There is in fact a need to look at the entire range of elements in the institutional culture of schools—the constraints and barriers to teacher ingenuity as well as the educational priorities set by building principals and in teacher education programs. In all these areas, emancipatory multiculturalism—as a form of what Henry Giroux (1985) calls critical literacy—is now suppressed.

Let us now look at the relationship of the textbook (and the textbook industry) to multicultural education. It is important to recognize from the outset that textbooks themselves embody relations of representation, production, and consumption that tend more or less to suppress minority identities and reproduce inequalities that exist in society. By 'representation,' I am not simply referring to the presence or absence of pictures of minorities in textbooks. By representation, I mean the whole process of who gets to define whom, when, and how. Who has control over the production of pictures and images in this society? I believe that textbook production is an important dimension of a much broader social and political context in which minorities, women, and the physically and mentally disabled have little control over the process of producing images about themselves. For example, when incidents like Howard Beach and Bensonhurst occur, black people do not have equal access to the media to tell their side of the story. So is it true in the case of textbooks.

In an essay entitled "Placing Women in History: Definitions and Challenges" (1975), feminist historian Gerder Lerner maintains that, with respect to the treatment of women, contemporary textbooks can be described as presenting 'compensatory,' or 'contribution' histories of the experiences of women in the United States. By compensatory history, Lerner refers to the tendency of dominant history textbooks to identify and single out what she calls 'women worthies.' This kind of history of notable women celebrates the achievements of individual women such as Jane Addams, Elizabeth Cady Stanton, Harriet Tubman, and so on. But compensatory history of this kind still tends to marginalize the agency of the broad masses of minority and working-class women. As such, these compensatory textbooks, while more inclusive than earlier books, are not exemplars of emancipatory or transformative scholarship.

This notion of compensatory history is also pertinent to the treatment of minorities in textbooks. In history, social studies, literature, and other discipline-based textbooks, minorities are added to an existing 'order of things' (Foucault, 1970). A half page here and a half page there discusses slavery, Harriet Tubman, or 'The Peaceful Warrior,' Martin Luther King. But there is no systematic reworking or restructuring of school knowledge, no attempt to present history from an alternative minority perspective. This fragmentary approach is also evident in the treatment of the third-world peoples of Africa, Latin America, and Asia. For instance, the editors of *Interracial Books for Children Bulletin* (1983), in an in-depth review of a 'representative sample' of seventy-one social studies textbooks used in American schools in the 1980s report the following:

> Central America is entirely omitted from many of the most common world geography, history, and 'cultures' textbooks used in U.S. classrooms. Thirty-one U.S. history texts were checked for their coverage of Central America. Seven of these do not even mention Central America. Fifteen texts limit coverage of Central America to the building of the Panama Canal, and most of these books ignore or mention only in passing the U.S. military intervention that led to the acquisition of the canal. . . . Not one of the 31 texts discusses the continuing involvement of the U.S. government—sometimes overt, sometimes covert—in Central America. (Editors, 1983, p. 12)

The editors of *Interracial Books* also found that among those textbooks that do attempt to address U.S.–Central America relations, such as the popular *Mexico, Central America, and the West Indies* (1971) by Robert Clayton, there is a tendency to portray the United States as:

> The 'benevolent' helper aiding the backward people of Panama [and other Central American countries] who need the U.S. to do such things as run the canal for them, because of their lack of skills, money, and military force. (Editors, 1983, p. 10).

This highly ethnocentric approach to textbook history and social studies is stabilized by a language of universality and objectivity. In this way, the textbook is a central site for the preservation of a selective tradition in the school curriculum—one that pushes minorities and third-world peoples to the outside, to the edge, to the point of deviance. But perhaps the most pernicious feature of this dominant approach to school knowledge and textbook preparation is the tendency to avoid complexity and conflict. For example, in King and Anderson's *America: Past and Present* (1980), a fifth-grade social studies text used in Wisconsin's elementary schools, the only sustained discussion of African-Americans is in the context of slavery, and even that is done in a perfunctory manner, with the relations between whites and blacks on the slave plantation described in benign terms, free of the symbolic and physical violence that characterized the slaves' daily existence. Supporting illustrations make life on the slave plantation look like a California wine orchard, with the slaves living comfortably and snugly in their cabins. The authors of *America: Past and Present* describe plantation life in the following terms:

> On any plantation you visited in the South you would find that all of the farm workers were black slaves. Southern plantations came to depend on slavery. By 1750 there were more slaves than free people in South Carolina. On the plantation you visit, the slaves live in cabins near the fields. Since the slaves get no money for their work, they depend on their owners for clothes and food. The food is mostly salt pork and corn. Some of the slaves have tiny plots of land where they can grow vegetables. (King & Anderson, 1980, pp. 149–50)

It is interesting to compare this description with writings about the slave plantation by indigenous authors such as Vincent Harding in his *There is a River* (1983) or C. L. R. James in *The Black Jacobins* (1963). For example, in his discussion of slavery in Haiti, James draws on this eyewitness account:

A Swiss traveller has left a famous description of a gang of slaves at work. 'They were about a hundred men and women of different ages, all occupied in digging ditches in a cane-field, the majority of them naked or covered with rags. The sun shone down with full force on their heads....A mournful silence reigned. Exhaustion was stamped on every face, but the hour of rest had not yet come. The pitiless eye of the Manager patrolled the gang and several foremen armed with long whips moved periodically between them, giving stinging blows to all who, worn out by fatigue, were compelled to take a rest—men or women, young or old.' This was no isolated picture. The sugar plantations demanded an exacting and ceaseless labour. (James, 1963, p. 10)

In *There is a River,* Harding draws attention to another dimension of plantation life that is given short shrift in history textbooks used in our schools—the topic of black liberation struggles. He makes the following contention about the impact of black liberation struggles on the planter-mercantile class in colonial America:

But it was not in Virginia and South Carolina alone, not only among white Southern society, that the fear of a black quest for freedom existed; the same attitude permeated much of Northern colonial life. In the Northern colonies blacks had already given evidence of their struggle for freedom. As early as 1657 Africans and Indians in Hartford 'joined in an uprising and destroyed some buildings' in the settlement. Such incidents were regularly repeated. (Harding, 1983, p. 31)

In sharp contrast to the works of Harding and James, the bland, nonconflictual writing one finds in many textbooks is in part a product of the highly routinized approach to textbook production used by the textbook industry. As publishers work to maximize their markets (and profits), textbook writing becomes more and more like an assembly line, with multiple authors producing submissions that are checked for quality control, readability, and overly conflictual issues by keen editorial staffs. When the textbook finally becomes a finished product, we have a tool for teaching that is often uninteresting and unchallenging to students and teachers alike. By bargaining away issues that might offend state adoption committees and conservative interest groups, publishers and textbook writers contribute to the marginalization of cultural diversity and the suppression of minority history and identities in textbooks.

Multicultural Reforms

As I have indicated, the textbook is only one aspect of a broad set of practices that impact on the institutional environment of the school. School critics and government officials are now talking about curriculum reform without recognizing the pivotal role of the classroom teacher. Curriculum reform proposals such as 'critical thinking,' 'scientific literacy,' and 'problem solving in mathematics' are coming from the outside, from researchers, politicians, and the business sector to teachers as slogans, in some cases already packaged and teacher-proof (Apple and Beyer, 1988). No matter how well-meaning many of these new proposals are, we run the real risk of precipitating a loss of teacher autonomy in the classroom.

Mobilization for multicultural education reform must therefore follow a very different path. Initiatives in the area of multicultural education must be situated in the context of broad structural and organizational reform in schooling. In most urban centers in this country, teachers work in school settings in which:

a)   They are underpaid (McCarthy, 1990).
b)   The principal, except in a number of exemplary circumstances, is subject to enormous administrative demands that impact on his or her effectiveness as an instructional leader. Excessive administrative demands directly limit the building principal's involvement in instructional improvement—whether it relates to critical thinking or multiculturalism or some other curriculum reform (McCarthy & Schrag, in press).
c)   There is considerable institutional isolation. Teachers complain that they don't have time to meet and plan and that such collaboration is not explicitly encouraged or materially supported (McCarthy, 1990). As a result, there is very little peer supervision or collegiality.
d)   Despite the rhetoric of 'restructuring,' school district offices are driven by a narrow sense of excellence, accountability, and educational achievement. Critical issues such as the need for multicultural reform in education are not given priority status (McCarthy & Schrag, in press).

Of course it is important to recognize, as Steven Purkey and Robert Rutter (1987) argue, that not all urban schools are beset by these barriers to critical teaching and learning. Some schools do have dynamic and progressive learning environments in which teachers pursue critical and emancipatory goals (Bastian, et al., 1986). But in a general sense, it can be said that teachers and educators in urban centers in this country have been presented with a crisis of legitimacy with respect to the project of multicultural reform. In a society where the government has clearly reneged on the promise of racial equality raised during the Johnson and Kennedy administrations in the 1960s, teachers and educators are being bombarded with new and contradictory demands. They are being asked to generate an ethos of harmony and equality at the same time that they are having to respond to increasing governmental pressure to foster competitive individualism in schools. This emphasis on competition reflects itself in the dominant role of standardized testing in pedagogical practices and the narrow range of classroom knowledge that actually gets taught in the urban setting. Teachers feel compelled to be conservative about what they teach, and in this context, multiculturalism is regarded as something of a supplement to a school curriculum that is oriented toward the so-called basics.

In other ways, too, the federal policy within the last decade of cutting back on financial support for the education of low-income students at all levels has sent out a message destructive for the education of minorities. The message is: *To hell with equality; we want to compete with the Japanese.* With resources becoming scarce, the gap between winners and losers is widening. Black and Hispanic youth have fallen victim to a system that says: *You are not a priority; you do not really matter.* These developments are part of the bitter legacy of the Reagan era, but in many respects the current Republican administration in Washington has not offered any respite from the pattern of disinvestment in the urban centers that was initiated by Nixon and Reagan.

Ironically, this is occurring at the same time that school populations are becoming more ethnically diverse. In the twenty-five largest school systems in the country, the majority of students are now minorities (*Education Week,* 1986). Indeed, current demographic projections indicate that by the third decade of the next century, one-third of the American population will be minority. These demographic changes raise profound questions about school knowledge, particularly the wisdom of maintaining the rather unventilated dominance of the Eurocentric curriculum in our educational institutions. The Eurocentric curriculum is, in a manner of speaking, being overtaken by events.

These developments should not lead to paralysis but to action for comprehensive reform in schooling. Multicultural proponents should not merely focus on curriculum content but should introduce broader brush strokes of educational reform that would promote structural reorganization in schooling. Such structural reorganization should involve as a first priority the restoration of the professional space of the teacher as well as the full integration and the guarantee of equality of access to instructional opportunity for minority and underprivileged children. For the multicultural curriculum to be fully realized in the school the following specific initiatives are absolutely critical:

1) Preservice teacher education programs at the universities and colleges across the country must systematically incorporate multicultural objectives into their curricula and field experiences.

2) School districts and school principals must set diversity as an explicit goal and seek ways to integrate the notion in the organization of the curriculum and the institutional life of schools. Right now multiculturalism is treated as a side topic that gets mentioned only during Black History Month and on International Women's Day.

3) Multiculturalism should not be limited to the present under-standing—that is, the idea that all we need to do is to add some content about minorities and women to the school curriculum. Multiculturalism must involve a radical rethinking of the nature of school knowledge as knowledge that is fundamentally relational and heterogeneous in character. In this sense, for example, we cannot get a full understanding of the civil rights movement in the United States without studying its multiplier effects on the expansion of democratic practices to excluded groups in Australia, the Caribbean, Africa, England, and in the United States itself. For that matter, we can not properly understand the development of European societies without a proper understanding of the direct link of Europe's development to the underdevelopment of the third world. For example, at the time that the French were helping to bankroll the American Revolution, two-thirds of France's export earnings were coming from its exploitation of sugar cane plantations in Haiti (James, 1963).

4) Such a reworking of school knowledge must go a step further toward reconsidering the privileging of Eurocentric perspectives and points of view in the curriculum as reflected in, for example, the 'famous men' approach to history. The new multicultural curriculum must go beyond the "language of inclusion" toward a "language of critique" (Giroux, 1985). This would centrally

involve the affirmation of minority identities and perspectives as the organizing principles for school knowledge. In this manner, schools would be sites for multicultural curriculum reform and pedagogical practices that are truly liberatory.

5) Teachers must be centrally involved in the reworking of the curriculum and the reorganization of the school in ways that give them a sense of professional autonomy and ownership over curriculum changes.

6) There is a vital need in this country to revise the K–12 exam system which now places an overwhelming emphasis on standardized, multiple choice, and short answer tests. Also, it is absolutely critical that these exams begin to reflect the emphasis on multiculturalism that I have argued for in this essay. At present, there is little incentive for teachers to teach and for students to learn more about minorities and women because these topics are not reflected in testing.

7) As far as textbooks are concerned, there is a need to involve indigenous minority and third world scholars and teachers in the production of school knowledge in the textbook industry at every level—that is, from the level of textbook writing right through to editorial and managerial decision making.

8) Finally, let me return to a theme that I stressed at the beginning of this essay: *The multicultural ethos in schools will only be fully realized when minority and underprivileged students have access to an academic core curriculum on par with their middle-class and white counterparts.*

Multicultural curriculum reform must therefore mean that we think about all these things. It should not mean simply incremental changes in curriculum content but should involve a wider scope of educational, pedagogical, and curriculum reforms that would enhance the participation of indigenous scholars and classroom teachers in the production of school knowledge and facilitate equal access to an academic core curriculum (that is multicultural) for minority and underprivileged youth—youth who are now significantly excluded from these critical educational experiences.

Conclusion

I have sought here to call attention to the urgent need to rethink the current privileging of Eurocentric ideas in our contemporary American school curriculum. I believe that this emphasis is misplaced in light of the rapid diversification now taking place in school populations across the United States. A fundamental place for rethinking to begin is the school textbook and the process of textbook production on the whole. But this alone is not enough to insure that our students will have a genuinely emancipatory, multicultural school experience. As I have maintained, multiculturalism must involve a wide range of educational change that would address the professional needs of classroom teachers and the burning issue of equal access for minorities to an academic curriculum. The needs of teachers and minority students must be understood as critical organizing principles in the movement toward multicultural curriculum reform.

References

Apple, M. & Beyer, L. (Eds.) (1988). *The curriculum: Problems, politics and possibilities.* Albany: State University of New York Press.

Arnold, M. (1888). *Civilization in the United States: First and last impressions of America.* Boston: Cupples and Hurd.

Arnold, M. (1971). *Culture and anarchy.* Indianapolis: Bobbs-Merrill Company.

Bastian, A., et al. (1986). *Choosing equality.* Philadelphia: Temple University Press.

Bloom, A. (1987). The closing of the American mind. New York: Simon and Schuster.

Cesaire, A. (1983). *The collected poetry.* (Trans. C. Eselman & A. Smith.) Berkeley: University of California Press.

Czitrom, D. (1982). *Media and the American mind: From Morse to McLuhan.* Chapel Hill: University of North Carolina Press.

Clayton, R. (1971). *Mexico, Central America, and the West Indies.* London: John Day.

Editors. (1983). Central America: What U.S. educators need to know. *Interracial Books for Children Bulletin, 3,* 2–3.

Education Week (1986). Here they come, ready or not: An *Education Week* special report on the ways in which America's population in motion is changing the outlook for schools and society. *Education Week* (May 14), 14–28.

Foucault, M. (1970). *The order of things: An archeology of the human sciences.* New York: Pantheon.

Giroux, H. (1985). Introduction. In P. Freire, *The politics of education*. Boston: Bergin and Garvey.

Grant, C., & Sleeter, C. (1989). *Turning on learning: Five approaches for multicultural teaching plans for race, class, gender, and disability*. Columbus: Merrill Publishing Company.

Grant, L. (1984). Black females' "place" in desegregated classrooms. *Sociology of Education, 57,* 98–111.

Grant, L. (1985). *Uneasy alliances: Black males, teachers, and peers in desegregated classrooms*. Unpublished manuscript.

Harding, V. (1983). *There is a river*. New York: Vintage.

Hirsch, E. D. (1987). *Cultural literacy: What every American needs to know*. Boston: Houghton Mifflin.

James, C. L. R. (1963). *The black Jacobins*. New York: Vintage.

Jordan, J. (1985). *On call: Political essays*. Boston: South End Press.

Jordan, J. (1988). Nobody mean more to me than you and the future life of Willie Jordan. *Harvard Educational Review, 58* (2), 363–374.

King, D., & Anderson, C. (1980). *America: Past and present*. Boston: Houghton Mifflin.

Lerner, G. (1975). Placing women in history: Definitions and challenges. *Feminist Studies, 3,* 1–2, 5–15.

McCarthy, C. (1988). Reconsidering liberal and radical perspectives on racial inequality in schooling. *Harvard Educational Review, 58,* (2), 265–279.

McCarthy, C. (1990). *Being there: A math collaborative and the challenge of teaching mathematics in the urban classroom* (monograph). Madison: Wisconsin Center for Educational Research.

McCarthy, C. (1990). *Race and curriculum*. London: Falmer Press.

McCarthy, C., & Apple, M. (1988). Race, class and gender in American educational research: Towards a nonsynchronous parallelist position. *Perspectives in Education, 4,* (2), 67–69.

McCarthy, C. & Schrag, F. (in press). Departmental and principal leadership in promoting higher order thinking. *Journal of Curriculum Studies*.

Morrison, T. (1989). Unspeakable things unspoken: The Afro-American presence in American literature. *Michigan Quarterly Review, 38,* (1), 1–34.

O'Connor, J. (1990). On TV, less separate, more equal. *The New York Times* (April 29), Arts and Leisure, 1.

Purkey, S. & Rutter, R. (1987). High school teaching: Teacher practices and beliefs in urban and suburban public schools. *Education Policy, 1* (3), 375–393.

Ravitch, D. (1990). Diversity and democracy: Multicultural education in America. *American Educator, 14* (1), 16–48.

Swartz, E. (1990). *Cultural diversity and the school curriculum: Context and practice.* Paper presented at the Annual Meeting of the American Educational Research Association, Boston.

Viadero, D. (1989). Schools witness a troubling revival of bigotry. *Education Week* (May 24), 1.

Will, G. (1989). Eurocentricity and the school curriculum. *Baton Rouge Morning Advocate* (December 18), 3.

Culture, Pedagogy, and Power: Issues in the Production of Values and Colonialization

Thomas S. Popkewitz

We live in a period in which the value of cultural diversity is politically sanctioned and legislatively mandated. Throughout the industrialized world, people have been given the right to have their children instructed in the language of their parents when that counters the dominant language of the country. In the Soviet Union, there was a long tradition of instruction in indigenous cultures; riots ensued when those traditions of language and culture were threatened by policy at the center. Dominant political thought in the United States celebrates pluralism, reflected in schools by pedagogical theories that valorize individualism. The federal government supports centers around the country to help school districts develop programs in language diversity and cultural pluralism; at universities, chancellors and presidents are giving special attention to recruitment of minority faculty and students, arguing that diversity improves the quality of education.

This essay recognizes these practices as part of political struggles. But, at the same time, my comments do not celebrate what is variously called multicultural education, bilingual education, or pluralism. Rather, I explore the relations of politics, power, and culture that underlie these pedagogical programs.

While not denying the importance of participation, I want to focus on a different layer of constructing educational programs: the ways in which choice, will, and desire associated with culture are socially formed and subjugated. To identify culture as a problem of pedagogy is to ask questions such as: Whose cultures are appropriated as our own? How is marginality normalized? Our definitions of "our" culture and views of "self" are constructions that occur in relation to structures of power and issues of dominance.

What we define as "our," and what is seen as culturally different, are based on distinctions and categorical hierarchies that constitute power relations. What culture is brought into schooling is an important social and political issue; the relation between culture and groups has to be understood as a problem of power. Very often the notion of culture is part of a dynamic struggle of inequality that is produced through the relations of the discourse. What is viewed as black, minority, or "ethnic" cannot be understood without considering racial and class formation. It is never clear which elements of culture belong to the dispossessed as "original" elements of their styles of life and which have been formed in response to dominant cultures and power relations. When we speak of our diversity, the past we defend may not be our cultural heritage.

The institutional processes of identification and selection compel us to consider how our subjectivities are formed and internalized. To identify "culture" or to study the rituals, ceremonies, and knowledge of "others" is to engage in a discourse that has rules of selection, organization, and privileged relations. Our task here is to examine the social fields that give order and distinctions to curriculum—to make these social fields themselves into objects of inquiry.

The Transformation of Culture and the Tensions of Modernism

The current political and pedagogical emphasis on pluralism can be understood, in part, in the context of a crisis about identity. It holds political potency for those with different ideological agendas in society. In a variety of nations, both the left and the right have championed the problem of culture as a major issue of contemporary society.

The issue of cultural diversity can be viewed in relation to the tensions of a heightened search for identity produced by the material and mental structures of modernity. The tendency of modernism is toward diversity and fragmentation of the social body. There is an increasing social mobility that has disturbed our sense of communal ties. The social and physical complexities of life make it difficult to locate the origins and causes of our patterns of conduct. Dominant social science methodologies deny commitment to any values except those of process while, at the same time, focusing on procedures of inquiry that stress the individual over the collective. Reason and rationality, where tied to the norms of science, produce a tension as both history and social community are assumed to be transcended.

The failure of contemporary reason and rationality is that the transformation of the sacred into notions of modern science and technology has stripped away a prerequisite for community. Everything seems scattered and rootless. In our mobility, there is a cultural redefinition (some call it breakdown) and loss of collective traditions and futures. The inclusion of culture into pedagogy provides a strategy for redefining community and collective identity.

At the same moment, the identification of culture as a problem of pedagogy raises issues of power. It is seen by disenfranchised groups as challenging existing power relations through the assertion of pluralism. Cultural pluralism can legitimate a construction of a past to gain social and political benefits for those who had been marginal to dominant society. For others, the "new" or modern is viewed with some suspicion, the "old" remembered as holding a key to a more golden age. Pluralism enables a belief in multiple pasts as part of creating a consensus for the present.

The pressures to create new systems of relations and new forms of solidarity through cultural diversity are also a problem of state building as older notions of governability no longer seem viable. The "cultural" crisis is one of the nation-state, as the economy is no longer controlled within one's national borders. The slogan "1992," the year when the 12-nation Western European community is supposed to abolish its frontiers, symbolizes pan-Europeanism and the loss of national sovereignty. Multinational corporations create contexts of production and labor that transcend older borders of a nation; accompanying these changes is an internationalization of culture as Headline Cable News, McDonald's hamburgers, Honda, and Benetton's help create a worldwide market.

The homogeneity and fragmentation is itself a product of modernization (see Berger, Berger, & Kellner, 1973). The multirelationality of consciousness that occurs with the development of rational thought encourages people to consider themselves as both unique and anonymous. People live in a universal system of economy and politics that contains Japanese cars, German medical equipment, French wines, and glasnost while, at the same time, defining themselves as ethnic or multicultural. The similarities and fragmentation of culture are unified in the modern conception of culture as new organic connections are created.

In fundamental ways, schools are bound in these tensions of violation, production, and reproduction. Schooling is a social creation to deal with the ruptures of cultural production and reproduction (see Lundgren, 1988). For many in our contemporary landscape, schooling is part of the modern quest to eliminate inequality and injustice; at the same time, there are the larger tensions of the structure of inequality that occurs in the cultural debates of school. While certain groups in the United States call for cultural pluralism as a way to give focus to the integrity of disenfranchised groups, others are calling for a new nation-building effort for United States schools. For the former, pedagogy is to make distinctions and difference as a valued category of society. The latter fears the increasing minority population in schools and suggests that schools strive to help create a national consensus and social solidarity. For these people, recognizing cultural differences is a tactic for arriving at more varied (and in the aggregate more effective) methods of putting across the traditional curriculum. With scores on standardized tests as the measure of success, schooling retains the particular cultural discourses that are embedded in the standardized testing industry.

To this point, I have argued that the identification of culture in pedagogy is never free-floating but occurs in a context of power relations. Issues of culture and diversity are, at the same moment, struggles to gain control and technologies to produce control. The idea of culture is itself only a hundred years old, an invention of Europe to help control the processes of colonization in a way not previously practiced. In our current affairs, the public rhetoric focuses on culture as a form of liberation and assertion of group power in the larger society. At the same time, dominant groups seek to interpret cultural differences in a way that preserves existing inequality. The tension of empowerment and subjugation is one we need to be continually aware of as we consider the issue of culture and schooling.

Ordering Fields and the Impositions of Modernism

Pedagogy is not only a system of information or subjects that are organized for students but an ordering of social fields. The organization of school knowledge defines the categories and distinctions that legitimate what is to be thought about and interpreted in social affairs. In this deeper sense, pedagogy is a system of discipline by which hierarchies—markers of social distinction and aspirations—are established.

Pedagogy as the production of distinctions and hierarchies that privilege certain interests can be given attention in the relationship of art and anthropology.[1] The Museum of Modern Art (MOMA) exhibit in 1984–1985 on modernism was formed as didactic experience that has affinities to curriculum designs. At first glance, the Museum exhibit seems a celebration of multiculturalism and global cultures. The show sought to illustrate the affinity of the modern and the tribal by juxtaposing the work of early 20th-century artists, such as Picasso and Leger, and non-Western objects from Africa. The purpose of the exhibit was to identify aesthetic principles that transcend culture, politics, and history. The exhibitors selected affinities by focusing on qualities of abstractness found in both modern art and Third World objects.

The system of appreciation and interpretation that took place conferred certain values on the objects and, at the same time, withheld others. The search for universal qualities and affinities involved a selection and representation that transformed non-Western arts to modernist terms of the Western world.

The museum exhibit made the relation of the Western and non-Western objects seem natural by ignoring the historical contexts in which the objects of art were produced. The display of tribal objects in the museum exhibit positioned the non-Western art as non-historical objects and those in the position to classify the objects as existing within a different and dynamic historical site. Western conceptions of shape, line, or color as formal elements of design were interjected by the MOMA exhibitors to explain the relation of the different objects. If one looks at the emergence of Western interest in non-Western art at the turn of the century, however, we see that it occurred at a moment when Europe was asserting political, economic, and evangelical domination in the "primitive" spaces of the world. The tribal cultures were seen in need of preservation, redemption, and representation, denying any concrete inventiveness to their existence.

The categories and hierarchical distinctions in the art exhibit and its history celebrated the different objects of culture as part of a universalized discourse. A dynamic and complex African conscious-ness was replaced with a technical discourse that contained a modernist allegory of redemption and of making things whole. Music instruments of a group became "a system of sound in man's aural environment"; community was seen as "an important function of organized sound" (Clifford, 1988, p.204). The words of anthropology in the exhibit denied the African view in which there is an acceptance of an endless seriality and a desire to keep things apart.

The particular ideological qualities of the show were reinforced by the form of display used. The museum explanations created illusions of adequate presentation of the world by cutting out the specific context and making particular objects stand for the abstract whole. The museum's "boutique decor" lighted the objects of different cultures in a manner that made the objects appear as isolated artifacts that could serve to represent formal qualities of aesthetics, such as the use of shape or color.

The emphasis on particular formal qualities reinforced a particular cultural description of collecting. The ordering of objects gave a definition of social life that reproduced particular ideologies of the Western world—that of possessive individualism, engendered relations, and racial domination. It gave value to a view of the self as an owner of objects rather than part of a historical process. The objects were to be owned and possessed in a static world. The Bandara Mask stood for the Bandara people. The objective world was seen as given, not produced; historical relations of power in the world of acquisition were occulted. The classification systems vivified the relational position of the West to others.

Aesthetic theory and social science became a dynamic in that reformulation. The discursive practices separated the objects from their occasions of production, with the distinctive features of the art classified according to a universe that was in line with those who had power to do the defining.

The significance of the discourse about culture in the museum exhibit was that it served to discipline cognition for those who saw the show. In fundamental ways, the discourse to illustrate affinities establishes relations that colonialize the other. What seemed to be merely a technical explanation of objects amounted to a wrenching of the art out of its social context and into a Western framework of individualism. Likewise, time was redefined in terms of progress, improvement, and development, concepts of Western utilitarian thought. The subjugation through discourse is a more significant technology of control than the older forms of physical occupation faced by Third World countries and indigenous minorities.

The Language of Empowerment as Control

When we approach the problem of school pedagogy, similar issues of decontextualization and reformulation occur. Curriculum generalizes and categorizes in a way that distances objects from their cultural and social context, transforming the experiences and communication patterns of particular cultural groups and refocusing experiences in ways that respond to dominant structures and power relations. This transformation occurs through the linguistic forms that are used to talk about diversity, differences, and marginality. The "other" is represented through the categories of time and space that incorporate particular Western values while distancing the "other" from what is defined as superior. In this process, "voices" of opposition and alternatives are often recast in relation to social fields that obscure the power relations and control mechanism of pedagogy.

The relation of pedagogy and culture is one of continual tensions and contradictions. These tensions can be told in the efforts to produce racial equality in the United States: of minorities obtaining a voice in social affairs while the discourse of participation draws on linguistic codes and rituals of civil politeness that redefine social and political interests. Legitimacy is given to particular notions of participation, progress, and social identity in a way that transforms cultural struggles to coincide with rules of existing institutional arrangements (see Popkewitz, 1979). Cultural differences become matters of degrees from what is assumed the norm.

We can focus upon this contradiction in the language of empowerment in school reform. At one layer, empowerment responds to social strains to include more people in the political process; at another level, the discourse of empowerment transforms cultural conditions in a way that introduces new systems of control.

Empowerment is a central part of the current rhetoric in United States educational reforms. The public discussions focus on the ways in which teachers and community can assume responsibility and autonomy in their practices. These practices are sometimes contradictory. State legislatures have redesigned certification requirements to increase parent participation in school policymaking and teacher certification while teacher reforms have focused on ways in which the organization of schools can increase teacher responsibility. For parents and minority communities, the increased involvement in school practices makes schools more responsive to local values and issues in an important cultural institution. Increased teacher participation is thought to improve the quality of teaching and professionalism by providing greater responsibility and autonomy.

As soon as we begin to examine the notions of autonomy and power, it becomes clear that there are certain cultural imperatives and rules that underlie these notions. Cultural distinctions are transformed and constrained by the norms and patterns of bureaucracy. Priority is given to a sense of abstract relations and functional anonymity. Teachers are to make decisions that concern the administrative and organizational requirements of schooling, often requiring them to recast the folk knowledge and craft skills associated with teaching into more rationalized systems that can be more readily monitored (Popkewitz & Lind, in press). Older forms of community solidarity based on face-to-face communication are denied, as pedagogical emphasis is given to unitary patterns of social relations.

Many of the efforts to produce empowerment of minorities and marginal cultural groups are tied to an administrative concept of politics. Politics is believed to be a network of associations that represent diverse ethnic, occupational, economic, and regional interests. Interest groups compete for support of policies. Within this context, government supports and promotes an exchange between groups. Justice and fairness are bound to adequate representation of groups, providing them access to decision making, which is defined as essentially rational and altruistic. Planning is conceived as primarily technical and considered to bring needed resources to bear on identifiable social needs.

In this administrative approach to politics, rituals of community involvement give plausibility to the social ordering of school failure and success. Participation creates an impression of a political system designed to translate individual wants into public policy. At the same time, the rituals of participation are bounded to the discourse contained in institutional relations. The systems that define not only what is learned but how learning is to be effected are left unscrutinized.

A Case Study

How pedagogy appropriates images and meaning of power relations can be understood by focusing on a project designed to include Native American culture and interests in school decision-making (Popkewitz, 1976). Under general guidelines of a federal anti-poverty agency called Teacher Corps, the project existed in three rural Native American communities. To plan and organize the programs in each community, there was a central decision making body composed of school administrators, university professors, and people from the local reservations.

The Teacher Corps project was consistent with the ideology of the federal War on Poverty that began in the mid 1960s. Participation in school policy would produce a greater responsiveness by bureaucracies to a minority and poor population. The project had multiple strategies within the school districts. It was to improve the self-image of children in school by including a curriculum of local history and culture. The teaching of basic skills was to be made more effective through use of the native language and experiences of the children. A special teacher education program was to produce more effective teachers of Native American children through a program that included studying the cultural heritage and "needs" of the minority population. The project existed into the late 1970s, although the data discussed here were collected in 1974–1975.

While the purpose of the project was to give community people representation in school policymaking, the discourse about change legitimated the status, privileges, and initiative of those who could authoritatively define the content of schooling. In part, there was a highly technical jargon that tended to set apart those who had been initiated (teachers, university professionals, student teachers) from those who were outsiders, members of the Indian community. A language of "competencies," "sites," and "modules" replaced a common-sense language about the priorities and strategies of schooling. The new language distanced Native Americans from those who administered the program but, at the same time, made them dependent on experts for interpretation of school experience. Further, group differentiation was produced by a recognition of credentialing: university folk were called professors; school professionals were addressed as "Mr." and "Mrs."; Indian representatives were called by their first names.

The "shared responsibility" of the project governance sustained background assumptions of the school educational process. Teachers tended to view Indians as lazy, lacking in ability and initiative, and having poor social habits. School labeling of "discipline problems," "remedial," "slow learner," and "culturally disadvantaged" tended to support the school ideology. The reform discourse also redefined cultural horizons of native American communities into categories of pedagogy that contained a linear conception of progress and a deficit model of learning that has its origin in Protestant views of salvation and missionary work (see Popkewitz & Pitman, 1986). The organization of change was seen as a rational procedure which could be outlined in flow charts of segmented time and sequences that represented progress. Embedded in the discussion was the belief that school failure derived from lack of hard work and from refusal to accept norms of delayed gratification and inner discipline. By focusing on community participation as implementing procedures, the dialogue between school and community effectively screened out the implications of school experience.

There was a redefining of cultural interests for the Native American community. Reading curriculum used community "vocabulary" but put it in a framework drawn from standard methods of curriculum reorganization. Craft projects were developed to explore Indian culture and find aspects that could be drawn into the curriculum. Thus, particular elements of the community's culture were brought into the classroom, but in a manner that redefined the order, priorities, and standards of the culture according to the presuppositions of the school. Moreover, student teacher volunteer work within the community followed the same pattern, with volunteers working as coaches on athletic teams or as aides in after-school centers. The school activities, teachers thought, would help uplift the moral and intellectual fiber of Indian life and move Indians out of the pronounced poverty syndrome. The Indian community was thought of as pathological and in need of reform toward dominant white values.

Ironically, in a program to bring empowerment to local communities, the strategies to respond to pluralism brought deviant interest claims and socio-political orientations under control. The emergent pedagogy drew on the vocabulary relevant to the arts and crafts of native American culture, but it redefined those experiences into a taxonomical structure that made Western, Protestant conceptions of time, space, and hierarchy seem natural and reasonable. Further, the psychological orientation in the curriculum transformed communal and social relations into systems of individualizing learning that made it possible to normalize the school conceptions through a focus on the minute behaviors of individuals that could be more readily observed, supervised, and disciplined.

The social, cultural, and political context in which American Indian systems of meaning are constructed was decontextualized by the curriculum discourse and reformulation in a manner that represented different sets of values and relations from those of the original setting. The system of classifications defined a set of relations that classified the community as deviant and in need of remediation.

The Discourse of Pedagogy:
Decontextualization and Reformation of Culture

The Museum of Modern Art exhibit and the Teacher Corps project enable us to consider the problem of language, representation, and distinction as implicated in issues of power. The pedagogical structures exist within a social field that imposes unequal relations and social regulation that are not always what appears on the surface or in the public expressions about purpose and intent. The relation of representation and power has important implications for the patterns of discourse that are used in the construction of multicultural education.

Let me pose this problem of pedagogy and power in relation to a current discourse about improving teaching and teacher education. As with the Museum of Modern Art exhibit and the Teacher Corps project, there is a tendency to decontextualize social, political, and cultural elements of school affairs by focusing upon abstract and universal qualities of teacher learning and thinking (see Popkewitz, 1988). Models of teaching and learning are posed as particular skills or attributes of individuals and knowledge. In the process, the problem of teaching is reformulated into concepts that stress a rational, individualized, and sequential development that ties the social organization of schooling with particular middle-class notions of civility, progress, and salvation. Let me explore this further, for this form of social regulation is deeply hidden in our accepted ways of thinking about and organizing school practice.

A "commonsense" view of schooling is to think of pedagogy as a problem of learning. The concern of learning, however, is historically constructed and tied to problems of the institutional development of American education (O'Donnell, 1985). The focus upon the psychological attributes of mind emerges with the earlier behaviorist psychologists who sought to relate "learning" to liberal political theories which sought to define the duties, obligations, and rights of individuals as the British confronted industrialization and the development of a strong bourgeoisie. In much of the writing of the 18th and 19th centuries, the individual was believed to be the proprietor of his or her own capabilities. Society was conceived of as free and equal individuals who entered into a social contract. The order of society was often cast in the metaphor of the machine. The interests of the individual were to be harmonized by natural market forces. Time and space were made into a unity that was to be hierarchical, linear, and taxonomical (see Fabian, 1983).

The language of learning in current curriculum is drawn from the economic and political theories of 18th- and 19th-century Britain and recast as a way to provide practical solutions for the socialization of children. Knowledge and people were to be treated as "things" or commodities that would be manipulated in an orderly and efficient manner as one could in the marketplace. The logic is one of the machine but transposed on social life.

The psychological discourse of pedagogy *as* learning crystalizes this particular structure of thought through its linguistic forms and makes it seem universal and appropriate for all. The everyday experiences and communication of diverse groups are decontextualized and reformulated according to a different set of rules, obligations, and values. Individual perceptions, cognitions, and interpretations are re-coded into stages of learning, attributes, or skills of learning or achievement that appear abstract, objective, and "natural." "Stages" assumes a biological conception of growth as evolution, but at the same time posits a philosophical foundational view of knowledge as having essential or universal truths about the world that underlie each stage.

Even in our notions of "problem solving," we find a particular orientation and disposition toward the world and its relations. Much of current cognitive psychology assumes that problem solving entails a mediation of symbols between the representations of the world and the knower. That mediation is thought to occur in which time and space have no consequence. But in fact, time is defined as consisting of discrete, logical, and sequential elements. A view of progress is incorporated that builds upon a conception of the sum of the parts producing the whole. This conception emerges from a particular Protestant middle-class notion of society as based upon social contacts and an individualism which ties salvation to personal effort. Linear relations, taxonomic categories, and universal sequences, such as are found in discussions of "problem-solving," exclude consideration of how structured relations of class, gender, race, and ethnicity produce distinctions and differentiations in society.

The decontextualization and reformulation of cultural systems are embedded in most discussions of a multicultural education. The cultural and social distinctions of different racial groups are expressed as a stylized system of checklists and formal categories that make differences universal rites rather than historical constructions. Black culture is transformed into "styles of learning" or learning from concrete rather than the abstract. With checklists of cultural principles, teachers are to plan strategies "for important differences in the way in which children perceive, classify and calibrate information and their preferred modes of motivation, for example whether oral, verbal or visual" (Lynch, 1987, p. 134).

With these principles of multicultural education, general sentiments are expressed, e.g., that teachers should accept the backgrounds of children, have open communication, and be open to new ways of thinking and behaving. Yet these normative preferences have practical technologies which organize practices into discrete and taxonomic qualities that give multicultural education a particular way of thinking about knowledge, society, and the individual. Reference to sequencing instruction, stages of learning, or levels of thinking create a system of thought that seems to have no context, removing knowledge from its sources. A particular notion of taxonomic time and space establishes linear relations and differences as discontinuous and fragmented.

The assumptions of a discourse about multiculturalism are not only to represent the world. Discourse practices have the potential for disciplining the individual to the sets of rules, norms, and relations that are implied. By this, I am concerned that pedagogical practices, while phrased in the most noble humanist concerns, also contain practical technologies that break social interactions into more discrete tasks that make the individual more open to observation, supervision, and control. The individual, as Michel Foucault (1973) has argued, is made the object of scrutiny and regulation. The strategies of education discipline the "self" into a self-management that enables power to operate through individuals as they monitor their own thought and practice. The individual is made visible to observation, scrutiny, supervision, and control, while, at the same time, the power arrangements that underlie our practices and relations are made more invisible.

The power relations are more difficult to discern as an institutional discourse translates political concerns into scientific problems that make the regulations of human affairs appear value-free and technical in nature. The most intimate behaviors and thoughts are made into objects of cultural definition that can be measured and manipulated through human sciences. By focusing on teachers' behaviors, or a psychology that has no explicit notion of society, we no longer see teachers or students as the objects of political concern, but as recipients of learning.

The strategies of curriculum design fail to realize that our questions are themselves part of a historical process; that data always refer back to a social field of "theory" which allows us to place the "data" and make sense of phenomena. The so-called revolution of cognitive science is itself an elaboration and extension of behavioral methodologies that were to supervise and control the individual (see O'Donnell, 1985). It incorporates values, priorities, and visions of the social world that are shaped and fashioned by a discourse that circulates power. Differences are transformed into a particular style of reasoning that provides for social integration and success according to norms that are historically bound to dominant bourgeois, Protestant conceptions of salvation and earthly success. The data of perceptions, attitudes, and belief need to be continually placed in the social and cultural horizons.

We need to recognize that the issue of power is not only "who chooses" but the distinctions and differences that are structured in and out of discourse patterns. Schooling is an essential element in the production and reproduction of the social fields. Our rules of curriculum classification about culture are distinctions that normalize and provide technologies that can discipline our hopes, desires, and wants. Education entails choosing categories and making distinctions as an ordering of the social field. The processes of selection and omission privilege relations and create fields of power through the organization of knowledge. The discourse about school knowledge can shape not only what is to be represented but the space in which we articulate our own sense of identity and esteem.

Conclusion

What seemed at first glance a way to give dignity, distinctiveness, and public space to "others" was explored in this essay as having contradictory moments. The Museum of Modern Art exhibit was to establish an equality between African and Western art, but the manner of presentation decontextualized the primitive and refocused attention upon categories and distinction that gave priority to the Western. The Teacher Corps project maintained sets of practices and rituals that defined a social field in which the multicultural education carried discourse practices that defined Native American culture as pathological and the role of the school as a morals-enforcing institution.

The rules of constructing pedagogy about multiculturalism also contain contradictions. It can decontextualize the culture of the "other" and reformulate experiences to respond to particular forms that hide moral, political, and social imperatives of schooling. In defining curriculum as a psychological problem, sets of values and social regulations are formulated. The dynamic sets of elements that underlie the social construction of culture are decontextualized and made into seemingly universal characterization. Where different cultures do make distinctions about the organization of time and space, the organization of curriculum discourse redefines and reformulates all experiences into universal, logical, and seemingly disinterested categories.

It is at the layer of discourse that the issues of control and colonialization are fundamental. As thought, feeling, talk, and "seeing" of others and ourselves are redefined through pedagogy, the patterns of control are no longer external but part of the discipline and self-governance of the individual. The prison can become ourselves as the reformulations are assumed as natural to our "self."

Studying the problem of culture and control enables us to reorder our tasks in understanding the issue of culture in schooling in a number of ways. First, we should direct our attention to how the labels of schooling are neither neutral nor disinterested. Second, we are continually compelled to give attention to power relations in society that become embedded in our institutions of discourse about teaching and learning. Third, we are placed in a position of not accepting the official categories and rhetoric of our public institutions but in making the languages and practices of everyday life the problem of research. Fourth, we are drawn to understand the tension between our hopes and desires for equitable institutions and the recognition that our hopes, desires, and notions of equality may themselves be socially formed and contradictory. The tensions, struggles, and contradictions do not mean we should forego the challenge. Rather, we should recognize the need for trust with skepticism.

Note

1. The following discussion is drawn from Clifford (1988).

References

Berger, P., Berger, B., & Kellner, H. (1973). *The homeless mind: Modernization and consciousness*. New York: Vintage.

Clifford, J. (1988). *The predicament of culture: Twentieth-century ethnography, literature and art*. Cambridge: Harvard University Press.

Fabian, J. (1983). *Time and the other: How anthropology makes its object*. New York: Columbia University Press.

Foucault, M. (1979). *The order of things: An archaeology of the human sciences*. New York: Vintage Books.

Lundgren, U. (1988). *Culture, reproduction and education*. Paper presented at the symposium Challenge the Future Through Culture, Lulea, Sweden, June 12–15.

Lynch, J. (1986). *Multicultural education: Principles and practice*. Boston: Routledge & Kegan Paul.

O'Donnell, J. (1985). *The origins of behaviorism: American psychology, 1876–1920.* New York: New York University Press.

Popkewitz, T. (1976). Reform as political discourse: A case study. *School Review, 84,* 43–69.

Popkewitz, T. (1979). Schools and the symbolic uses of community participation. In C. Grant (Ed.), *Community participation in education* (pp. 202–223). Boston: Allyn & Bacon.

Popkewitz, T. (1988). Educational reform: Rhetoric, ritual and social interest. *Educational Theory, 38*(1), 77–92.

Popkewitz, T., & Lind, K. (in press). Teacher incentives as reform: Implications for teachers' work and the changing control mechanism in education. *Teachers College Record.*

Popkewitz, T., & Pitman, A. (1986). The idea of progress and the legitimation of state agendas: American proposals for school reform. *Curriculum and Teaching* 1(1–2), 11–24.

II

Pedagogies of Possibility

Decentering Discourses in Teacher Education: Or, the Unleashing of Unpopular Things

Deborah P. Britzman

There is something fundamentally scary about pedagogy because pedagogy references the unknown. Despite our best authorial intentions, no guarantees mediate our private lesson plans or the public effects of the pedagogical encounter. More often than not, things do not go according to plan: objectives reappear as too simple, too complicated, or get lost; concepts become glossed over, require long detours, or go awry; and evaluation rarely delivers its promise of closure. In fact, what seems most certain is that after the pedagogical encounter we must return to our plans, rethink our expectations, and theorize the tensions of multiple performances that compete for our attention. In short, pedagogy is filled with surprises, involuntary returns, and unanticipated twists. For this reason, we can conclude that pedagogy ushers in an intangibility that we can identify as 'the uncanny.' That is, enlightenment may well be our destination, but the journey is fraught with creepy detours.

Critical and feminist pedagogies can help us return to these tangles in ways that move beyond the impulse to manage techniques, discipline bodies, and control outcomes. Such pedagogies are meant to interpellate, or beacon, teachers and students with new discursive practices and new identities. The intent is to decenter the obvious and create the semiotic space for cultural critique. Given such uncharted terrains, those who advocate, construct, and practice these newer traditions are obligated to analyze the discursive moments that mark these pedagogies as both different and desirable. We are also required to grapple with the unfinished, the puzzling, and the awkward. For when powers shift, hierarchies invert, and certainty crumbles, and when boundaries are transgressed in voluntary and involuntary ways, the new dilemmas, tensions, and contradictions must be accounted.

My purpose is to explore the feminist pedagogical experiments of a team of student teachers in a tenth-grade literature class and attend to some of the engendered tensions that emerge when decentering pedagogies work to return participants to involuntary places. The concerns of postmodern theory—notions of the uncanny, of parody, of the play of meanings, and of the contradictory effects of discourse—frame my analysis. Elizabeth Wright suggests that "postmodern theory provides feminism with an additional framework, enabling it to articulate diversity and contradictions that spring up not only *between* various positions but also *within* various positions" (Wright, 1989, p. 146). Problems arise when we are unable to situate the contradictory effects of the positions we take or believe our positions can somehow transcend the contradictions we attempt to address. Thus my goal in this exploration is to narrate a sort of contest over the authorization of official and unofficial meanings that circulate in the feminist classroom. The reason, however, is not to point out winners or losers. In this contest, power and the boundaries of pedagogy are continually shifting. Moreover, the normative dualism of success and failure cannot intelligibly render the discursive qualities that mark this lesson and the identities of its participants. This analysis, then, should be read as a way into theorizing the tensions and the effects of pedagogies that intend to be critical and as a way of rethinking how pedagogy always makes available particular identities at the cost of others.

Pandora's Pedagogy

Behind critical pedagogies are critiques of the normative that work to assert what Bakhtin (1981) called "authoritative discourse." Authoritative discourse signifies the received and institutionally sanctioned knowledge that demands allegiance to the status quo and authorizes stereotypes as if they were unencumbered by ideological meanings. Such discourse is compelling: it persuades and is persuaded by relations of power, and it depends upon a style of narration that works to cover its own narrative tracks. This is because authoritative discourse positions the speaker as author. Anyone can take up authoritative discourse as if it were one's own. The problem is that this discourse never originates from the speaker. In actuality, the speaker merely borrows it without an awareness of serving as its bearer and without an understanding of what it means to carry its effects. This is the insidious nature of authoritative discourse: it asserts the unitary meanings we desire at the expense of recognizing the complicated constructs we live.

The development of pedagogies that are critical is meant to help students and teachers consciously concern themselves with the ways authoritative discourses interpellate or 'summon' the subject. 'Interpellation' refers to the unconscious ways in which authoritative ideas become infused with personal investment and thus become a part of who we are. Such a process suggests that there is more behind our desires and fears than individual choice. Ideally, critical pedagogies expose such operations by providing the strategies, the narratives, and the discursive positions that might support creative interventions in the process of coming to know. The goal is to call into question the authoritative discourses and the recipe knowledge that work to sustain the obvious. However, in doing that, pedagogies that are critical, in turn, must interpellate the subject. Nor can these pedagogies transcend authoritative knowledge. Indeed, every pedagogy is always dependent upon interpellation and upon the power to authorize particular discourses.

Recent writing about critical pedagogies (see, for example, Aiken, et al., 1987; Brodkey and Fine, 1988; Cohen, 1988; Ellsworth, 1989; Miller, 1990; Mohanty, 1986; Hall, 1981; and Williamson, 1981) has moved from a moralizing posture of advocacy and the promise of transcendence to a more self-reflexive stance. The actual difficulties of practicing critical theories, the uncomfortable ways teachers are implicated in any pedagogical encounter, and the tensions that are already embedded in critical practices are now admitted and theorized. For example, antiracist and feminist pedagogies have begun to address the uneven relation of theory and practice—the daily problems of transforming curriculum, students, and the self—as well as the complicated resistances students and teachers bear when they confront the imperatives of social change, social control, and radical agency. In this research, pedagogy is not just about encountering critical knowledge but also about constructing contextually dependent relations that recognize the power of lived experiences and of ideology. Methods of specifying one's pedagogy, identifying one's interests and investments, and resisting totalizing claims of transcendence are the contributions of this new scholarship. Equally important is the admission of the limits of the teacher and the contradictory desires she holds.

Incomplete attempts at social change are now being documented. Three related concerns mark this literature: (1) the problems unleashed by negative critique; (2) the contradictory effects of self-transformation; and (3) the tensions engendered when the political is coupled with the personal. Each of these concerns addresses the discursive boundaries of social relations, the local knowledge determined there, and the contradictory possibilities offered when critical pedagogy structures learning and teaching. For example, Aiken and colleagues catalog the "hydra-like" resistances male academics offer when asked to integrate feminist scholarship into the mainstream curriculum and how these resistances act upon feminist practices (Aiken, et al., 1987, p. 258). When one problem seemed to be resolved, another sprung up, reminding these feminists that "the scripts that underwrite masculinist culture are well learned and intensely resistant to change" (p. 272). Linda Brodkey and Michelle Fine (1988) analyze the contradictory sources of reluctance university women students hold when confronted with the painful dynamics of sexual harassment. Their work on narratives points to the need for understanding how history and social structure fashion the stories that can and cannot be told.

From another vantage, Judith Williamson addresses the dissonance of negative critique with the following warning to teachers: "It seems downright irresponsible to me to try and make students understand concepts like ideology without also showing understanding of how terrifying they are" (Williamson, 1981, p. 85). Concepts that threaten to throw students into emotional and social disarray are likely to be unpopular and viewed as yet another instance of the teacher's authority if the teacher asserts the critical without regard to the threats it poses. As Elizabeth Ellsworth (1989) argues, critical pedagogy implies that teachers are already liberated and students need liberation. To address issues of power, teachers must ground their pedagogical stories in the real and contradictory relations of race, class, and gender. Similarly, S. P. Mohanty (1986) critiques the difficulties of taking up new theoretical perspectives and the need to always understand pedagogy as overdetermined by radically contingent relations.

From another perspective, Philip Cohen argues that the rational basis of antiracist and feminist pedagogy is built upon the illusion that sentiments can be persuaded logically by merely replacing bad stereotypes with good ones. Yet the sources of stereotypes are not rational. Moreover, despite the fact that stereotypes work to freeze identities, there is still the potential to recuperate and redefine negative meanings. An excessive dependence on the power of positive role models cannot address this contradictory process. "What in one context is a term of racial hatred communicating a violent intent," Cohen points out, "may, in another, signal the message 'this is play' promoting a brand of inter-ethnic humor which can serve as a powerful diffuser of tensions" (Cohen, 1988, p. 28). In other words, to act as if meanings are stable is to already undermine the more difficult work of social change.

What must be addressed are the deep investments teachers and students have in the available discourses, and the ways they are borrowed, taken up, and reinflected with subjective meanings. With this in mind, Stuart Hall offers the example of teaching about race and warns of the necessity and the difficulty of creating:

> an atmosphere which allows people to say unpopular things. . . . What I am talking about here are the problems of handling the racist time-bomb and doing so adequately so that we connect with our students' experience and can therefore be sure of defusing it. That experience has to surface in the classroom even if its pretty horrendous to hear: better to hear it than not because what you don't hear you can't engage with. (Hall, 1981, pp. 58–59)

Yet the double problem of engaging with "unpopular things"— an engagement that is necessarily a part of any pedagogy that is critical—and what it might mean to the teacher is just beginning to be explored. For the gay or lesbian teacher and students who must listen as their cohorts work through or become more entrenched in their heterosexism, for the ethnic racial teachers and students who must listen to racist and sexist discourse as a precondition to convincing those to do otherwise, or, for that matter, for any teacher or student who attempts to deconstruct any kind of repressive ideology of the obvious, the unleashing of "unpopular things" always has the potential to not only colonize social imagination—that is, bring many back to the place of departure—but also to disorganize the efforts of those who attempt to intervene.

The question 'Why pedagogy?' is central to any practical discussion about the agency that joins teaching and learning. Pedagogy should both address the messy process of producing knowledge and suggest strategies for interpreting the knowledge that can and cannot be produced. Once Pandora's box is opened, we have to find ways to make sense of its cacophonous beckoning. In the context of English education, the site that borders the analysis of this article, and a place where unpopular things are often masked and unmasked by literary works, we need to think about practices of reading and interpreting that help students and teachers rethink the effects and beckonings of desire and power. This requires deconstruction of obvious reading strategies, such as practical criticism, that work—through their assertion of the tyranny of plot, theme, character, engendered conflict, and authorial intent—to legitimate fixed and essential meanings, and through their myth of attentiveness, couple textual authority with the teacher's authority. Pedagogies in English education, if they are to be critical, must begin to admit what it is that structures the authorization of meanings in ways that move beyond obdurate notions of textuality and linguistic essentialism. What follows is an exploration into the contradictory effects of a team effort of student teachers who attempted to help high school students read differently.

Unpopular Narratives

Unpopular narratives unleash ambiguous effects. A story may be deemed unpopular if it goes against the grain of the acceptable in ways that either offend sensibilities or challenge the comfort of clear boundaries. The unpopular disorganizes questions of morality, civility, and subjectivity. It can grate on the nerves or expose what might have been repressed. In any case, unpopular things call into question what is taken as already settled. They set loose unanticipated and rebellious meanings that throw into question our very agency. In tracing one brief incident in the lives of two student teachers, boundaries between the popular and the unpopular blur. In this classroom, at one moment ideas become unpopular when they challenge received knowledge or force people to consider how they are implicated in conditions that are oppressive. At another moment, unpopular ideas assert oppressive denials and subvert the fragile coalition that depends upon concern for others.

My narration of classroom practice traverses multiple contexts. The first context is an English education graduate student teaching seminar. The students were simultaneously enrolled in a student teaching internship and in university coursework. In the mornings they taught in high school settings and in the evenings they attended graduate education courses. I had the dual role of teaching the seminar in English methods and supervising the student teachers in their classrooms. Thus two contexts were always competing for attention—the university context where student participation was voluntary, and the high school context where student participation was compulsory.

My decision to attempt two kinds of decentering made this semester different from previous years of teaching and supervising. First, I wanted to disrupt the isolation of learning to teach by structuring the collaborative work of team teaching. Graduate students paired together, visited each other's classes, and chose a site for the team teaching assignment. Then, teams of student teachers collectively created, taught, and critiqued their lessons. Team teaching efforts were videotaped for the seminar to watch and to analyze. Second, I wanted to disrupt the hegemony of practical criticism in high school English classrooms and in my own seminar by working with newer theories of literary criticism. Over that semester, I worked to persuade graduate students to decenter received discourses of teacher education and English education. In doing so, the students and I collectively built contexts where our own recipe knowledge could be called into question. However, the tension between persuading graduate students to complicate their textual practices in a college seminar and then transform their understanding into meaningful pedagogy appropriate to the compulsory context of high school classrooms opened contradictions we neither anticipated nor resolved. Indeed, as succeeding drafts of this paper were circulated, read, and commented upon by seminar participants, I came to understand that at best, my version of what happened when a team of student teachers attempted to work with the complexities of race, gender, and power can only be partial. This is because multiple stories were always colliding and new meanings arose from this discursive rubble.

Erica and Kathleen chose to work with each other for the team teaching assignment. Their efforts were videotaped by a third member of the university seminar, and this tape was viewed by the seminar participants. Both of these young women identify themselves as feminists, are concerned with issues of social justice, and are articulate about the perplexing social relations that make up any classroom. Erica, an African-American woman, entered graduate school with a focus on English education, determined to introduce African-American literature to high school students. Her own school biography lacked not only African-American literature but any admission of the dynamics of race, gender, and class. In an assignment that asked students to examine their 'English autobiographies,' Erica identified in poignant terms the contradictory terrain of her own lived experience.

My English 10x class was full of rich kids, and I felt a bit out of place being the only black person in the class. . . . As a young teenager, I felt that I was not accepted as equally bright among white students, neither by my peers nor by my teachers. Yet,

I was considered too smart to be "cool" by most of my black peers, the majority of whom were non-Regents tracked due to behavior, not ability (my theory).

That year I...did a report on Gwendolyn Brooks. It had embarrassed me that of all her work, we read "We Real Cool," when I was the only black person in the class. I had a very awkward feeling that all eyes were on me, that such a poem was supposed to reflect my experiences or one typical of my race (opposed to the human race).

Kathleen, a bilingual Anglo-American, is an avid participant in theater and decided that English education would provide opportunities to explore the performative and expressive arts. Before attending graduate school, Kathleen had worked in a battered women's shelter, and she brought to her graduate work a commitment to the process of consciousness raising.

These women decided to teach, for two consecutive days, in Kathleen's tenth-grade upper-track English classroom. Erica usually taught in the town's junior high school and was eager to work with high school students for she believed that high school students were more mature and thus able to take on difficult material. The high school, situated in a small town, served the children of a lower-middle-class community. While only approximately 20 percent of the students were African-American, Asian, and Puerto Rican, this school represented the most racially diverse school in the area and had the aura of an urban high school. However, Kathleen's class did not reflect the school diversity and thus was similar to the classes of Erica's school biography: of the twenty-odd students in Kathleen's class, only one was African-American.

During their planning session, Erica and Kathleen decided to focus on how positions of power and desire are constructed in literature and in the student's world. This theme was central in the university seminar. To help their high school students work with the concepts of power and desire, the student teachers reintroduced Roland Barthes' (1974) narrative codes. Prior to their teamed lesson, Kathleen's class had worked with Barthes' codes. Three codes were discussed: the hermeneutic code, or the puzzles and questions the reader must answer when reading a text; the cultural code, or the knowledge of time, place, people, and cultural geography that readers draw upon to construct pictures from the narrative; and, the communicative code, or the study of how characters talk with one another, what it is that structures their talk, and the rules governing the said and the unsaid. These codes, according to Barthes, structure the unconscious work readers do to make sense of a text. In making these codes conscious, the teachers hoped that students could begin to theorize about what it is that sutures intertextual meanings and explicitly examine the classroom dialogue that realizes meaning.

As a way to apply Barthes' codes, the teachers presented visual slides of photographs that questioned gender and then presented Ann Petry's naturalist story, "Like a Winding Sheet." Erica had studied this story in an undergraduate course on black women's writing, and in that seminar the story spurred lively debate. Thus Erica believed that this text would provoke serious discussion on race and gender. Moreover, both Erica and Kathleen were pleased to create an opportunity to introduce an African-American writer and, in this small way, intervene in a curriculum that absented issues of race and gender.

"Like a Winding Sheet" complicates the uneasy dynamics of race, class, gender, power, and desire. It magnifies one day in the life of a black working-class couple. Although the narration is omnipotent, the story trails the point of view of the black man called Johnson. Johnson and his wife, Mae, work the night shift at different factories. On the late afternoon of Friday the thirteenth, they reluctantly leave for work. Johnson arrives late and his boss, a white woman, chastises him and calls him "a nigger." With clenched fists, Johnson tells the boss, "You got the right to get mad. . . .You got the right to cuss me four ways to Sunday but I ain't letting nobody call me a nigger." He realizes how easy it would be to beat her, yet despite the "curious tingling in his fingers," he suppresses his physical anger. However, for the rest of his shift he embodies "the queer feeling that his hands were not exactly a part of him any more—they had developed a separate life of their own over which he had no control." When his shift ends, Johnson walks to the subway and stops at a diner for coffee. He waits in line, but when it is his turn to be served, the white girl at the counter tells him the coffee urn is empty. Again Johnson feels the sensation of wanting to hit the girl for refusing a black man a cup of coffee but reasons with himself and walks out, not seeing the girl behind the counter make a new urn of coffee. He returns home exhausted, as does his wife, Mae. They begin to argue about small things and Mae tries to cajole him: "You're nothing but a old hungry nigger trying to act tough and. . ." Seized again by the tingling in his hands, Johnson "sent his fist shooting straight for her face." Although the idea of hitting his wife appalls him, he can't stop himself. "Like a Winding Sheet" ends with Johnson repeatedly hitting Mae.

Upon entering the classroom for the first day of this lesson, the tenth-grade students found their desks arranged in a large circle, a slide projector positioned in the center of the room, and a video camera (operated by another student teacher) recording their arrival. Students chose their seats and quietly waited for the class to begin. Unlike other days, when the students animatedly entered the room, this day they appeared subdued and self-conscious. Later, upon viewing this segment of the tape, the graduate seminar students attributed this tone to the presence of the video camera, Erica's status as a visiting teacher, and the day's material.

Kathleen had assigned "Like a Winding Sheet" the night before, so she began the class by asking the students to rethink the story and focus on its assumptions—the beliefs it took for granted. This question did not solicit anything but more self-conscious silence. Indeed, the entire period was marked by the two student teachers asking a series of literal and interpretive questions, cajoling barely audible responses from some very reluctant students. After approximately five minutes of unanswered questions, Erica provided a different context. She projected a photograph depicting an early twentieth-century white male washing clothes with a scrub board. Seated next to him was a white woman reading a magazine. The slide was titled "Washday." More students participated in this form of interpretation: they identified their surprise at viewing a man washing as a woman read, but they had difficulty exploring what it was that surprised them. One male student said the woman was reading *Sports Illustrated,* slyly introducing the notion of 'gender-bending.' When asked, the students could identify the narrative codes. Despite their initial surprise, however, they could not admit that the photograph addressed any problem when Erica asked, "Is there a problem here?"

A few minutes before the class ended, the student teachers tried to return to the Ann Petry story. The students resumed their reluctant state. They did respond, however, when Erica and Kathleen asked them about their own experiences with displaced anger and their views on the cultural rules of addressing and communicating with people in their lives. They began to discuss the different rules they use when speaking to teachers, bosses, parents, and friends, and they implied that their voices were more authentic when speaking to people in similar positions as opposed to speaking with people who hold power.

Watching the first part of this tape with the graduate seminar participants, I wondered aloud if the students had read the story and, if they had, what prevented them from participating in the discussion. As the graduate students watched this segment of the tape, everyone seemed to identify with the difficulties of helping students enter into the story. We had all experienced 'deadly' discussions from the perspective of teacher and student.

On the second day, when the high school students walked into their classrooms, the desks were arranged in groups of five, a handout of small-group discussion questions was placed on each desk, the schedule of the period's activities was written on the chalkboard, and the video camera had not yet started filming. Evidently, Erica and Kathleen had decided to structure the class in more explicit ways and provide opportunities for students to work with one another. Earlier that morning, Erica and Kathleen had arranged to begin the class with a surprise role play, where a female student walked into the classroom after the bell, and both Erica and Kathleen responded to her late entrance with anger, wielding their teacher authority for all to see. The fracas was such a surprise and tapped into such real fear that the student teacher responsible for the videotaping chose not to record the argument. That spectacle made everyone look bad. The camera began rolling only after the cameraperson realized the ploy, so the second segment of the tape began with Kathleen and Erica explaining about power and the rules that structure communication between students and teachers.

A few minutes before group work began, the whole class participated in a lively discussion of power. "When do students have power?" Kathleen asked. One student argued that students who receive the grade of 'A' have more power than students who receive the grade of 'C'. Another student disagreed: "You don't have power over a teacher no matter what grade you get." Erica admitted that, although it seemed as if teachers had power, they too were constrained by the system. "I'd change everything if I could," Erica said, and she seemed for a moment to be overwhelmed by the immensity of the problem. Both student teachers encouraged the students to define what they meant by power, and a few students expressed the idea of having control over what one does and being able to control others.

Each small group had two tasks. First they were to answer a series of questions about the story and come to a consensus about these answers. Second they were to rewrite the story's ending. In Erica's words: "Not to just add on to it but to change it." Their endings would then be read aloud to the entire class. During this small-group work, Erica and Kathleen circulated around the room, helping, listening, and supporting individual groups. The small groups were lively and the room, in startling contrast to the previous day, was filled with animated voices. A few minutes before the bell rang, students were asked to report on their progress and then to read their endings. "Let's just read the endings!" a young woman called out twice. "No," Kathleen said, "I want to hear your answers to the questions first."

A very short discussion initiated by Erica began with the question of what was 'bugging' Johnson. The only black student in the class, a young man, said he thought racism hurt Johnson. A white female student disagreed: she did not think that the story was about race. "What made you think it was a race issue?" Erica softly asked the young man. "She called him a nigger," he replied in a barely audible voice. Carefully, Erica responded, "Yes, so that's something that could point to race." Yet Erica did not pursue this point with the female student who did not view the story as a racial one. Instead—partly due to lack of time, and partly due to the painful experience of dealing with the denial of race—Erica asked another question: "What does it mean that all of Johnson's confrontations were with women?" That question was lost because of the time. The students were restless and wanted to listen to each others endings more than discuss the story, and because this was Erica's last day as a visiting teacher, both teachers needed to draw the lesson to a close.

About five minutes before the dismissal bell was to ring, four groups read their endings aloud. The third group, which included the young woman who had been overeager to read the story she had composed for the group, raised the most distress. Although this ending was not representative of the other groups' (and in fact was mainly an individual as opposed to a group effort, and thus diverged from the group assignment), it was this story and the way it was received by the high school students that haunted the graduate student seminar. The seminar's collective fascination and horror with this particular videotaped narrative was partly because it was a story overpopulated with offensive things, partly because it challenged so much of the team teaching efforts, and partly because almost everyone felt the same thing could happen in their classes.

The graduate seminar watched the video tape in horror as the young white girl read aloud rather gleefully:

> He overdosed on PCP that he has been taking all along (that he bought from Lester). Then he proceeded to the local pub and got rather drunk. He then returned home. Mae was rather perturbed because he was quite late. She started complaining. He yelled, "Shut up ——— ." He then went crazy. Pulled out a

butcher knife, stabbed her 69 times, raped her because she was still warm. Took her and threw her over the bridge to get into the river and then decided to jump to be with her because he really did love her, but before he did he savagely and brutally murdered 7 white nuns with a razorblade studded garden hose.

At the end of this performance, the high school students broke out in wild laughter. In the midst of this uproar, Erica said to the student who had written the story: "That's really sick." But the student teachers felt compelled to quiet the class in order for the last group to read their ending. And this last group had in fact created an alternative ending—Johnson talked through his frustrations, threw objects around instead of beating Mae, and then found a job that made him feel good—but their narrative was hardly heard because the other students were still stuck in the previous narrative. The tape ends with both student teachers looking distraught and the students, still excited about the slasher story, quickly fleeing the room at the sound of the bell. Later, Erica expressed her shock to me: "After hearing that story, I just didn't have any words."

Realizing that they could not end the lesson in that commination, Erica and Kathleen spent the afternoon talking about ways to intervene. Both teachers found the narrative fantastically disturbing and were puzzled that a young woman had constructed such a violent scenario. Indeed, they initially felt that had a young man produced that narrative, reasons for it might have been neatly drawn. Regardless of author, however, the narrative provoked complicated feelings.

Erica was extremely distressed about the entire tenor of the class—that students were unwilling to discuss race and that the narrative returned students to the racist stereotypes she was trying to deconstruct. Moreover, she felt that the narrative was offensive to herself and the only black student in the class in a way the white students and Kathleen could never understand. Indeed, upon further discussion of this incident a few weeks later with both student teachers, Erica felt that a significant problem was that she and Kathleen should have discussed their individual views of what it means to work with the concept of race *before* trying to work with students. The entire incident conjured up her own educational biography—the double pain of being singled out and rendered invisible, of having to listen to the stereotypical images of black culture, and of being confronted with the triple refusal of white students unable to understand their own complicity in racism, view themselves as raced, and of white teachers never intervening in their students' racism.

Kathleen recognized Erica's pain and a few weeks later understood that she should have told the students what her investment was in teaching the story and why she cared so much about fighting racism and sexism. Kathleen believed she should have initiated public dialogue with Erica during class time to demonstrate the power of dialogue and their friendship. This understanding of the power of dialogue is reminiscent of Bell Hooks' discussion of "difficult dialogues" and the need for black and white women to publicly talk about race and thus build solidarity. "Despite the growing body of work wherein white women feminists talk and write about race," Hooks states, "we need to know more about how and why white women develop anti-racist consciousness. We need to hear white women talk about what happens when they challenge white supremacy. How does this challenge transform the feminist practice?" (Hooks, 1990, p. 43) Kathleen also had a relationship with this white girl and identified her behavior as another instance of the girl as actress, staging her own text. The different pain of both teachers motivated them to plan one last lesson which Kathleen would have to teach alone. (Unfortunately, Erica had to return to teach her own class.)

The next day, without the video camera, Kathleen handed back the students' endings and asked them to return to their small groups. She then asked them to re-read their own endings for the embedded narrative codes, and identify the cultural, communicative, and hermeneutic codes. Later, Kathleen described the students' surprise at having to return to their endings. While the students expected to apply these codes to literature, they seemed shocked that, as Kathleen described, "they would be held accountable for their own stories." Kathleen paid special attention to the small group of girls who produced the most unpopular narrative. The young woman who staged her own text still refused to explore how her narrative constructed race and gender. Of the three codes she was asked to identify, she could only admit that her story assumed one: "Conflicts aren't really resolved, they're taken out in violence." As for the cultural code, which the young woman read as the moral, she asserted patriarchal imperatives: "The man should be the head of the house." Crossed out on her paper was the last sentence: "A raving maniac will always rape a warm body."

The Unpopular as Uncanny

To name an experience as uncanny is to identify it as oddly familiar and strangely estranged.[1] Perceptual borders are transgressed, and this opens a conceptual and psychic uncertainty between the phantasm and the real. Elizabeth Wilson describes the uncanny as "the persistent re-enactment of past unresolved conflicts in the present" (Wilson, 1989, p. 42). "Repetition," Constance Penley writes, "is the source of the uncanny" (Penley, 1989, p. 149). What gives the uncanny its eerie feeling may be found in Freud's famous dictum of "the return of the repressed." Secrets are enacted despite attempts to keep them hidden, and their reappearance feels creepy. The uncanny is a revisited place, and because of this it is an appropriate metaphor for the classroom. In the case of the student teacher, who returns to the familiar classroom in an unfamiliar role, and who attempts to educate others while being educated, uncanny feelings of acting in involuntary ways are quite common. This is partly due to the disconcerting fact that our educational biographies are haunted by both good and bad teachers (Britzman, 1991).

Central questions become unleashed if we read the narrative produced by this young white girl as uncanny—as overpopulated with repetitious violence, culturally taboo linguistic markers, and a relentless inversion of the student teachers' pedagogy. What kinds of conflict are being re-enacted and repressed? What investments, identifications, and refusals structure such conflict? To theorize about these kinds of questions, I will first return to the borders of the narrative—a tenth-grade English class taught by two young feminist teachers. Then I will consider some of the contradictory meanings that circulate both within this narrative and within the pedagogy of the student teachers.

Inscribed in any pedagogy are the tensions of the social. Every pedagogy is overburdened with relations of power, techniques of social control, and institutional mandates. Thus pedagogy articulates imperatives of particular discourses and enacts specific styles of interpellation. There are always claims of knowledge, regimes of truth, and the deployment of discursive rules that render communication and conduct intelligible and unintelligible. Feminist pedagogy is no stranger to these tensions. In fact, according to Paula Treichler (1986), the feminist classroom should become the site where such tensions, even if they cannot be resolved, are made explicit. Yet this mandate, to work with the personal as if it were overburdened by the political, requires serious persuasion and a willingness to share one's own stories. Such a willingness is difficult because both teachers and students are adept at masking their feelings and views. Moreover, many believe that to work with the personal as if it were political means claiming an identity overdetermined by social constructions or as an effect of discursive regimes. Judith Butler thoughtfully disputes this myth:

For an identity to be an effect means that it is neither fully determined nor fully artificial and arbitrary. . . . Construction is not opposed to agency; it is the necessary scene of agency, the very terms in which agency is articulated and becomes culturally intelligible. (Butler, 1990, p. 147)

Such an approach may help us get beyond the dualistic argument that to be a construct one cannot be an agent. In other words, the problem of interpellation can be thought about differently if we recognize the range of subject positions made available to the student teachers and the students in school contexts and consider the terms the classroom students employed to make these positions culturally intelligible.

The physical arrangement of the classroom suggests an odd combination of coercion and willingness. Recall that before the students' entrance, the desks were arranged in a large circle and later, in clusters of small groups. Particular seats were not assigned, but the circle—a strategy meant to challenge the traditional hierarchical order of learning and teaching—was as compulsory as the students' class attendance. Like rows of desks, the circle lends itself to easy surveillance. Yet this was not the goal. In arranging desks in this way, these student teachers wished to signal to their students that face-to-face encounters were desirable. The tension was that although the student teachers were a part of this circle, they were painfully aware that they were the ones who initiated and authorized discourse. This self-consciousness made them hesitant to reveal their own agenda.

Within this arrangement, students were invited to reflect on the curriculum by way of their own personal experiences. The tension was that while students were asked to be the experts in their own lives through the admission of the personal as evidence of the Petry story, both teachers and students had difficulty extending such experiences beyond the confines of the students' personal world. And the student teachers, evidently not wanting to influence the students with their own stories, suppressed their views. So, like a reluctant guest, subjective moments of the students were invited, briefly acknowledged by the student teachers, but then left unattended. Inviting subjectivity is always difficult, especially in contexts where the personal is not valued. Feminist pedagogy is meant to redress this lack. On the one hand, feminist pedagogy begins with the acknowledgment of subjective experience, and it is through this experience that voices are welcomed and solidarity is built. On the other hand, feminist pedagogy must come to terms with the fact that experience is neither transparent nor a guarantor of access to understanding. These student teachers did value the students' voices. The problem they faced, however, was what to do once the voices arrived and how to engage and extend these voices in dialogue.

On the second day, the students worked with each other in small groups and then read their works aloud. Presumably, the students became teachers while the student teachers took up the role of facilitator, another position common to feminist pedagogy. As facilitators, they listened, encouraged, and suggested ways to think about the story and to collaborate in small groups. But the student teachers also had a symbolic presence in that the list of questions students were to address embodied the teachers' agenda. These questions structured the students' return to Ann Petry's story and focused on Johnson's actions, perceptions, and problems. Then each group was asked to "write a different ending for the story." The first task, by way of the questions, had ordered student discourse, whereas the second task—writing a different ending—seemed to ask students to order their own discourse. It must be admitted here that these student teachers—concerned as they are with feminism and with social justice—actually desired their students to intervene in the story in particular ways. The implicit expectation was that students use their 'good' voices and interrupt Johnson and Mae's cycle of oppression.

There is, in all of this, an odd combination of coercion and willingness, of the persuasive power of feminist morality and the rebellious subjectivities of those who resist it. There is both the hope that students will say what they think and the fear of insensitive thoughts, the desire for students to take up concerns for social justice and the dread that they will hold onto repressive discourses as if they were their own. In such a combination, the boundaries of persuasion—of who persuades whom—blur. Such a tension unravels the supposedly seamless essentialism of cultural feminism—the belief that the experience of female gender implicitly confers insight into the dynamics of women's oppression; that women have a core experience; that "ontological givens" (Wright, 1989) lead one to particular conclusions; and that feminist subjectivity can be unified through narrative strategies (Cocks, 1989; Alcoff, 1988). The unadmitted tension in cultural feminism is that there has never been a neat correspondence between one's place in the social hierarchy and one's political commitments. This tension affects everyone. Yet the essentialist narrative of social change can only pose the following dualism: on the one hand, if teachers are persuasive, students may take on the desires of teachers as if they were their own; on the other hand, if teachers are successful, students will find their own voice. In this dualism, the only 'true' voice is the teacher's, and thus willingness can only be realized through coercion.

A different way to think about pedagogy begins with the dialogic that teachers and students work hard interpellating and changing each other. In this process, identities are offered and refused. And as a means of self-understanding, identities are tried on, refashioned, and even left behind. We must begin to understand the inevitability of interpellation and the endless struggle to disengage oneself from it. Shoshanna Felman in writing about ignorance, complicates this point:

> Teaching... has to deal not so much with lack of knowledge as with resistances to knowledge.... [The refusal to know] is not a simple lack of information but the incapacity—or refusal—to acknowledge *one's own implication* in the information. (Felman, 1982, p. 30)

Thus, to begin unraveling all that beckons us requires that we admit how we are implicated—or, how we take on, yet re-inflect—the intentions of others as if we were the author, not the bearer, of ideology. Teachers and students are continually trying on narrative identities that attempt to persuade as they are persuaded by relations of power. To think of pedagogy in dialogic ways is to concern ourselves not just with what it means to know and be known, but with how we come to know and come to refuse knowledge.

The student teachers in this complicated story were implicated on a number of levels. They tried to invite student voices yet felt the tension of moving the students to new and perhaps terrifying and thus unpopular places. They created contexts where dialogue was valued but seemed disconcerted with the dialogue produced. Finally, their lesson was one where students were asked to think about power and desire in contexts that pushed to extinguish the contradictions that circulate within it. That is, schooling, as a site of power and desire, rarely admits these dynamics in ways that empower students or teachers. And it was not until the 'terrible' narrative was read that these student teachers began to reevaluate the difficulties of feminist pedagogy.

The young white girl also seemed to struggle with multiple and contradictory interpellations—of feminist discourse, popular culture, and her own series of denials, identifications, and stagings. In discussing the contradictory relations between pedagogy and psychoanalysis, Constance Penley observes:

> The teacher is not a smooth mirror in which the student-subject can see the reflected structure of its own demand and desire. This is because the student can always sense the hidden demands of the teacher... The student, like the child with the parent, is almost *clairvoyant* when it comes to understanding the desire of the Other and how best narcissistically to mirror the Other's desires. (Penley, 1989, p. 169)

It may well be that this girl asserted her own unpopular narrative precisely to let the teachers know that although their feminist desires were at least recognized, they would not be granted. On the other hand, if we return to Shoshanna Felman's concern with ignorance as the refusal to know, this girl's "unpopular" narrative may be a refusal to identify with the vulnerability of women. Recall, for a moment, the girl's ending. The identity of Mae was reduced to a complaining voice. She was stabbed sixty-nine times and was, in essence, obliterated. And although Johnson held the butcher knife, he too was erased by drugs and alcohol. The power of the story, then, rests in the narrator who freely asserts phallic symbols without the signifier. Such an odd and contradictory narrative defies easy interpretation or interpellation.

Still, this narrative is uncanny in what it does. It recalls the Willie Horton narrative popularized by George Bush's presidential campaign.[2] Positioned by a conservative discourse of law and order, Willie Horton doubly signified the failure of liberal reform and the white racist's construction of the black male (Walton, 1989). Although the narrative of Willie Horton differs somewhat from this white girl's narrative of Johnson, her 'choice' to extend the violence of Ann Petry's story may have been an attempt to reject a feminist narrative (thereby asserting the failure of reform) and to return to popular racist narratives which may have been more persuasive to her. These intentions were almost admitted when she was asked to return to her story and identify the cultural codes working through it. The girl could admit that "conflicts aren't really resolved, they're taken out in violence," but she was unwilling to explore her own implication in this construction of race. She may well have felt protected by parody in that this trope can work to construct racist and sexist ideology without claiming to do so.[3]

The spectacle of the teenage slasher films populates this fantastic narrative as well, but in ways that rewrite the rules of this genre. For example, Carol Clover's provocative analysis of forty slasher films leads her to conclude that, "rape is practically nonexistent in the slasher film. . . violence and sex are not concomitants but alternatives. . . ." (Clover, 1987, p. 196). Moreover, according to Clover, the 'hero' of the slasher genre is not the mutilated guy who is always returning to reek bloody havoc on unsuspecting teenagers and their suspecting (and largely male) teenage audiences. Rather the 'hero' is actually what Clover calls the "Last Girl," who not only stays alive but is the only person who can stop—and not without amazing moments of trauma and not without participating in—the repetitive murderous rampage. Perhaps on the figurative level, the narrator positioned herself as the "Last Girl." But on the literal level, in both the girl's narrative and in the slasher films, we only have the victims, those who are usually not smart enough to read the cultural codes, and even if they read them the codes are of no use because there are no stable signifiers in this world and no real lessons to learn. At first glance, then, the sheer viscerality of terrifying, grossing out, and appalling her classroom cohorts and teachers may well have been the purpose. Indeed, such intentions most disturb the ostensible rational purposes of school and most disrupt any movement toward a feminist narrative. The irony is that traditional pedagogies would have never created the space for such a narrative, and the tension is that feminist pedagogy created the conditions for such a narrative to be unleashed.

One problem, then, is that this narrative met the student teachers' pedagogical dare: to voice one's own ending despite the authority of the teachers. Yet as we shall see, questions of power are central to the authority these student teachers created. The girl's narrative offered a pastiche of discourses, a tacky fixing of fragmented copies that work to regulate what is taken as the real. On the one hand, this borrowed narrative asserts cultural taboos that decenter obdurate notions of rationality. On the other hand, this kind of decentering depends upon popular racist images that provoke hurt and shame in some students yet help other students bond. Its effects are even more contradictory than the shifting meanings that antiracist pedagogies attempt to address. In this white girl's construction, she must reject feminism in order to create a masculinist solidarity with the majority of her white peers. So while her discourse decenters, it also firmly entrenches the girl in cultural authority. She positioned her political imagination as colonized by the narrative of Willie Horton and her aesthetic imagination as colonized by the slasher genre.

Is this lesson an instance of "the uncanny"? What familiar secrets are being unleased? What are the sources of ambiguity, of dread, of what Freud called "creepy terror"? One must consider whether the girl's narrative takes us into the real world of racism or constructs a horrendous fiction that depends upon the obviousness of popular racism, the parody of feminism, and the assertion of the phallic. The narration is both familiar and overpopulated with secrets. Like the hermeneutic code, it suggests puzzles, incongruence, and the question; 'But then what happened?' Cultural codes are traversed; the critical agency, so desired by these student teachers, goes awry. From the perspectives of the student teachers, there is the return to an 'involuntary place,' for on some levels this unpopular narrative seems to bring the class back to where they began—a struggle with feminism and a refusal to consider how each of us is implicated in the vulnerabilities and constructions of gender, race, and class.

In his essay, "The Uncanny," Freud provides some revealing personal examples. In one instance he recounts a time when he became lost.

> Once, as I was walking through the deserted streets of a provincial town in Italy, which was strange to me, on a hot summer afternoon, I found myself in a quarter the character of which could not long remain in doubt. Nothing but painted women were to be seen at the windows of the small houses, and I hastened to leave the narrow street at the next turning. But after having wandered for a while without being directed, I suddenly found myself back in the same street, where my presence was now beginning to excite attention. I hurried away once more, but only to arrive yet a third time by devious paths in the same place. Now however, a feeling overcame me which I can only describe as uncanny. (Freud, 1958, pp. 143–144)

Involuntary returns are unsettling, particularly when one's efforts manufacture such returns. In the case of Freud, lost in what seems to be a neighborhood of "painted women," there may be the additional fear of being identified as a john, of losing one's anonymity, and of being coupled with an identity that at once disrupts and constructs one's sense of place, time, and desire. Thus, part of our reflection about what it means to teach and learn must concern the problems of being lost, of being mistaken, of appearing as someone other than one desires or supposes: even the ways our efforts produce creepy detours or dreaded destinations. The unpopular narratives that are unleashed and that do coexist uneasily with feminist pedagogy, then, must not be read as failures but as part of a process that necessarily blurs the certain boundaries between coercion and willingness. To think about the "uncanny" in pedagogy is to consider this terrifying underside and to reflect upon how pedagogy has as much to do with fashioning desires, investments, and identities as it does with constructing and interpreting knowledge.

But once we admit the terrible underside, how might pedagogy address it? Can pedagogy decenter authoritative discourses without unleashing unpopular things? The answer is no. The social categories of race, class, and sex are what Stuart Hall calls, "combustible materials" (Hall, 1981, p. 59). They incite so easily because everyone embodies these categories and through these categories identity, investments, and desires are made. Race, sex, and class—already overburdened by social meanings—are the conceptual lenses through which people are recognized. Thus, on the one hand, teachers must acknowledge "the strong emotional ideological commitments" (Hall, 1981, p. 58) everyone has to positions about race, class, and sex. On the other hand, if these commitments are to be made explicit, they must be understood beyond the discourse of human relations and individual attitudes. To undermine the obvious requires pedagogical practices that address how the obvious is historically constructed and how it is sustained through discursive practices.

The student teachers in this study did create strategies for students to excavate their discourses. In returning to Barthes' codes and in applying these codes to their own narratives, students were challenged to undermine their assumptions about how social life is lived. And although this strategy was not totally taken up by every student—indeed there was the phenomenon of the "Last Girl"—what seems most significant is that these student teachers' efforts were not disorganized by unpopular things. In some ways, unpopular things mobilized their practices. This dialogue between the conditions of pedagogy and the knowledge and identities produced there must become a central consideration in critical pedagogies. Familiarity with postmodern concepts such as the uncanny, parody, and the contradictory play of meanings may help teachers rethink their pedagogical efforts in ways that can take into account the subjective world of students and the deep investments students hold in the ready-made discourses that live in schools and in the larger social world. Such concepts may help those who practice critical and feminist pedagogies to reexamine whether moralizing postures are in fact automatically emancipatory. Clearly, it is not a question of using 'good' voices, but rather that feminist and critical pedagogies become most significant when teachers and students can first examine how any voice mobilizes deep investments, discursive positions, and contradictory identifications. Only then can we evaluate whether the subject positions offered construct possibilities for understanding how people work and attaching received realities to possible ones.

Notes

1. I am grateful to Professors Waren Wager and Jean Quataert for their translation of the German word *unheimlich*. In his essay on "The Uncanny," Freud examines the etymology of the work *heimlich,* which can mean 'home,' and *unheimlich,* literally 'unhomely'. Freud quotes a German dictionary: "From the idea of 'homelike', 'belonging to the house', the further idea is developed of something withdrawn from the eyes of others, something concealed, secret, and this idea is expanded in many ways. . . . (Freud, 1958, p. 130). The idea here is that the home, as the private sphere, is also a place of secrets.

2. Willie Horton, a black man, was sentenced to life imprisonment in Massachusetts for murder in 1974. In the early 1980s Horton, while working in a prison day work release program, raped a white woman in front of her fiance, who was also attacked. One of the supporters of the prison release work program was Michael Dukakis, Governor of Massachusetts and presidential candidate for the Democratic party in 1988. During the 1988 presidential campaign, George Bush, the Republican candidate, ran on a law-and-order platform which exploited the Willie Horton case as an example of the liberals' inability to control crime. A mug shot of Willie Horton became a commercial for George Bush's "get tough" campaign. The entire episode symbolized the racialization of crime in Republican discourse.

3. Racist and sexist humor, for example, is often defended by its form. If it is only a joke, the reasoning goes, then no one will take it seriously. For example, male standup comedians such as Andrew Dice Clay, Dr. Dirty, and Eddie Murphy fall back on this rationale to defend offensive humor.

References

Aiken, S., et al. (1987). Trying transformations: Curriculum integration and the problem of resistance. *Signs, 12*(2), 255–275.

Alcoff, L. (1988). Cultural feminism versus post structuralism: The identity crisis in feminist theory. *Signs, 13*(3), 405–436.

Bakhtin, M. M. (1986). *The dialogic imagination.* (Trans. C. Emerson & M. Holquist.) Austin: University of Texas Press.

Barthes, R. (1974) *S/Z: An essay.* (Trans. R. Miller.) New York: Hill and Wang.

Britzman, D. (1991). *Practice makes practice: A critical study of learning to teach.* Albany: State University of New York Press.

Brodkey, L. & Fine, M. (1988). Presence of mind in the absence of body. *Journal of Education, 170*(3), 84–99.

Butler, J. (1990). *Gender trouble: Feminism and the subversion of identity.* New York: Routledge.

Clover, C. (1987). Her body, himself: Gender in the slasher film. *Representations, 20* (Fall), 187–228.

Cohen, P. (1988). Tarzan and the jungle bunnies: Class, race, and sex in popular culture. *New Formations, 5,* 25–30.

Cocks, J. (1989). *The oppositional imagination.* New York: Routledge.

Ellsworth, E. (1989). Why doesn't this feel empowering? Working through the repressive myths of critical pedagogy. *Harvard Educational Review, 59*(3), 297–324.

Felman, S. (1982). Psychoanalysis and education: Teaching terminable and interminable. *Yale French Studies, 63,* 21–44.

Freud, S. (1958). The 'Uncanny'. In B. Nelson (Ed.), *On creativity and the unconscious: papers on the psychology of art, literature, love, religion* (pp. 122–161). New York: Harper and Row.

Hall, S. (1981). Teaching race. In A. James & R. Jeffcoate (Eds.), *The school in the multicultural society* (pp. 58–69). London: Harper and Row.

Hooks, B. (1990). Feminism and racism: The struggle continues. *Zeta Magazine, 3*(7/8), 41–43.

Miller, J. (1990). *Creating spaces and finding voices: Teachers collaborating for empowerment.* Albany: State University of New York Press.

Mohanty, S. P. (1986). Radical teaching, radical theory: The ambiguous politics of meaning. In C. Nelson (Ed.), *Theory in the Classroom* (pp. 149–176). Urbana: University of Illinois Press.

Penley, C. (1989). *The future of an illusion: Film, feminism, and psychoanalysis.* Minneapolis: University of Minnesota Press.

Treichler, P. (1986). Teaching Feminist Theory. In C. Nelson (Ed.), *Theory in the classroom.* 57–128. Urbana: University of Illinois Press.

Walton, A. (1989). Willie Horton and me. *New York Times Magazine* (August 20, 1989), 52–53, 72.

Williamson, J. (1981). How does girl number twenty understand ideology? *Screen Education, 40*(2), 80–87.

Wilson, E. (1989). *Hallucinations: Life in the post-modern city.* London: Hutchinson Radius.

Wright, E. (1989). Thoroughly postmodern feminist criticism. In T. Brennan (Ed.), *Between feminism and psychoanalysis.* 141–152. New York: Routledge.

The Politics of Race: Through the Eyes of African-American Teachers[1]

Michèle Foster

Research on teachers, though extensive, has generally disregarded the experiences of African-American teachers.[2] 'Wisdom of practice' studies and other studies of teacher thinking have generally ignored the experiences of teachers of color, particularly those who teach African-American students (Shulman, 1987). And though African-Americans are more prominent in sociological and anthropological studies of teachers, they are frequently portrayed in this literature as uncaring, unsympathetic, rigid individuals who, regardless of their class origins, neither identify with or relate well to their working-class, African-American pupils (Spencer, 1986; Rist, 1970, 1973; Conroy, 1972). While some of this scholarship has been more inclusive, sympathetic and balanced portrayals of African-American teachers such as those by Sara Lightfoot (1978), Philip Sterling (1972) and Gerda Lerner (1972) are rare.

The experiences of African-Americans are rarely encountered in the first-person teacher narratives despite countless examples of this genre. Of sixty-five first-person teacher narratives written in this century reviewed by this author, fewer than six were authored by African-Americans. A number of first-person teacher accounts deal specifically with the instruction of African-American pupils, but most of these were written by socially conscious white teacher-activists and reformers (Kohl, 1967; Herndon, 1968; Decker, 1969; Kozol, 1972). Although first-person accounts by African-American teachers are few, perhaps characteristically of the genre, when these teachers do write about their own practice, many of them reveal information about their political views and how these views influence their teaching practice. Narratives by Fannie Jackson (1913), Septima Clark (1962), James Haskins (1971), Dorothy Robinson (1974), and Mamie Fields (1985),

all works by African-American teachers written in this century,
provide some insight into the political orientation of their authors.

Compared to portrayals of white teachers, positive character-
izations of black teachers are infrequent. In the same way that
researchers have planted the idea of the culturally deprived child,
so too (perhaps unwittingly through omission, distortion, and negative
portrayals) have they sown the idea that African-American teachers
are indifferent, uncaring, and lacking the political perspective
required to teach African-American students effectively. But, not all
African-American teachers are guilty of holding the perspectives
suggested by earlier studies. In fact, this unflattering portrayal of
African-American teachers contrasts sharply with the views held by
the African-American community of its teachers as revealed in essays,
narratives, and sociological studies written by and about African-
Americans.[3] According to these accounts, not only have African-
American teachers developed productive relationships with their
pupils, but they have been capable teachers who, despite overwhelming odds, have challenged the status quo by encouraging black
students to achieve beyond what society has expected of them
(Blauner, 1989; Fields, 1985; Kluger, 1979; Murray, 1970; Clark,
1962).

Historically paid less than their white counterparts, rarely
employed except to teach African-American pupils, opposed by unions
seeking to preserve seniority rights of largely white constituencies,
dismissed in large numbers following the *Brown v. Board of Education*
decision, and denied access to teaching positions through increased
testing at all levels—the lives and careers of African-American
teachers have been seriously affected by racism (Tyack, 1974;
Franklin, 1979; Curry, 1981; Anderson, 1989; Ethridge, 1979;
Dilworth, 1984). This paper, which focuses on the politics of race,
emerges from a larger ongoing study of African-American teachers.
It examines the attitudes and views of sixteen African-American
teachers on issues related to race. It considers the racism they
encountered in their own schooling, their experiences in both
segregated and desegregated school systems, and their understanding
of the structural constraints imposed by race; and it examines how
these experiences have shaped and influenced their teaching practice
and pedagogy. The paper contends that these teachers have been
exploited, victimized, and marginalized by the larger society as well
as by the educational institutions in which they work. As a result
(as I have argued elsewhere [Foster, 1989]), they understand the
structural constraints of race in their own lives and on their teaching

practice better than they do those imposed by gender and class. The purpose of this paper is twofold: first, it will document the noteworthy but often overlooked work of African-American teachers, thereby offering a view of them rarely encountered in the research literature; and second, it will show by their example that, despite the difficult circumstances in which teachers often find themselves, it is possible to consciously embrace an educational philosophy and fashion a pedagogy designed to counteract oppression and foster empowerment.

Listening to African-American Teachers Tell Their Own Stories

I interviewed sixteen exemplary teachers, twelve female and four male, who were chosen by community nomination.[4] Using open-ended life-history methods, I asked them about their childhoods, family and community lives, schooling experiences (at the elementary, secondary, and postsecondary levels), current and previous teaching positions, and personal philosophies and pedagogies of education. These teachers ranged in age from forty-five to eighty-four (the majority were in their forties and fifties), and their years of teaching experience ranged from twenty to sixty-six. Seven have been employed as elementary teachers for most of their careers, eight as high school teachers, and one as a junior high teacher. All began their careers in predominantly black schools, and thirteen still teach in predominantly low-income black schools in urban or rural communities.

All of the teachers interviewed grew up and most began their professional lives during the time that 'separate but equal' was the law in the United States. Eleven spent their entire childhoods in officially segregated communities where laws dictated separate schools for blacks and whites. Four grew up in communities not segregated by law, and one woman spent half her childhood in a legally segregated community but by early adolescence had moved north where she completed school.

Experiences in Communities of Orientation

Raised in different environments, each teacher experienced the brand of racism peculiar to his or her region. Many who grew up in segregated communities recalled walking to school while white children rode buses, attending school in buildings in disrepair, and studying from books handed down from white schoolchildren. Despite these negative aspects of their schooling experiences, the teachers also remembered African-American teachers who lived or boarded in their communities, who often acted as surrogate parents, and who were involved with them outside of school in church and community life and activities. In contrast, although most of the teachers from northern communities began their schooling in racially isolated schools, by secondary school they all attended majority-white schools, which employed few, if any African-American teachers and in which there were only a handful of African-American pupils enrolled. In fact, none of the teachers raised in northern communities was taught by an African-American teacher before attending college. Thus, while the teachers growing up in segregated communities were firmly anchored in their African-American communities and their community life reinforced by their schooling experiences, the northern teachers were forced to leave their communities of origin to secure favorable schooling.

The differences in the northern and southern schooling experiences of these teachers is captured best by the account of one woman who attended school in Austin, Texas through grade six before relocating with her family to Boston.[5]

> I don't really feel that I had the closeness of the teachers there (in Boston) that I had of those in the other school, because they were black teachers in Austin. I don't remember a black teacher until. . . I'm trying to think. One does not stick out in my mind. Yeah, in Roxbury. I think when I was in the South, I felt closer to my teachers. I also knew some of them as human beings, and where they lived, and some of them were even part of the churches. I don't think I knew the teachers there (in Boston) as well. I kind of feel, too, that as I look back with the teachers that I had in Austin, they were even involved in afterschool activities and some other kind of things with kids. That was not the case (in Boston). I'm not saying they weren't good teachers, but I remember so many kinds of things that in elementary school. . . as I told you the PE teacher who taught us to dance, the programs. I remember the little drill team that she had and I remember the soccer games we had in elementary school and the PE teacher even had some little cheerleaders, although in her own way even with what she had to work with. I didn't have that (in Boston).

At issue here is that, regardless of the setting in which they were raised, all of these teachers were aware of the marginal position that they and other African-Americans held in the larger society.

Experiences Before Desegregation

At the time these teachers entered the profession, between 1928 and 1968, teaching was one of the few jobs available to college-educated African-Americans. Though the period during which these sixteen teachers began their careers spans forty years, in keeping with the laws of de jure segregated school systems and the practices of de facto segregated school systems of the times, all except two of the participants in this study began their careers in all-black or majority-black schools. For those who began their careers in legally segregated communities, the place of African-American teachers was unambiguous. Although all African-American teachers were concentrated in separate schools, within these confines the range of teaching and administrative opportunities was open to them. Northern communities, on the other hand, employed unofficial and more subtle practices to concentrate African-American teachers in certain schools and to keep them out of certain grade levels. Three teachers who began their careers in the Boston and Hartford public school systems in the 1950s remember the unofficial placement practices of central offices that resulted in the concentration of African-American teachers in certain schools and at specific grade levels:

Because at the time I started teaching, black teachers were assigned to just that strip going from the South End into Roxbury, between, let me see, Tremont Street and Washington. You didn't get any choice. That's where you were sent and most of the black teachers had a very hard time out of town (the area where black teachers were assigned).

Then I came to Hartford. Did not get a job immediately. I applied. This was in 53. I applied each year that I went back to West Virginia, but they didn't have any openings, or they never called me. . . . I subbed at the Noah Webster School which was in the Northwest section of the city which was predominantly white—it was white. I was a long term sub for two months because the teacher there was on maternity leave. At the end of June the principal asked me what was I gonna do next year. I said I didn't know. She said, "Well, why don't you put your application in. I told her it had been in, so she called downtown and she said, "I want Bobbie here." They say, "We don't have an application." 'Course, I know where the application went. When I applied, it went in the waste basket. Because of the color of my skin. This was in 1953. I don't know how many black teachers it might have been, maybe six or seven in the city. I'm not sure of how many at the time, but there weren't that many black teachers.

A certified high school English teacher with several years of experience in Florida recalls that she was denied a position in Hartford because she was not licensed for elementary school, where the majority of African-American teachers were placed. Not until she acquired an elementary certificate was she able to secure permanent employment in the Hartford Public Schools.

Although there are some documented exceptions (Jones, 1981; Sowell, 1974, 1976), the inferiority of segregated black schools is a widely accepted fact. Detailed descriptions of black schools in segregated southern school systems make this point (Kluger, 1975). There is no doubt that segregated schools were severely underfunded and lacking in supplies and equipment. Even so, it cannot be unilaterally assumed that students enrolled in segregated schools were automatically deprived of an academically challenging curriculum.[6] Everett Dawkins, a retired teacher who taught in a rural North Carolina school district for forty-one years (twenty-seven in segregated and fourteen in desegregated schools), agrees that segregation had a deleterious effect on the amount and quality of materials available to his county's black public schools. Nonetheless, it was Dawkins who introduced the first advanced math class in the county, which he taught to his students in the all-black segregated school. When the county school board learned of the course, they forced him to stop teaching advanced math until the white schools in the county could implement a similar course. Although forced to comply, Dawkins recognized the cancellation of the course as a political struggle over who was to control the content of black education.

The theme of controlling the education of African-American children surfaces repeatedly in the life histories of teachers who began teaching in legally segregated schools. Another instance is evident in the incident recounted by Miss Ruthie, an eighty-year-old South Carolina teacher. Remembering the fight waged by teachers and parents when Georgetown County tried to force a local Episcopal parochial school known for its excellent academic curriculum to close, she describes how African-American parents and teachers actively resisted the county's efforts to exercise control over their children's education:

The county had just built a new school and they wanted all of us to go together to the new school. So we told them no. So they said that they were gonna see that this school closed down. My husband told them, "We'll see that it stays open." So that was the argument between the superintendent and us. So they stirred the people up telling them how they felt. They said if the children came here to school that when they finished here they couldn't go into public school for a higher education. And that's when the parents started to roll and we started keeping Columbia hopping. We got the Department of Education hopping. To answer the questions that they were putting out. We kept on going, but some of the parents, you know how they can frighten some off. The next year, the Diocese said they couldn't support the school, but if we wanted to keep it open we could do it. They did everything they could to make us close the school. And we didn't. So then the Diocese said if we wanted to keep it and the community wanted it we could do it without support and that's what we've been doing ever since.

Experiences in Desegregated Schools

Teachers

The civil rights movement, most notably the struggle for desegregated schools, had a profound impact on the professional lives of African-American teachers. A number of the teachers in this study were involved in the early desegregation efforts undertaken in their school districts. This fact notwithstanding, twelve of the teachers are currently employed—ten as teachers—in schools where students of color make up the majority. Only one teacher works in a school system where pupils of color are not the majority.[7]

African-American teachers who have been transferred to desegregated schools have experienced conflicts with colleagues, administrators, and white parents—the latter often challenging their competence as teachers solely on the basis of race. A teacher in the Boston Public Schools since the 1950s describes white parents' hostility when, during the first year of desegregation in 1974, they found out that she would be teaching their children. Their animosity increased even further when, in an attempt to add diversity to her curricular offerings, she taught her pupils the Langston Hughes poem, "I am the Darker Brother," to recite at a school assembly.

Other teachers reiterated this theme, noting similar conflicts with white parents. A veteran teacher with thirty-five years of

experience, one of only four teachers transferred from the segregated
school in an east Texas town and currently the only African-American
teacher in the town's elementary school, described the confrontation
she had with a white parent who tried to remove her daughter from
class:

> One morning I came up three years ago. I didn't realize it was
> people still that prejudiced. I knew they were prejudiced. And
> she came up. And Mr. Wooten (the principal) had come up here
> and got me and he said he wanted me to come and go to my room
> and have a parent conference. And I said, "This morning? You
> mean I got a parent in my room this early?" So he said, "You
> can handle it." Well, I came in here and she has her hands on
> her hip and they had opened my room, and that had made me
> mad, too. And, she said "I want my kid out of your room." I said,
> "Is there a problem?" "Yes, I want my daughter to have a college
> education. And I don't want her in your room." And I said,
> "Don't we all want our daughters to have a college education?"
> I said, "Is there a problem?" "No, I just want her out of your
> room." I said, "Oh, it's a racial issue, is it?" And she said, "Yes."
> I said, "In that case, lady," and she had her husband with her,
> "I think we ought to go to the office." And we went to the office
> and I slammed that door. And I said, "Mr. Wooten, this lady
> wants her kid out of my room." And he said, "What's the
> problem?" And I said, "This, my color."

In the end, in accord with this teacher's wishes, the principal
refused to transfer the child to another class. Though frustrated by
conflicts with white parents, some of the teachers recognize that their
presence and ultimately their success forces white parents and
students to confront their own feelings of superiority.

In a few cities, voluntary interdistrict programs have been used
to achieve desegregation. Boston and Saint Louis are two such cities.
Believing that such programs benefit suburban districts at the
expense of city districts, two teachers who work in cities which
participate in urban-suburban desegregation comment that the
programs in their communities subtly discriminate against African-
American teachers. One high school teacher, the 1974 Missouri
Biology Teacher of the Year, recalls how she and another African-
American science teacher were recruited to work in two suburbs
participating in desegregation. After learning she was being hired
to teach only black students from the city and white students in the

lowest tracks, she declined. Unaware of her teaching assignment, the other teacher transferred to the suburbs only to find that all of the black students were placed in one of her five classes. In keeping with the custom set during desegregation, these school districts are continuing (if slightly altering) the practice of siphoning off the most competent black teachers from all-black schools to desegregate the faculty and, in this case, enlisting them to teach 'undesirable' suburban students.[8]

Earlier I argued that, irrespective of region, African-American teachers have been victimized by racist hiring practices. In Boston, for example, where before the 1974 desegregation order, African-American teachers were severely underrepresented among the teaching force, the Boston Teachers' Union (in order to maintain the privileged status of its largely white membership) attempted to further restrict the number of blacks entering their ranks by shrouding the issue in the cloak of seniority. Even though they support improved pay and working conditions for teachers, many of the northern black teachers in this study avoid the combative actions of unions, which in their estimation do not give equal emphasis to strengthening relationships with parents and community and ensuring accountability for students' academic achievement. Although she thought that the union concerns for better working conditions were valid, a retired teacher with thirty-two years in the Hartford Public Schools refused to join a strike, recalling her experiences with the union:

A lot of teachers felt it is for their own good that they would be in those kind of organizations, because they were the ones who got the ball rolling as far as salaries and things like that are concerned. I was a member of both (organizations). I joined both. I never struck though. They had three strikes while I was there, but I never went out on strike. But I would never cross their picket lines. What I would do was go to school before the picket lines started and wait until after school then when they left, then I would leave. Well, that was respect for them. I just didn't feel that as a teacher I should strike. The school had to stay open as far as I was concerned. The kids had to be taught. It never caused me any trouble because I just told them in the very beginning that I was not going to strike.

In southern and border states before desegregation, because of laws mandating dual school systems, African-American teachers were employed in far greater numbers than in northern cities with unitary

school systems such as Boston (Tyack, 1974; Franklin, 1979). One
result of desegregation, however, was that the ranks of African-
American teachers in southern and border states were decimated
(Ethridge, 1979). In many southern school systems, African-American
teachers were simply dismissed. Negative and unfair evaluations
resulted in the firing of many others, and in other cases the most
competent African-American teachers were reassigned to white
schools. Obscured by these grim statistics are the untold stories of
large numbers of African-American teachers. The experiences of two
of these teachers who began teaching in segregated schools in small
southern towns and were later transferred to desegregated schools
tell the partial story, but more importantly, their stories expose the
racism that eliminated large numbers of African-American teachers
and thwarted the careers of many others.

A retired male teacher from rural North Carolina explains how,
in a newly integrated high school, he and another African-American
teacher were assigned to coach the football, basketball, and baseball
teams, forced into stereotyped roles even though neither had participated in any kind of college athletics. The continuing racism
experienced by African-American teachers in small southern towns
is expressed in the account of another teacher.

Ella Jane was raised in an east Texas community, attended the
consolidated K–12 for black pupils, studied to be a teacher at Prairie
View A. & M., then returned to teach for nine years in the same school
she had once attended. Summoned from her classroom to the superintendent's office in the spring of 1964, she was informed that she
was one of four black teachers to be sent to the newly desegregated
school:

> I got in the car, left the school which was about eight miles out
> and came over to the administration building. I was sandwiched
> between a high school principal on one side and on the other
> a secretary to the superintendent. And they carried me through
> the wringer. That's how I got here. The questions they asked
> were ridiculous. They said, "Ella Jane, did you know that we
> have to have some black teachers?" And I said "Yes." And he
> said, "Did you know that you are going to be very fortunate
> because you are going to be one of the black teachers that we're
> going to hire?" And he said, "You're the best teacher I have in
> the system, black or white. I did not have to tell you that and
> if you tell anyone I said that, I'm gonna tell 'em you lied." He
> says, "Do you get my meaning?" And he said, "It should make

you feel very proud whether you do or not that you're going to be one of the ones who are retained." That's how that happened.

Ella Jane went on to say that though she and her cousin, each of whom possessed master's degrees, reported to school each day, neither of them was given a class. Instead, because the white towns-people were unwilling to accept them as teachers for their children, they sat in a classroom for half of the school year without teaching a single student. Finally, after the white teachers complained, the school board created classes of remedial reading students—composed of nine to twelve students, all of them black or poor white—for them to teach. For three years, they continued teaching remedial reading classes. During this entire period, the other teachers showed their contempt for them and the black students. Ella Jane speaks about how they were treated:

We were just glorified students. Incidentally, I couldn't use the bathroom with the teachers and everything. I would use the bathroom with the students. I didn't eat with them (the other teachers). You know, they just kind of treated me like dirt. We brought our black students. The teachers, the white teachers, would put the black kids, this is the truth, on one side and white ones on the other so they wouldn't touch, and so they wouldn't mingle and that's the truth. This was starting in '64. This went on for a long time.

For twenty-six years, Ella Jane has found herself caught between the institutional racism of the school system and her belief that she is both qualified and entitled to teach. Realizing that "everywhere blacks were getting flak and that it was hard after integration for us to get jobs," she has resisted the school system's effort to push her out and has chosen instead to confront the racist behavior of some school administrators who use the authority of their office to antagonize and intimidate her and the individual racism of many of her white colleagues who resent and challenge her position as grade leader by remaining in her job.

In their own ways, all of these teachers have resisted the institutional racism they have confronted in their lives and pro-fessional careers. Although each story represents a personal triumph, their value lies in what they reveal about the institutional racism and structural conditions that continue to limit the professional lives of African-American teachers and strangle educational possibilities for African-American pupils.

Seeing Black Students Through the Eyes of Black Teachers

It is inarguable that *Brown v. Board of Education* dealt a necessary and final blow to legally sanctioned segregation in the larger society. With respect to schools, the specific target of the Brown suit, the benefits are less clear, leading some African-American scholars to question whether the costs exacted of the African-American community by school desegregation have been offset by the educational gains of black children (Cruse, 1987; Bell, 1987). Persistent problems, known as 'second-generation' desegregation problems, now impede the achievement of African-American students.[9] In many desegregated schools, blacks are suspended at much higher rates than whites. Over-enrollment of blacks in special education and low tracks and under-enrollment in advanced placement has often led to resegregation within desegregated schools. And even though in northern states desegregation opened up the teaching and administrative ranks to more African-Americans, in southern and border states, where some thirty thousand black teachers and numerous administrators lost their jobs, it decimated the black teaching force (Ethridge, 1979).

By demanding only inclusion, the Brown decision did not challenge structural inequalities in American society. Thus, as currently implemented, school desegregation has merely rearranged—not changed—the power relationships in public schools. Consequently, it has been unable to reverse the racism in the schools or in the larger society.

There has been a longstanding debate in the African-American community over whether its children would be better served in segregated or desegregated schools. Today a number of African-American scholars concede that there was a certain naivete in the assumption that simply allowing African-Americans to attend school with white students would significantly alter the educational achievement of African-American pupils. But this assumption was challenged twenty years before the Brown case was decided. In a 1934 essay entitled "Does the Negro Need Separate Schools?" W. E. B. DuBois provided a prophetic and insightful analysis of today's school desegregation outcomes. He argued that:

> The Negro needs neither segregated school nor mixed schools. What he needs is Education. What he must remember is that there is no magic, either in mixed schools or in segregated schools. A mixed school with poor and unsympathetic teachers,

with hostile opinion, and no teaching of truth concerning black folk, is bad. A segregated school with ignorant placeholders, inadequate equipment, poor salaries and wretched housing is equally bad.

Embedded in the interviews with these teachers is the paradox of desegregation alluded to by DuBois. On one hand, these teachers acknowledge the improved material conditions that resulted from desegregation. At the same time, they describe the tracking, lowered expectations, and unprincipled support of athletically inclined black students in desegregated schools. Though he did not pinpoint specific examples, one high school teacher spoke about the negative expectations that white teachers had for African-American students:

I saw a lot of my little black brothers get into classes that were taught by white instructors who went into the class saying, not very loudly, but very clearly, the black kids can't make it. And I think that bothered me to no end.

Describing the treatment of black students in her school system, an elementary teacher in the south expanded on this theme:

The black kids are really pushed back. The only thing that they can excel in here is athletics. And, if you're a good athlete, they'll try and keep your GPA up enough for you to participate in the athletic program, but if you're academically inclined and black you'll only get a C. We have a gifted and talented program here. There's only one black kid in the entire gifted and talented program. He's good. I don't know how he got in there.

Another teacher described what happened to two of her students who transferred from the parochial school to the local public school in South Carolina Though they had earned the highest average coming out of eighth grade, these African–American students were almost denied the honor of being valedictorian. According to this teacher, this incident crystalizes the discrimination in desegregated schools, where faculty rarely expect or promote academic achievement among African-American students:

The teachers won't give you one point. I remember because I had two that finished valedictorian over at the public school there. Some of the teachers would not vote for her to get

valedictorian. But, she got it. She got it. And she came to me
and said, "Miss Ruthie, some of the teachers wouldn't vote for
me." The same thing happens with her sister. The commence-
ment was on Thursday, but they waited until Tuesday to tell
her to get something to say.

An African-American Teaching Philosophy

These teachers share the perspective that the effective teaching
of African-American students involves more than merely imparting
subject matter. They reason that African-American teachers' ability
to talk with African-American students in terms they understand
about the personal value, collective power, and political consequences
of choosing academic achievement has been sharply curtailed by
desegregation. As a result, they contend that not only has desegregation weakened their solidarity with black students, but it has also
limited their ability to engage in critical dialogue with African-
American students, dialogue necessary to engage students in their
own learning. A male high school teacher comments on the difficulties
of achieving this goal with African-American students in mixed
classrooms:

The big difference was that I can see we were able to do more
with the black students. In other words, if I wanted to come in
this morning, have my kids put their books under the desk or
on top of the desk and I'd get up on top of my desk and sit down
and just talk to them. "Why are you here? Are you here just
to make out another day? Or are you here because the law says
you must go to school? Are you here to try to better yourself?"
This kind of thing I could talk to them about. "Well, now I'm
here to better myself. Well, what must you do? What are the
requirements? Do you know where your competition is?" And
I could talk to them about things like that. "Your competition
is not your little cousin that's sittin' over there. Your competition
is that white person over there in that other school. He's your
competition. He's the one you've got to compete with for a job.
And the only way that you're going to be able to get that job
is that you can't be as good as he is, you got to be better." And
I could drill that into their heads. But once you integrated, I
mean you didn't feel, I didn't—I don't feel comfortable really in
a mixed setting to really get into the things that the whites did
to us as black people. I don't really feel too comfortable doing
that in a mixed group because I think I know how I felt when

they talked about me. And surely they have feelings even though
sometimes I didn't think they had any, but that kind of thing
we, I mean I, couldn't do. I didn't want to pull them aside because
then they would feel that they had been moved out of the
mainstream because then you were just talking to just blacks.
But this is the big difference that I saw, that you couldn't do.
Well, I guess another thing, I got disillusioned with integration
because of that type thing, because I could not get to my people
and tell them all the things that they needed to know. I could
not beat into their minds that they had to be better—that to
compete with that white kid on an equal basis was not enough.
I couldn't tell them that. I couldn't stop my class and tell him
that so that he would understand. I think this is one of the things
that they miss, black kids, in general.

Another teacher repeats this theme, noting that desegregation
has hindered the ability of African-American teachers to adopt the
multifaceted and protean roles of admonisher, urger, and meddler:

I think that integration, when I'm talking I could talk about
it two ways. It's like integration is great and we need to know
each other, but they miss the big picture. I know that in one
way integration is worthwhile because you're going into the
work force. But, on the other hand, it's been so detrimental to
kids. I mean maybe it's great for white people. Because I don't
think the kids even know where they're supposed to be themselves. The kids say, "Well, I've got a C, so hey, that's
wonderful." But, see nobody black would let him get away with
that. They would say, "You know you're supposed to do better
than that." In the olden days. What integration as a whole has
done to the black teacher. In the olden days where you could
just stand there in front of your class and just tell 'em, you can't
do that. I mean, I can't do that when I got blacks and whites,
you know what I mean? I mean you could do it in your own little
way, but you can't just stand there and say, "You're being hurt
by this, wake up and smell the coffee," kind of thing. They really
don't understand what's happening to them. That's the
sad part.

These teachers have a clear understanding of the contradictions
inherent in the equal educational opportunity ideology of desegregated schools, especially as it has affected the motivation and

consequent achievement of African-American students. A North Carolina high school teacher with experience in both segregated and desegregated schools commented on African-American students' reactions after the schools were desegregated:

> Black kids are not hungry now. There are some few of them that want to be on top, but they're not really hungry. They want to be there because they heard somebody say that it's nice to be on top, but they do not hunger and thirst after righteousness, if I can use that expression from the Bible. They don't hunger and thirst for it and the reason they don't is because nobody tells them that they need to hunger and thirst for these things. And I'm talking about that kid out there whose parents maybe get up in the morning and maybe go to work and they don't see them any more until six or seven o'clock at night. There's nothing that's pushing them. When they went into an integrated situation, they looked back. They look at Martin Luther King's address and he said, "I have seen the promised land." They say, "I have reached the promised land. Now that I'm here I don't need to be concerned anymore."

These interviews are infused with the theme that teaching African-American learners effectively demands knowing more than subject matter and the accompanying pedagogical skills. It is evident from what these teachers say that undergirding their practice with African-American students is a 'hidden curriculum', one they believe has been severely compromised in desegregated schools and that has negative consequences for many African-American students. This research corroborates findings from my earlier ethnographic study of an African-American teacher (Foster,1987). The comments in these interviews as well as the behavior and speech events of the teacher in the previous study illustrate a pattern of interest and concern demonstrated by African-American teachers that both urges students to invest in learning and explains the political reasons for doing so. In both studies, the teachers assert their connectedness to and identification with black students and the larger black community.

Communicating and teaching across ethnic and cultural lines is complicated by the sociopolitical relationship between dominant and subordinate groups. Ray McDermott (1974, 1977) maintains that teachers and students from different cultural and ethnic backgrounds often collude in maintaining the status quo. Using their shared racial consciousness and their experiences with racism illustrated earlier, these teachers consciously work to undo the status quo. In the following excerpt, Pam Owens, a high school teacher, explains why lack of trust often results in counterproductive relationships between white teachers, black students, and their parents.

> The black kids have just been hurt. They've bought into a lot of the things that white people have told them. You know if you're black you can't do this, you can't do that. I mean, we talk about high expectations and this, I think for the most part they (white teachers) don't have 'em. I mean for God's sake, they're victims of their own society and their own upbringing. Like I was saying, why should they want some black child to achieve? What is in it for him? But, then on the other hand, there are only so many things black parents are gonna let white teachers do to their children, as well. Just because they don't have that kind of faith. They might put their lives into a black teachers hand. We have some kind of community in terms of knowing what's going on in this person's head.

Combined, the comments above suggest that though unfamiliar with McDermott's argument, these teachers understand its essence.

So far, because desegregation has merely rearranged and not changed the power arrangements in American schools, it has failed to stop the socialization of racism through the school system. In fact, in desegregated schools, it is often assumed that African-American students rather than institutional racism or unequal power relations are the problem. One teacher recalls an in-service workshop that reinforced that view:

> In 1970 we had a workshop, a three day workshop. They paid us to go to this workshop, black and white teachers; we were integrating the school. So the first day, they came in and they had these experts who knew everything. They told these white teachers, now this is what you can expect from black kids. Whatever it was, don't expect them to come in and say, yes mam' and no mam' to you; they're gonna say yes and no and so you're going to have to accept that even though you're not used to it. I mean this is basic. They're not going to bring all their homework in everyday even though that's what you're kind of accustomed to from these white kids, which was a lie by the way. But the first day we spent a whole six hours and they were

telling that white teacher how to get along with that black kid. Came in the second day, we spent six hours telling that white teacher how to get along with that black kid. Another six hours. We came in that third day and the first three hours we spent with these so called experts telling these white teachers how to get along with black kids. So when we came back in after lunch break on the third day, they started the same stuff again. And I stood up and said, now wait a minute, we have spent two and a half days here, and you have told these white teachers how to get along with these black kids. You have not told me yet how to get along with that white kid. I said, you got some of them out there just as nasty as any black kid you ever seen, so far as conduct is concerned this is what I'm talking about. They're not coming in that classroom to sit down and be little angels. And I see it as something wrong if they did; they are children just like the black child is. But you have not said anything to me as to how to get along with the white kid. Why was that white teacher told how to deal with the problems that he was going to face with the black kid? Why wasn't I told how to deal with the problems that I'm going to have face in dealing with that white kid? When I was a youngster, fortunately or unfortunately, my parents drilled into me when you go to Miss Ann's house you go to the back door and knock. Now, I got this little stinker in my class who is gonna try and run me out and I am not going anywhere. Now, I got to go and visit that parent. You haven't told me whether or not I should go to the front door, the back door, the side door or anything. I mean this kind of thing that I thought was very important, that white kids are going to give you problems too. But the basic premise that they were dwelling on is that you going to have trouble with black kids. I know he was a problem. I had problems with black children, and I'm black, but I did. But don't tell me that because he's black that he's automatically going to be a problem and that white child because he's white he's not going to be a problem. You going to have some problems with them.

What teachers working in integrated schools complained about most was not the loss of personal autonomy, nor the individual or institutional acts of discrimination aimed at them, but their diminishing ability to influence positively the educational futures of African-American students.

Structural Conditions in Society

When I asked these teachers to discuss the changes that have occurred during their careers regarding teaching African-American pupils, most often they commented on the changing societal conditions that continue to limit students' futures by robbing them of meaningful participation in the economic system.

Miss Ruthie, who has been teaching since 1938 on a South Carolina sea island that has fallen victim to the 'recreation explosion,'[10] a version of gentrification, commented on the systematic and deliberate land taking schemes by which African-Americans have lost their lands:

There were blacks all over there back in times before. (The land) Not owned by all whites. But now, it's all white, understand. All this over here—we call it Palmetto Beach. Blacks owned it. All right, the whites wanted it. So they put the taxes up so high that their heirs couldn't pay it. So after they wouldn't sell it to them, they put it on auction. Blacks got together—a group of men and women who were in business—got the money together and were determined they were going to save it. The blacks had brought $75,000.00 and they were willing to go. So all right, they bid, and they bid and they bid and they bid. Every time the blacks would outbid them. Finally they quit at $50,000.00 and the Negroes got the beach. But you know they wouldn't give'em a fair deed so they can develop that beach.

Continuing this theme, Jean Vander, a Boston elementary schoolteacher with thirty-five years experience, discusses displacement along with other problems facing many of the first graders who attend her school:

They (the city) have ideas of moving those people right out of Orchard Park (the housing project where many of her children reside). They will move poor people into areas where they will not be able to survive—just survive the situation, but they'll be out there someplace. Orchard Park is full of drugs. That is a given. It is full of drugs. One mother met me in the supermarket. She said, "Mrs. Vander, I have my children with me all the time because of the drugs." They haven't got the money. They see no way out, and this is true, Michèle. Things cost. Do you know what that's going to mean? Total loss for black kids. Because

some of those kids are dealing with so much. They'll say, "I
didn't come in yesterday because my cousin got shot or my father
went to jail," or you know, they have some pretty serious
situations. Really. Because the kids have so many more health
problems. A lot of kids come in hungry. Because I think that
the sixties encouraged the use of drugs too along with building
up of black self-image. I think the business of drugs has a strong,
definite stronghold in poor neighborhoods. Because that's the
only way of subsisting for some of these people. They are selling
the shit. They are selling drugs. And they are selling to whom-
ever will buy. Because they have to live, too. People weren't
outside of the law as much before. People are more and more
outside of the law. Women are hustling, Michèle, to make money
'cause they can't make it out here with collard greens a dollar
a pound.

While all of these teachers believe they are competent and have
influenced the lives of most of the students who have been in their
classrooms, they agree that changes in schools without the
corresponding societal changes will not change the prospects for the
majority of African-American pupils. When asked what happens to
the children from her school once they leave her, an elementary
teacher with thirty years in the same Philadelphia school describes
the life chances of students in her community:

Yeah, they (the students) come back all the time. Or they send
word or whatever. But there's nothing in the middle. They either
do very well, or poorly. There's nothing in the middle. I don't
mean just college. I mean they graduate from high school, and
they get responsible jobs, and they're fine people, and they read,
that's important. And then you know, so many of them graduate
from college, lawyers, doctors, all that. I haven't had a doctor,
but I had two lawyers. And some in jail. No middle. That's the
way of the neighborhood. They have to get out of it. They have
to get out to do better. Then if they want to come back, well,
that's OK. But they have to go away to school or go away to
the army, or just go away, because it'll just eat you alive.

An English teacher who for thirty-one years has worked at
Philips High School, a school whose students come from Chicago's
Robert Taylor Homes, echoes this theme, noting that the obstacles
facing African-American students growing up in the large urban cities

are so intractable that he has concluded, based on his experiences, "that only three out ten students are likely to escape." What is significant about all of these comments is that they do not blame parents or students for the societal conditions not of their making.

Conclusion

There are a number of conclusions that can be drawn from these interviews. An obvious one is that despite the critical role that *Brown v. Board of Education* played in dismantling segregation, it has had little effect on the schooling of large numbers of African-American students because it could not attack the structural inequalities or suppress the racism in the larger society. A tragic and unintended consequence of desegregation is that it has created significant problems for African-American teachers and relegated them to having little voice in the education of African-American pupils. There are other conclusions that may be less obvious. Admittedly, this article has documented teachers' beliefs and does not include observation of their practice. Nonetheless, teachers are unlikely to teach students effectively if they blame them instead of society for their condition. What characterizes these expert teachers is that they understand the structural conditions, but are not totally overwhelmed by them. And despite the limitations imposed by the schools and larger society, they have been able to fashion a teaching philosophy and pedagogy that enables them to act as social agents in ways that both change and construct their own and their pupils' realities. As noted earlier, these teachers share the belief that teaching African-American students successfully requires more than merely mastering subject matter and the accompanying pedagodical skills, but consists of engaging these students in dialogue that continually questions and seeks to change the status quo. Consequently, they are neither overly optimistic nor pessimistic.

Unfortunately, school personnel often armed with findings from the research community blame the victim, her family, or the larger society rather than acting in ways that challenge the status quo. In fact, a recent survey of The Great City Council of Schools, made up of forty-four of the nation's largest cities, has concluded that these districts are more likely to blame parents' and students' attitudes and external conditions than they are the internal schooling conditions over which they have the most control (Lytle, 1990). Likewise, a recent study by King and Ladson-Billings (1990) of largely white pre-teaching majors in an elite Jesuit university reveals the extent to which they were likely to blame African-Americans' problems on supposed cultural deficits rather than on institutional racism and structural inequities. This is not to minimize the pressing social problems or the restrictive structural arrangements that constrain many who work in schools. What this article has attempted to demonstrate is that, despite structural constraints of segregation and desegregation, it is possible for teachers to act in ways that challenge the status quo and chart alternative courses for their own lives and those of their pupils. It is my contention that certain societal changes, in particular the dismantling of the separate but equal laws, have created an illusion and convinced many Americans that institutional racism is a thing of the past. But, as noted earlier, the power arrangements have merely been rearranged, not changed.

In conclusion, failure to include the voices and perspectives of experienced, exemplary African-American teachers not only denies these teachers the right to be recognized for their impressive achievements, but it also means that researchers may be cutting off an important source of understanding about how to improve the education of poor African-American children. Because teachers of color are more likely to work in school districts with greater proportions of low-income pupils of color, this omission could have serious consequences for educating students currently least well served by schools (Metropolitan Life, 1988).

Notes

1. I acknowledge funding from the University of Pennsylvania Research Foundation, and the Spencer Small Grant Program. A Spencer Postdoctoral Fellowship from the National Academy of Education, a University of North Carolina Minority Postdoctoral Fellowship and a Faculty Fellowship from the Smithsonian Institution provided me with the funds that enabled me to work full-time on this research. I would also like to thank Joyce King and Kathleen Weiler who commented on earlier drafts of this article, and I am grateful to Jeanne Newman for her careful transcription of the interviews.

2. In this paper, the terms black and African-American are both used. I use black only to refer to students' or teachers' physical characteristics without regard to historical or cultural background. African-American refers to black students and teachers who are Americans of African heritage.

3. Elsewhere (Foster, 1989) I offer an explanation for the discrepancy.

4. Community nomination, a term coined by this author specifically for this study, means that teachers were chosen by direct contact with African-

American communities. Periodicals, community organizations, and individuals provided the names of the teachers.

5. All informants' names are pseudonyms. The place names remain unchanged.

6. From the beginning, many have assumed that schools staffed by black teachers would be inferior. However, this was not necessarily the case. James Anderson (1989) refers to an 1867 report by Frank R. Chase, the Freedmen's Bureau Superintendent of Education for Louisiana which noted that "many of the most prosperous schools in the State are taught by competent colored teachers."

7. Two teachers were retired when interviewed. Since the first interview, one teacher has taken a position as a district level multicultural curriculum coordinator.

8. For an excellent discussion of the way suburban districts have benefited by interdistrict plans at the expense of urban districts and students, see Daniel Monti (1985).

9. A recent survey conducted by a major black periodical indicates that many in the black community are dissatisfied with the outcomes of school desegregation. Asked about the impact of desegregation, 58.8% of those polled felt that the education of black children was worse or the same as it had been before the Brown decision.

10. For a discussion of the term "recreation explosion" with respect to the development of coastal South Carolina, see Russell & Silvernail (1966).

References

Anderson, J. (1989). *The education of blacks in the South, 1860–1935*. Chapel Hill: University of North Carolina Press.

Bell, D. (1987). *And we are not saved: The elusive quest for racial justice*. New York: Basic Books.

Black Enterprise (1990). Black Enterprise Survey. August.

Blauner, B. (1989). *Black lives, white lives: Three decades of race relations in America*. Berkeley: University of California Press.

Clark, S. (1962). *Echo in my soul*. New York: E.P. Dutton.

Conroy, P. (1972). *The water is wide*. Boston: Houghton Mifflin.

Cruse, H. (1987). *Plural but equal: Blacks and minorities in America's plural society*. New York: William Morrow.

Curry, L. P. (1981). *The free black in America, 1800–1850.* Chicago: University of Chicago Press.

Decker, S. (1969). *An empty spoon.* New York: Harper and Row.

Dilworth, M. (1984). *Teachers' totter: A report on certification issues.* Washington: Institute for the Study of Educational Policy, Howard Univerity.

DuBois, W. (1934). Does the Negro need separate schools? In M. Weinberg (Ed.), *W. E. B. DuBois: A reader.* New York: Harper and Row.

Ethridge, S. (1979). Impact of the 1954 Brown v. Topeka Board of Education decision on black educators. *Negro Educational Review, 30*(3–4), 217–232.

Fields, M. (1985). *Lemon Swamp: A Carolina memoir.* New York: The Free Press.

Foster, M. (1987). *"It's cookin' now": An ethnographic study of a successful black teacher in an urban community college.* Unpublished doctoral dissertation. Harvard University.

Foster, M. (1989). Plus ça change, Plus c'est la même chose: Constancy, change and constraints in the lives of black women teachers. Paper presented at the Annual Meeting of the American Anthropological Association. Washington, November.

Franklin, V.P. (1979). *The education of black Philadelphia: The social and educational history of a minority community, 1900–1950.* Philadelphia: University of Pennsylvania Press.

Goodson, I. (1988). Teachers' lives. *Qualitative Research in Education: Teaching and Learning Qualitative Traditions.* Proceedings from the second annual conference of the Qualitative Interest Group, Athens, GA.

Haskins, J. (1971). *Diary of a Harlem schoolteacher.* New York: Grove Press.

Herndon, J.(1968). *The way it spozed to be.* New York: Simon & Schuster.

Jackson-Coppin, F. (1913). *Reminiscences of school life and hints on teaching.* Philadelphia: AME Book Concern.

Jones, F. (1981). *A traditional model of excellence: Dunbar High School of Little Rock Arkansas.* Washington: Howard University Press.

King, J. & Ladson-Billings, G. (1990). Dysconscious racism and multicultural illiteracy: The distorting of the American mind. Paper presented at the meeting of the American Educational Research Association, Boston: April.

Kluger, R. (1975). *Simple justice.* New York: Vintage.

Kohl, H. (1967). *36 children.* New York: Signet.

Kozol, J. (1968). *Death at an early age: The destruction of the hearts and minds of Negro children in the Boston public schools.* Boston: Houghton Mifflin.

Lerner, G. (1972). *Black women in white America: A documentary history.* New York: Vintage.

Lightfoot, S. (1978). *Worlds apart: Relationships between families and schools.* New York: Basic Books.

Lytle, J. (1990). Minority student access to and preparation for higher education. Paper presented at the Annual Meeting of the American Educational Research Association. Boston: April

McDermott, R. (1974). Achieving school failure. In G. D. Spindler (Ed.), *Education and cultural process.* New York: Holt, Rinehart & Winston.

McDermott, R. (1977). Social relations as contexts for learning in school. *Harvard Educational Review, 47* (2), 198–213.

Metropolitan Life (1988). *Strengthening the relationship between teachers and students.* New York: Metropolitan Life Insurance Company.

Monti, D. (1985). *A semblance of justice: St. Louis school desegregation and order in urban America.* Columbia: University of Missouri Press.

Murray, A. (1970). *Black experience and American culture.* New York: Vintage.

Provenzo, E. (1988). Black and white teachers: Patterns of similarity and difference over twenty years. Paper presented at the Annual Meeting of the American Educational Research Association. New Orleans: April.

Rist, R. (1970). Student social class and teacher expectations: The self-fulfilling prophecy in ghetto education. *Harvard Educational Review, 40,* 411–451.

Rist, R. (1973). *The urban school: A factory for failure.* Cambridge: MIT Press.

Robinson, D. R. (1974). *The bell rings at four: A black teacher's chronicle of change.* Austin: Madrona Press.

Russell, J. & Silvernail, R. G. (1966). The impact of recreation on coastal South Carolina. *Business and Economic Review, XIII,* 3–8.

Shulman, L. (1987). The wisdom of practice: Managing complexity in medicine and teaching. In D. Berliner & B. Rosenshine (Eds.), *Talks to teachers: A festschrift for N. L. Gage.* New York: Random House.

Sowell, T. (1974). Black excellence—The case of Dunbar High School. *Public Interest, 35,* 3–21.

Sowell, T. (1976). Patterns of black excellence. *Public Interest, 43,* 26–58.

Spencer D. (1986). *Contemporary women teachers: Balancing school and home.* New York: Longman.

Sterling, P. (1972). *The real teachers: 30 inner-city schoolteachers talk honestly about who they are, how they teach and why.* New York: Random House.

Tyack, D. (1974). *The one best system: A history of American urban education.* Cambridge: Harvard University Press.

The Art of Being Present:
Educating for Aesthetic Encounters

Maxine Greene

This is a moment in our history when persons are described as "resources," when changes in education are being called for in the name of economic productivity and national defense. The values of process and choicemaking are being repressed or set aside. Human energies are to be channelled and controlled in the "national interest"; no longer is there talk of what is not yet, of imagined possibility. Along with this comes a sense of petrifaction. Publics are asked to accommodate to an objectified "reality," marked off and demarcated in cost-benefit terms. It is reified, "given"; we are all being required to sublimate our private visions and confine ourselves to what Wallace Stevens called "the plain sense of things." (1964b, p. 502)

Those of us who are concerned for teaching rather than training, for persons in their pluralities rather than potential "job-holders and consumers," (Arendt, 1958) need to think again about what it signifies to pay heed to centers of human consciousness thrusting variously into a common world. We need to think about the creation of situations in which preferences are released, uncertainties confronted, desires given voice. Feeling and perceiving and imagining must, at least on occasion, be given play. Perhaps most important of all: students must be brought to understand the importance of perspective, of vantage point, when it comes to interpreting their lived worlds. The idea of interpretation seems to me to be crucial, that and the realization that "reality"—if it means anything—means interpreted experience. One way to move people from bland accommodations to what is offered as authoritative description, *the* description, is to acquaint them with the notions of multiplicity and incompleteness. There are, after all, alternative modes of structuring reality; there are, as some have pointed out, "multiple realities." (Schutz, 1967, pp. 207–259) Moreover, since everyone is located in space and time, since universal or God-like visions are inconceivable, every perspective is in some way incomplete, in some way provisional. There are always horizons to be breached; there is always a "beyond"— what is not yet.

It is with this in mind that I want to argue for increased attention to informed awareness of the several arts. I do not want to claim that the capacity to encounter poems or dance performances or musical pieces is the fundamental human capacity, nor even that it is available for everyone. I do want to say, though, that a deliberate effort to empower individuals to notice what there is to be noticed in works of art and to become familiar with the range of "languages" or symbol systems involved, can become an effort that moves people to the taking of initiatives. (Goodman, 1976) In other words, what is sometimes called aesthetic educating may provoke individuals to act rather than to behave in response to outside stimuli and cues. To act is to embark on a new beginning for oneself, a beginning generated by questioning, curiosity, wonder, restiveness. If, for example, an individual is in a museum along with others, he/she may well move through a room hung with Cezanne paintings and simply take note of which ones are hanging there and of the fact that they were painted by Paul Cezanne. Yes, he or she might recognize an apple here, a pitcher there, the slope of a mountain, the slant of a roof. But that might very likely be all—that and the mild pleasure associated with recognition or response to the richness of color or the spaces of the gallery itself. If the same person were somehow to be released by a teacher to understand the importance of uncoupling from the ordinary when entering the gallery, of trying to bracket out conventional seeing and expectation for a while, that individual (answering, perhaps, the appeal of one or two particular paintings) might take the time to stand in the presence, say of a still life or a portrait, and move (perceptually and imaginatively) inside the pictorial frame. Yes, he/she might have to know enough to see the picture as something other than a mere representation of a world that would have looked almost the same if photographed. He/she might have to know enough to notice the strokes of the paint, the ways in which those strokes created contours and jutting forms. Attending to light and color and form, he/she might be fortunate enough to see some dimension of the natural world actually taking on visibility before his/her very eyes. If so, the person as beholder would be understanding in such a fashion as to bring new orders into being within his/her experience, new connections in that experience never made before. He/she would (to put it otherwise) be allowing a work of art to emerge within his/her experience the more he/she attended to particulars, the more he/she allowed those particulars to compose and give rise to a shimmering, never entirely fixed totality. It would never be fixed or entirely finished, because the next time the individual came to the same painting (whether because he/she had lived a little longer, learned more, was in a different mood, or was enabled to look from another angle) the painting would show itself somehow differently, perhaps more fully or more abstractly. The point is that the work (the canvas once painted by a living Paul Cezanne) must be consciously realized by a person willing and informed enough to let his/her own imaginative and perceptual energy go out to it, if it is to come into being as an aesthetic object, not simply a neutral *thing*.

To be able to do this is to be able to respond mindfully—and, yes, with feeling and a kind of raptness—to something presenting itself to consciousness. "Mind," John Dewey once said, "is care in the sense of solicitude, anxiety, as well as of active looking after things that need to be tended. . . ." (1934, p. 263) Mind, as Dewey saw it, is a verb and not a noun; it is a mode of taking action, of attending; it is a mode of achieving and, yes, funding meanings. This is quite, quite different from a mere gathering of information or attempting to bring a pre-existing stock of knowledge into correspondence with a pre-existing world. To recognize this, to recognize that an encounter with a work of art can open windows in the presumably actual or the pre-defined, windows that open outwards to alternative visions of the world, is to break with the sense that reality is petrified. It may also be to realize how much depends on resistance to the taken-for-granted, on desire, on way of seeing, on the awareness of what is not yet.

Perhaps it might be called, in Heideggerian language, a realization of the "thought-provoking." By that Heidegger meant being moved to reach beyond towards what continually seems to withdraw. (1968, p. 23) He meant achieving the kind of relatedness to things the cabinetmaker achieves with respect to wood or "the shapes slumbering within wood." Such shapes are, as it were, possibilities; they are always *to be* realized; they can never be finally encompassed or disclosed. Something remains *to be* explored. Once provoked, the mind or the imagination keeps inclining itself, addressing itself to what is not yet. This is what can happen, I shall want to keep suggesting, when a person is empowered to be present to a Cezanne landscape or a Beethoven quartet or a Bergman film or a Wallace Stevens poem.

The difference between this address to the "thought-provoking" and technical or empirical knowing must be evident. But even as Heidegger recognized that "computing" would always go on even if "meditative thinking" were made possible, so we must recognize that the understanding we hope to nurture through and by means of encounters with works of art cannot be a substitute for the modes of inquiry intended to lead to closure when problems are solved or products secured. The calculative ways, the efficient ways, the "productive" ways have to be taught; and we can only hope that learners and their teachers can be brought to realize that these modes of knowing how are also grounded in lived worlds, in the pre-verbal, in what Michael Polanyi (1966) has called "tacit awareness." It may be that more informed encounters with art forms may make the idea of purely "objectivist" knowledge increasingly questionable. In any case, I think we have to keep celebrating and arguing for alternative modes of knowing or understanding, not solely to provide perspective on what people do when they strive for control, but to provoke increased attentiveness to the concrete and the lived. There is no doubt that a being present to Cezanne's rendering of apples and bottles in some manner alters the quality of attending to ordinary apples and bottles, makes shapes seem in some way more solid, makes the light more palpable as it strikes dusty glass. So does an engagement with patterned dance movements on a stage make somehow more visible the rhythms of bodies moving on the street. An active noticing of qualities in works of art, in other words, may make less likely an unthinking acceptance of disembodied, technicist ways of being in the world. People may at least come to realize that the technical or the abstract or the statistical is merely one of a range of possible interpretations, that every one must in time find validation in the actually lived.

As a teacher, I live in dread of the disembodied, depersonalized vision. I fear robotization and systematization and alienation. The arts, in and of themselves, are not necessarily remedies for these conditions. Pieces of music, painting, works of literature, plays exist neutrally, indifferently in cultural space. Without human consciousnesses to engage with them, to grasp them, they simply *are*. And, at this period of time, they are all too frequently made into commodities; they are fetishized; (Arato, 1978, pp. 185–224) or they are permitted to exist in a sheltered "preserve," (Berger, 1977, p. 32) protected from the seeking eyes and the questioning minds of the "mass." It is not enough to assert that there were long lines for the Manet exhibit in New York or for the American landscapes in

Washington, that people come in crowds to see classical ballet. All depends on the degree to which energies are moving out to the various works, on the quality and intensity of involvement, on the breaking of habitual frames. And this, I am convinced, does not come "naturally."

When we think of the arts in education, however, we do not ordinarily think of educating for informed and restless awareness of art forms, of empowering people to be personally and actively present in galleries, theatres, and concert halls. Nor do we ordinarily think of nurturing the kind of critical consciousness that will enable people to withstand the publicity, the "hype," the sense of coterie, the cooptive mechanisms that make it so difficult for individuals to make their own choices, their own appropriations, or to dare to speak for themselves. The arts in education ordinarily summon up certain creative and expressive activities fostered in art rooms and music rooms and dance studios. Too frequently, these are described as component parts of an "affective" realm, considered in antithesis to the "cognitive," the really serious concern of the schools. Because standard measurement devices cannot be used to evaluate what happens in the art rooms, they are treated as "frills," as basically irrelevant in a world where the important "outputs" are those subject to quantification.

There is no denying, however, the importance of—and the need to argue for—the explorations that take place or should take place in those spaces: the images and shapes and sounds discovered, the articulation of the hitherto unexpressed. Most of us recognize by now that work with a medium of whatever kind cannot but involve the cognitive as well as the affective, that mindfulness is as significant here as it is in the math room or the chemistry lab. The point is that capacities are displayed differently, that ways of being intelligent are expressed that are not usually expressed or encouraged in other classrooms. Howard Gardner (1983), developing a theory of "multiple intelligences," draws attention to bodily-kinaesthetic intelligence, for example, to literary intelligence, to a whole range of know-how generally ignored by school people taught to concentrate in a much narrower range. In my view, such intelligences must be recognized and heeded; so must the capacities relevant within each "frame of mind." Critico-creative thinking, for instance, can be nurtured in the course of enabling the young to play band music together, make paper-mache dolls, design an Indian village. Fidelity, persistence, originality, imaginativeness: all have as much part to play in art rooms as they do in the fields of more specifically cognitive study.

The point is to provide opportunities for them to be displayed. It may well be that, if expressive and creative activities are carried on within sight and sound of the various, problematic art world (whether discovered in museums, on television or in the auditorium of the school), there will be more occasions for the expression of a range of capacities than there are when attention is confined to the "right brain."

Many of us, looking back, can remember the feel of clay in our hands, the pleasure of painting yellow suns and green grass (or blue, or purple), the joy in pretending to be a witch or a lion or a king. I can recapture the almost physical delight that came with the discovery of how language could be molded and shaped and twisted, how words could release sparks of light and unsuspected meanings; and I can remember collecting words sometimes and admiring them on the page. That probably enticed me to read more than I might have; and the reading made me realize what could be done with language if you really knew how to play with it and transform it, as I (for a long time) could not. I think of Virginia Woolf saying how "I make it real by putting it into words." There are many young people, provided with paint or charcoal or clay (or with keys and saucepans and glasses on which to make percussive sounds), who feel similarly when they give the inwardly felt an outward expression. I am convinced that early familiarity with medium and its potentialities prepares the ground for the discoveries made available by the works of professional artists. They are continuous, after all, with the experience of finding an outward expression for what is tacit, has originally no words or notes or shapes.

Significant as such explorations and adventures with the "stuff" of the arts may be, they are not sufficient if the young are to find actual art forms thought-provoking enough to open new perspectives in their experience. There are, it is true, occasional efforts to nurture art appreciation in our schools; but, far too often, they do little more than expose the young to "important" works presented as part of an objective tradition or art-world. Sometimes it is assumed that a Rembrandt painting, say, or a Mozart sonata possesses enough intrinsic power to assure a rapt attentiveness, even on the part of the most disinterested. Sometimes it is considered enough to locate a given work in time and place or in the history of styles. Merely to take note of or to recognize a work is thought to be sufficient for entry into the "educated" or "civilized" community in part defined by its attachment to or investment in "good art." All that is asked of learners is usually a polite receptivity; as persons, each with his/her own distinctive way of grasping phenomena, they are not provoked to engage themselves, to become involved.

Strangely, this is seldom the case where imaginative literature is concerned (although imaginative literature is seldom identified as "art"). There may be some who are satisfied if students can simply decode the words of a piece; but most teachers realize that there must be personal participation in a text if it is to be grasped *as* a text, *as* an imaginary world. Surely, the same thing must be true of other art forms. "Reading" a painting, decoding a ballet are important; but more must be done than the teaching of what is, after all, "basic." People must be intentionally empowered to go beyond such basics in order fully to perceive, to engage, to bring to life. If they are not, paintings and dance performances and enacted plays are likely to be absorbed by their surroundings, to become parts of the taken-for-granted reality. Just as a cathedral or a pyramid may simply be "seen" or noted, so may *Giselle* be apprehended as a series of movements illustrating a story, or *The Glass Menagerie* as an acting out of events from Tennessee Williams' actual youth. In no case will ordinary, habitual vision be disturbed; conventional modes of paying heed will simply be confirmed. What is being experienced will be viewed as another way of being shown what is already known; there will be no sense of an alternative reality, no sense of something beyond.

Although I do not believe that aesthetics *per se* need be taught in schools in the effort to introduce students to the art-world, I do believe that certain kinds of questions should be posed and encouraged for the sake of keeping a reflectiveness about the role of the arts alive. The arts do, after all, create a specific "province of meaning," (Schutz, 1967) different from that of the natural or social sciences, different as well from the provinces of religious faith and dreams; and even play and the arts, like the other modes of awareness, require a distinctive "style" of directing attention to aspects of reality. Art is a transfiguration of the commonplace, one writer tells us. (Danto, 1981) Art is serious and beneficial, remarks another, a game played against chaos and death. Yes, comments still another, art opens a dimension accessible to no other experience. The languages, the images we find in art "make perceptible, visible, and audible that which is no longer or not yet perceived, said, and heard in everyday life." (Marcuse, 1978, p. 72) Indeed, art may make the petrified world "speak, sing, and perhaps dance. . . ."

None of these comments represents a firm definition of art; nor does any one identify an "essence" or common denominator setting art forms off from all other phenomena in the world. They are, in effect, descriptive of various people's responses to the arts or of their efforts to account for the impact of the arts on their lives. That may be the best anyone can do in these times; but it may be that an insistent questioning has something to do with the significance of certain encounters, certain high artistic moments in people's lives. In a time when the boundaries are obscured and certain of the old canonical "traditions" are being challenged as exclusive and elite, individuals in their communities probably have to decide for themselves what should be cherished as art and set apart from non-art. It ought to be part of the learning process to consider how a three-minute video differs from a filmed vignette, a painting, a fully developed film. Given the vast popularity of and admiration for Michael Jackson, can he be expected to transform experience as other great singers can—Pavarotti, say, or Milnes? Does Jackson require the same mode of listening, the same repeated hearings? If not, why not? In any case, what does liking something have to do with judging it to be a work of art? It must be clear, in a school committed to variety and diversity, that there is nothing illegitimate in enthusiasm for Michael Jackson, nothing wrong with enjoyment. But the young too can confront the question of whether it is possible to relish Jackson and at once go beyond to the Brandenburg, perhaps, when the time is ripe, to *Don Giovanni,* to Beethoven's quartets. Where are the stopping places, the side roads, the openings? The young can be freed to choose. What of horror movies and those suffused with gratuitous violence? What of works that demean minorities? That humiliate women and make objects out of them? What of the works that make voyeurs out of spectators or, as John Berger (1977) says, render them (under the eyes of certain figures in paintings) merely "specimens"? What, in any case, is the "good" of art when there is carnage in El Salvador, when missiles are being deployed, when official voices woo and mystify, when people starve? The arts and engagements with them have not been known to make people moral or humane over the course of history. How justify their presence in our lives?

The questions need to be kept alive in the realization that there are no final answers. Each person has to discover his/her own and choose himself/herself with respect to what is found. No one is likely to do this, however, in innocence. No one is likely to do it without having some art experiences, since it is only out of actual encounters that meaningful questions about the arts can arise. Keeping the discussions alive means providing room for the young to choose for themselves, rather than simply submitting to the voices of authority and orthodoxy. Yes, their teachers (like professional artists) can empower them to see, to read, to apprehend; but they are the ones who must "incline" in those moments when things seem to withdraw, when something seems to wait to be disclosed.

They will not incline without some capacity to uncouple, at least for a time, to move into an alternative space, an imaginary space; and this requires a narrowing and a focusing of attention, a taking of time. Here, too, the young can learn to learn; and it takes the delicate creation of situations that will move them—and give them the courage—to choose to learn, to become different from the way they are. Uncertainties will remain respecting the connections between the arts and the human condition and human consciousness at the various moments of growth. There are the difficult issues respecting distortions through the arts and by the arts; and there are the revelations of hitherto hidden faces and facets, unfamiliar dimensions of lived realities. I recall seeing a random pile of grey army overcoats in an exhibition of Joseph Bueys' work; and, because I knew I was in an art space and chose myself with respect to it (apart from the humdrum and routine), I saw what I had never seen about the drabness and weariness of war, and its random pointlessness. I recall a paragraph in Toni Morrison's *Sula* (1975) that altered my views of artmaking and the media of art, extended them in a direction I had never moved before. Morrison is describing her anti-heroine, Sula:

> In a way, her strangeness, her naivete, her craving for the other half of her equation was the consequence of an idle imagination. Had she paints, or clay, or knew the discipline of the dance, or strings; had she anything to engage her tremendous capacity and her gift for metaphor, she might have exchanged the restlessness and preoccupation with whim for an activity that provided her with all she yearned for. And like any artist with no art form, she became dangerous. (105)

Sula is a black woman, doubly oppressed, impelled to break through the confining frames of her community and its modes of perception. She is a pariah, yet a force for liberation; and that is why, in fact, she is "dangerous." When she is dying, she says she is "going down like one of those redwoods." And she goes on to say: "I sure did live in this world." No, she did not get "all she yearned for," and it may have been as well. So she becomes somehow paradigmatic for me. She makes me look upon all interpretive systems (even the ones I take for granted) as in some sense problematic. I am moved to think, once again, about the "web of relations" (Arendt, 1958) my associates and I have woven between ourselves and wonder how inclusive it is and what it means for my choosing, for our choosing, and what it means to be critical and to transform.

The experience, it must be said, is not wholly subjective, although the reader's subjectivity cannot but be involved. For one thing, a book or a visual work has a public presence; it has been and is being read and interpreted by a public of some kind, interpreted in the light of a particular social reality. Reading *Sula,* trying to achieve it as meaningful, I am bound to integrate a variety of perspectives, transcending my personal and limited one: the perspective of the narrative point of view, the perspective of the white people in Meridian and the black people on the "Bottom," the contesting and often irreconcilable perspectives of Sula's family and Nel's and Shadrack's and Ajax's, the perspective of the fictional "Reader" to whom the book is addressed. In a classroom, there might be dialogue and argument about the book; since diverse persons must read it from diverse vantage points, even though there is a form that is to some degree given, words that are (on the surface at least) the same for everyone. Out of the dialogue, out of the multiple and shifting vantage points, a richer presence may well emerge. But the questions are likely to remain unanswered; the book "appeals," as Jean-Paul Sartre (1961, pp. 64–65) once said, to each one's freedom. So it continually moves to what is not yet. And, as it does, it renders what is already known in some way new.

There can be no closure; there can be no final answers, as there might be for empirical questions. Neither *Sula* nor *King Lear* nor Picasso's *Guernica* nor the Hallelujah Chorus nor Ingmar Bergman's *Fanny and Alexander* solves anything, offers any guidelines. They do, however, make one see and hear and feel in such a fashion that one's questions sharpen, one's head aches. Marcel Proust once wrote that the writer and painter are like eye specialists for those who attend to their works. "The treatment—with the help of their paintings, their writings—is not always pleasant. When the treatment is concluded, they tell us: You can look now. And thus the world which hasn't been created only once, but is recreated every time a new artist emerges, appears to us perfectly comprehensible—so very different from the old." (Proust in Polanyi, 1964, p. 200) What he was describing was what Virginia Woolf called a "shock of awareness," an experience that shakes conventional certainties as it opens the way for something new.

An awareness of this, coupled with an awareness of the ambiguities and the open possibilities associated with art experiences, may have played into the persistent efforts to trivialize and sentimentalize the arts within the schools. I do not only have in mind the didactic and moralistic (yes, and patriotic) purposes the arts have been made to serve. I think of the Valentine's Day cards and Mother's Day cards that emerged when the "genteel tradition" began working in schools late in the last century. Most of all, I think of the figurative curtains that hid art forms from our view. There was a Velasquez reproduction in my high school (of "Las Meninas," I believe, with the eyes of the painter and the members of the Hapsburg family staring at the model, who is not rendered, who may be the beholder, any one of us who dares to look); and I am sure there was a Raphael Madonna; but that meant no more and aroused no more than did the painting of Washington crossing the Delaware or the picture of Abraham Lincoln or the photograph of the basketball team frozen in the past. Because no one paid heed, because no one ever mentioned the possibility of taking the time to look, and because few of us knew anything about how to look, Velasquez and Raphael were absorbed into the drabness of the corridors. Like so many other aspects of our reality, they were rendered invisible. I am reminded of how the winter trees and the ice-blocked river withdraw and become invisible until I take the time to attend, to notice, to release myself from the routine. And I think of how various and shimmering and multifaceted the envisaged world becomes in those few moments when I consciously attend.

That, really, is the point: to awaken persons to a sense of presentness, to a critical consciousness of what is ordinarily obscured. Without such experiences, we are all caught in conventional (often officially defined) constructs in such a fashion that we confuse what we have been taught to see with the necessary and the unalterable. Even if we grant, as we must, that we come to know the world by means of symbol systems, languages, *schemata* developed over time by our "predecessors and contemporaries," (Schutz, 1967, p. 23) even if we grant that we could not communicate with one another if we were not initiated into existing ways of knowing, the consciousness of our own consciousnesses, our own agency, remains important if we are not to be submerged. I would stress, however, that such consciousness seldom develops in isolation. It is most likely to develop in the context of dialogue, of communication, something of great consequence for schools. The pleasures offered by art experiences are enhanced by articulation in a speech situation, in which persons find out what they feel and what they think (after emerging from an encounter) by speaking with others in their own voices as *who* (to borrow from Arendt) (1958) not *what* they are.

For teachers, the obligation is to teach persons how to notice what there is to be noticed without imposing alien readings or interpretations. Perceptions of contours, colors, form-content relations can be shared without depriving students of their capacities to see and hear for themselves. They can be enabled to understand what it signifies to move into an illusioned world. They can be helped to realize that, when Tom (in *The Glass Menagerie*) tells the audience that they are about to see a "memory play," (Williams, 1961, p. 439) that truth will be masquerading, as illusion, those in the audience are being asked to release themselves by means of *their* imagination. Only as they do so, only as they place in parentheses grocery lists and domestic concerns and memories of case histories, will they be able to inhabit Williams' unreal world and achieve it as meaningful for themselves. And having done so, they can expect their worlds to be in some measure "recreated," as Proust said. Young people, in other words, can be released to perceive, to pattern by means of perceiving, to grasp by paying heed. And, in the case of all other kinds of educative experiences, they may begin to learn when they begin teaching themselves and going beyond where they are.

Arguing for the opening of significant art spaces in the school, I know I am arguing for altered schools. To enter such spaces, individuals must be empowered, each in a way appropriate to themselves—their background, their life story—to perceive differently, to hear and to see. Entering, it may be that such students are enabled to create their spaces as they move together "making music together." (Schutz, 1967) It may be that they will gain a new capacity to name themselves and name their worlds, as they come to see themselves and their worlds anew. We can affirm with some certainty that each individual has to be in an art space in person if any art works are to be achieved. There is no such phenomenon as a second-hand experience with a Cezanne landscape or a Stevens poem or a Woody Allen film. We can never send someone else to see it for us and come back and report. Not only are we required to be there; we are required to be there as active and conscious beings, allowing the energies of perceiving and imagining and feeling to move out to the works at hand, to bring them into life. Yes, and we are required to be there as open and reflective consciousness, empowered to resist fixed definition, the fetish, and the fraud. Wallace Stevens (1964, p. 183) wrote:

> Throw away the lights, the definitions,
> And say of what you see in the dark.
>
> That it is this or that it is that,
> But do not use the rotted names.

This is from "The Man with the Blue Guitar," and the blue guitar signifies imagination (among other things). At the end of the stanza quoted above, we find: "You as you are? You are yourself./ The blue guitar surprises you." The notion of surprise, like the notion of desire, is fundamental. Works of art, when attended to with some degree of discriminating awareness, cannot but surprise if persons are present to them as living beings who live with others and feel themselves existing in the world. That is because such works impel the awakened beholder (or reader or listener) to break with the habitual, the customary, the merely conventional, the given. Desire is evoked by the realization of what is not yet, expressed in the yearning towards possibility. Many works of art, when confronted by a yearning consciousness, are like those "slumbering shapes" in the carpenter's wood; they can never be exhausted, never finally achieved, never "done." There are boundaries, yes, edges, frames; but they are there to be transcended. And to transcend, each one himself or herself and at once along with others, is to transform the petrified world.

References

Arato, A. (1978). Esthetic theory and cultural criticism. In A. Arato & E. Gebhardt (Eds.), *The essential Frankfurt School reader.* New York: Urizen Books.

Arendt, H. (1958). *The human condition.* Chicago: University of Chicago Press.

Barthes, R. (1975). *The pleasure of the text.* New York: Hill and Wang.

Berger, J. (1977). *Ways of seeing.* London: Penguin Books.

Danto, A. C. (1981). *The transfiguration of the commonplace.* Cambridge: Harvard University Press.

Dewey, J. (1934). *Art as experience.* New York: Minton, Balch.

Gardner, H. (1983). *Frames of mind: The theory of multiple intelligences.* New York: Basic Books.

Goodman, N. (1976). *Languages of art.* Indianapolis: Hackett.

Heidegger, M. (1968). *What is called thinking?* New York: Harper Torchbooks.

Marcuse, H. (1978). *The aesthetic dimension: Toward a critique of Marxist aesthetics.* Boston: Beacon Press.

Merleau-Ponty, M. (1964). *Cezanne's doubt. Sense and non-sense.* Evanston: Northwestern University Press.

Morrison, T. (1975). *Sula.* New York: Bantam Books.

Polanyi, M. (1964). *Personal knowledge: Towards a post-critical philosophy.* New York: Harper Torchbooks.

Polanyi, M. (1966). *The tacit dimension.* Garden City: Doubleday.

Sartre, J. (1961). *Literature and existentialism.* New York: Citadel Press.

Schutz, A. (1967). *Common-sense and scientific interpretation: The problem of social reality.* The Hague: Martinus Nijhoff.

Schutz, A. (1964). Making music together: A study in social relationship. *Studies in social theory.* The Hague: Martinus Nijhoff, 159–178.

Steiner, G. (1967). *Language and silence.* New York: Atheneum.

Stevens, W. (1964). *The collected poems of Wallace Stevens.* New York: Alfred A. Knopf.

Williams, T. (1961). The glass menagerie. In *Six great modern plays.* New York: Dell Publishing.

Woolf, V. (1976). A sketch of the past. In J. Schulking (Ed.), *Moments of being.* New York: Harcourt Brace Jovanovich.

Schooling, Popular Culture, and a Pedagogy of Possibility

Henry A. Giroux and Roger I. Simon

Within the last decade educational discourse in North America has focused primarily on two related issues. On the one hand, educational reform has been linked to the imperatives of big business. Schools in this perspective are training grounds for different sectors of the workforce; they are seen as providing knowledge and occupational skills that are necessary for expanding both domestic production and foreign investment. This view links schooling to the demands of a technocratic and specialized literacy. Its offensive is less ideological than it is technicist and instrumental in nature. On the other hand, the late 1980s have witnessed the dramatic rise of the culturalist wing of the far Right, especially in the United States. This ideological detour in the conservative offensive has been legitimated and sustained in the United States largely through the influence of William Bennett, President Reagan's secretary of education since 1985. Bennett has broadened the conservatives' definition of schooling by reaffirming its primacy as a guardian of Western Civilization. Under the banner of excellence, Bennett has promoted a 19th-century brand of elitism by appealing to a narrowly defined "Western tradition," conveyed through a pedagogy unencumbered by the messy concerns of equity, social justice, or the need to educate a critical citizenry.

Bennett's redefinition of the purpose of education and the nature of teachers' work has set the stage for a number of ideological assaults against liberal and radical views of schooling. In this refurbished conservative discourse, the targets are modernity, democracy, difference, and above all, relativism. Classical Western traditions, in this view, are beset on all fronts by relativism. It is alleged to be running rampant in various academic disciplines; in the social protest movements of students; in the increasing cultural and ethnic diversity of the

United States; and in the expanding sphere of popular culture, which is viewed as a tasteless and dangerous threat to the notions of civility and order.

Although these positions defend various aspects of the conservative agenda for schooling, they share a common ideological and political thread. That is, they view schools as a particular way of life organized to produce and legitimate either the economic and political interests of business elites or the privileged cultural capital of ruling-class groups. More importantly, both positions represent an attack on the notion of culture as a public sphere where the basic principles and practices of democracy are learned amid struggle, difference, and dialogue. Similarly, both positions legitimate forms of pedagogy that deny the voices, experiences, and histories through which students give meaning to the world and in doing so often reduce learning to the dynamics of transmission and imposition.

We want to intervene in this debate by arguing for schools as sites of struggle and for pedagogy as a form of cultural politics. In both cases, we want to argue for schools as social forms that expand human capacities in order to enable people to intervene in the formation of their own subjectities and to be able to exercise power in the interest of transforming the ideological and material conditions of domination into social practices which promote social empowerment and demonstrate democratic possibilities. We want to argue for a critical pedagogy that takes into consideration how the symbolic and material transactions of the everyday provide the basis for rethinking how people give meaning and ethical substance to their experiences and voices. This is not a call for a unifying ideology by which to construct a critical pedagogy; it is a call for a politics of difference and empowerment as the basis for developing a critical pedagogy through and for the voices of those who are often silenced. It is a call to recognize that, in schools, meaning is produced through the construction of forms of power, experiences, and identities that need to be analyzed for their wider political and cultural significance.

With these issues in mind, we want to emphasize the importance of critical pedagogy by analyzing its potentially transformative relations with the sphere of popular culture. In our view, popular culture represents not only a contradictory terrain of struggle, but also a significant pedagogical site that raises important questions about the elements that organize the basis of student subjectivity and experience.

At first glance, the relationship between popular culture and classroom pedagogy may seem remote. Popular culture is organized around pleasure and fun, while pedagogy is defined largely in instrumental terms. Popular culture is located in the terrain of the everyday, while pedagogy generally legitimates and transmits the language, codes, and values of the dominant culture. Popular culture is appropriated by students and helps authorize their voices and experiences while pedagogy authorizes the voices of the adult world, the world of teachers and school administrators.

In addition to these differences, there is a fundamental similarity between popular culture and pedagogy that needs to be articulated. Both exist as subordinate discourses (Grossberg, 1986). For both liberals and radicals, pedagogy is often theorized as what is left after curriculum content is determined. It is what follows the selection of ideologically correct content, its legitimacy rooted in whether or not it represents the proper teaching style. In the dominant discourse, pedagogy is simply the measurable, accountable methodology used to transmit course content. It is not a mutually determining element in the construction of knowledge and learning, but an afterthought reduced to the status of the technical and the instrumental. In a similar mode, in spite of the flourishing of cultural studies in the last decade, the dominant discourse still defines popular culture as whatever remains when high culture is subtracted from the overall totality of cultural practices. It is seen as the trivial and the insignificant of everyday life, and usually it is a form of popular taste deemed unworthy of either academic legitimation or high social affirmation.

The dominant discourse, in short, devalues pedagogy as a form of cultural production and it likewise scorns popular culture. Needless to say, while popular culture is generally ignored in the schools, it is not an insignificant force in shaping how students view themselves and their own relations to various forms of pedagogy and learning. In fact, it is precisely in the relationship between pedagogy and popular culture that the important understanding arises of making the pedagogical more political and the political more pedagogical. Popular culture and pedagogy represent important terrains of cultural struggle which offer both subversive discourses and important theoretical elements through which it becomes possible to rethink schooling as a viable and important form of cultural politics.

Pedagogy and the Production of Knowledge

Pedagogy refers to a deliberate attempt to influence how and what knowledge and identities are produced within and among particular sets of social relations. It can be understood as a practice through which people are incited to acquire a particular "moral character." As both a political and practical activity it attempts to influence the occurrence and qualities of experiences. When one practices pedagogy one acts with the intent of creating experiences that will organize and disorganize a variety of understandings of our natural and social world in particular ways. What we are emphasizing here is that pedagogy is a concept which draws attention to the processes through which knowledge is produced:

> It enables us. . . to ask under what conditions and through what means we "come to know." How one teaches is therefore of central interest but, through the prism of pedagogy, it becomes inseparable from what is being taught and, crucially, how one learns. . . .What pedagogy addresses is the process of production and exchange in this cycle, the transformation of consciousness that takes place in the interaction of three agencies—the teacher, the learner, and the knowledge they produce together. (Lusted, 1986, p. 3)

Such an emphasis does not at all diminish pedagogy's concern with "What's to be done?" As a complex and extensive term pedagogy's concern includes the integration in practice of particular curriculum content and design, classroom strategies and techniques, a time and space for the practice of those strategies and techniques, and evaluation purposes and methods. All of these aspects of educational practice come together in the realities of what happens in classrooms.

But the discourse of pedagogy centers something more. It stresses that the realities of what happens in classrooms organize a view of how a teacher's work within an institutional context specifies a particular version of what knowledge is of most worth, in what direction we should desire, what it means to know something, and how we might construct representations of ourselves, others, and our physical and social environment. In other words, pedagogy is simultaneously about the practices students and teachers might engage in together *and* the cultural politics such practices support. It is in this sense that to propose a pedagogy is to construct a political vision.

The education organized by a critical pedagogy is one that must raise questions of how we can work for the reconstruction of social imagination in the service of human freedom. What notions of knowing and what forms of learning are required by such a project?

Required is an education rooted in a view of human freedom as the understanding of necessity and the transformation of necessity. We need a pedagogy whose standards and achievement objectives are determined in relation to goals of critique and the enhancement of human capacities and social possibilities. This means that teaching and learning must be linked to the goals of educating students: to understand why things are the way they are and how they got to be that way; to make the familiar strange and the strange familiar (Clifford, 1981; Clifford & Marcus, 1986; McLaren, 1986, 1988); to take risks and struggle with ongoing relations of power from within a life-affirming moral culture; and to envisage a world which is "not yet" in order to enhance the conditions for improving the grounds upon which life is lived (Giroux, 1988; Simon, 1987).

Education and the Popular

The development of cultural studies in the last two decades has produced an intense interest in the concept of "popular culture" and, correspondingly, a number of important efforts to theorize the idea of "the popular." Given our specific concern with popular culture and its relation to pedagogy, it is important to recognize that well over a century ago those who controlled the developing agenda of state schooling were implicitly, if not explicitly, theorizing a notion of the popular that has dominated the practice of schooling ever since.

At the dawn of Canadian confederation (1860–1875), Egerton Ryerson, social architect and then head of Ontario's emerging public school system, was writing and speaking against a particular form of "the popular." Addressing himself to educators, he warned against the "trashy and positively unwholesome literature which is so widely extended throughout the country in the shape of . . . novelette papers" (Ryerson, 1868, p.72). He was convinced that reading such material would help undercut Canada's "connection with the mother country" and that officials at the U.S.–Canadian border should intercept the "obscene" and "filthy" publications "now so abundant in the States." Ryerson thought that "persons who read little or nothing besides the trashy novels of the day would do better not to read at all." He complained that "the most popular and best thumbed works in any of our common reading-rooms are invariably those which are the most worthless—we might say the most dangerous" (Ryerson, 1870, p. 53).

What Ryerson was talking about was not material analogous to contemporary pornography. He was referring to relatively inexpensive publications of short stories and novels filled with local vernacular expressions and "republican ideas." It was in a context such as this that, for instance, Ryerson criticized Mark Twain's *Tom Sawyer* (Morgan, 1987). What is at issue in positions such as Ryerson's is not simply an attempt at aesthetic definition—a matter, for instance, of articulating the distinguishing features between a "high" and a "low" or "popular" culture. Rather, given the current control over the social field by individuals who express ideas similar to Ryerson's, what is more fundamentally at issue is which set of cultural forms will be acknowledged as the legitimate substance of state-provided schooling. In other words, how will state schooling be used as an agency of moral regulation? The issue here is very basic; it is a matter of what vision of future social relations a public school system will support. Such visions have always been defined by a few for the many. Examining what has been excluded as well as required in official curricula clearly reveals, in country after country, that such decisions have been dialectically structured within inequitable and unjust relationships. Indeed, Ryerson's invective against the popular was asserted from the assumption of a superiority and natural dominance he associated with his class, gender, and race.

The popular has been consistently seen by educators as potentially disruptive of existing circuits of power. It has been seen as both threat and profane desire, that is, as both subversive in its capacity to reconstruct the investments of meaning and desire, and dangerous in its potential to provide a glimpse of social practices and popular forms that affirm both difference and different ways of life (Rockhill, 1987). The year 1987 is no exception. Allan Bloom's best-selling book in the United States, *The Closing of the American Mind,* argues that popular culture, especially rock music, has resulted in the atrophy of both nerve and intelligence in American youth. Rock music, and more generally popular culture, represent in Bloom's mind a barbaric appeal to sexual desire. Not to be undone by this insight, Bloom further argues that since "Young people know that rock has the beat of sexual intercourse" (Bloom, 1987, p. 73), popular culture is simply synonymous for turning "life. . . into a nonstop, commercially prepackaged masturbational fantasy" (p. 75). Of course Bloom's sentiments about popular culture in general and rock music in particular have been shaped by what he perceives as indices of a serious moral and intellectual decline among American youth. Specifically, he fears the challenge to authority formed from the student movements of the 1960s, and the leveling ideology of democratic reform characteristic of the discourse of radical intellectuals. In effect, Bloom's book offers unsupported authoritarian ravings that appear to emulate the very convulsions he suggests characterize much popular culture. He writes:

The inevitable corrollary of such sexual interest is rebellion against the parental authority that represses it. Selfishness thus becomes indignation and then transforms itself into morality. The sexual revolution must overthrow all the forces of domination, the enemies of nature and happiness. From love comes hate, masquerading as social reform. A worldview is balanced on the sexual fulcrum. What were once unconscious or half conscious childish resentments become the new Scripture. And then comes the longing for the classless, prejudice-free, conflictless, universal society that necessarily results from liberated consciousness— "We are the World," a pubescent version of *Alle Menschen werden Bruder*, the fulfillment of which has been inhibited by the political equivalents of Mom and Dad. These are the three great lyrical themes: sex, hate, and a smarmy, hypocritical version of brotherly love. Such polluted sources issue in a muddy stream where only monsters can swim. (Bloom, 1987, p. 74)

Of course, the monsters who inhabit this terrain are contemporary youth, subordinate groups, and all those others who refuse to take seriously the canonical status that Bloom wants to attribute to the Great Books that embody his revered notion of Western civilization. More specifically responsible for this version of contemporary madness are leftists, feminists, and anyone who uses a Walkman radio. Bloom's discourse is based on the myth of decline, and its attack on popular culture is inextricably linked to the call for the restoration of a so-called lost classical heritage. Rather than a sustained attack on popular culture, this is the all-encompassing discourse of totalitarianism using the veil of cultural restoration. Its enemies are democracy, utopianism, and the unrealized political possibilities contained in the cultures of "the other"—that is, those who are poor, black, women, and who share the common experience of powerlessness. Its goal is moral and social regulation in which the voice of tradition provides the ideological legitimation for a ministry of culture. Its echo is to be found in Hitler's Germany and Mussolini's Italy; its pedagogy is as profoundly reactionary as its ideology and can be summed up simply in the terms *transmission* and *imposition*.

In mentioning Ryerson and Bloom, we are stressing the rather straightforward point that historically, state-regulated forms of schooling have viewed popular culture as a marginal and dangerous terrain, something to be inoculated against, or—at best—occasionally explored for the incidental motivational ploy that might enhance student interest in a particular lesson or subject. In other words, educators have traditionally viewed popular culture as a set of knowledges and pleasures which are distinguished from, properly subordinate to, and at times co-optable by, the agenda of schooling. And for our purposes, this traditional view cannot be completely dismissed. Despite all its repugnant aspects, it correctly places teachers' work at the center of its discourse. That is, useful notions of the concept of popular culture must be articulated to a particular notion of pedgogy.

Pedagogical Relevance of Popular Culture

Our interest is not in aesthetic or formal qualities of popular culture. Nor are we particularly concerned with the way in which various popular forms might be codified into subjects or themes for study in cultural studies programs. Rather we begin with more fundamental questions, including some that are raised by teachers: What relationship do my students see between the work we do in class and the lives they live outside of class? Is it possible to incorporate aspects of students' lived culture into the work of schooling without simply confirming what they already know? Can this be done without trivializing the objects and relationships important to students? And can it be done without singling out particular groups of students as marginal, exotic, an "other" within a hegemonic culture?

In asking these questions we have to assume that pedagogy never begins on empty ground. For this reason, a good starting point would be to consider popular culture as that terrain of images, knowledge forms, and affective investments which define the ground on which one's "voice" becomes possible within a pedagogical encounter (Giroux, 1988). In stating this it is apparent that we have a particular form of teaching and learning in mind. This form is a critical pedagogy that affirms the lived reality of difference and everyday life as the ground on which to pose questions of theory and practice (McLaren, 1988). It is a form that claims the experience of lived difference as an agenda for discussion and as a central resource for a pedagogy of possibility (Simon, 1987).

Such a discussion of lived difference, if pedagogical, will take on a particular tension. It implies a struggle—a struggle over assigned meaning, a struggle over the direction in which to desire, a struggle over particular modes of expression, and ultimately a struggle over multiple and even contradictory versions of "self." It is this struggle that makes possible new investments and knowledge beyond individual experience and hence can redefine the possibilities we see both in the conditions of our daily lives and in those conditions which are "not yet." This is a struggle over the very notion of pedagogy itself, one which constantly makes problematic how teachers and students come to know both within wider cultural forms and in the exchanges that mark classroom life. It is a struggle that can never be won, or else pedagogy stops (Lewis & Simon, 1986).

This position does not require teachers to suppress or abandon what and how they know. Indeed, the pedagogical struggle is lessened without such resources. However, teachers and students must find forms within which a single discourse does not become the locus of certainty and certification. Rather, teachers must find ways of creating a space for mutual engagement of lived difference that does not require the silencing of a multiplicity of voices by a single dominant discourse; at the same time, teachers must develop forms of pedagogy informed by a substantive ethic that contests racism, sexism, and class exploitation as ideologies and social practices that disrupt and devalue public life. This is a pedagogy that refuses detachment, though it does not silence in the name of its own ideological fervor or correctness. A critical pedagogy examines with care and in dialogue how social injustices work through the discourses and experiences that constitute daily life and the subjectivities of the students who invest in them.

What might a teacher need to understand in order to engage in such a struggle? Though we will take this issue up in detail at the end of this paper, we can suggest here several questions that a teacher might pursue in the effort to develop a critical pedagogy. If we further define popular culture as both a site of struggle between dominant and subordinate groups (Hall, 1981), and a reference for understanding how experience is organized, produced, and legitimated within cultural forms grounded in the dynamics of everyday life, there are several questions a teacher might pursue. For instance, what are the historical conditions and material circumstances within which the practices of popular culture are pursued, organized, asserted, and regulated? Do such practices open up new notions of identities and possibilities? Do they exclude other identities and possibilities, and if so, which ones? How are such practices articulated with the hegemonic forms of knowledge and pleasure? Whose interests and investments are served—and whose are critiqued and challenged—by a particular set of popular cultural practices? Finally, what are the moral and political commitments of such practices and how are these related to one's own commitments as a teacher? If there is a divergence between these two sets of commitments, what does this imply?

The importance of asking these questions is, in part, to remove the analysis of popular culture from simply a question of reading ideology into either commodity forms or forms of lived everyday relations. Rather, we are moving toward a position within which one could inquire into the popular as a field of practices that constitute for Foucault an indissoluble triad of knowledge, power, and pleasure (Foucault, 1980a). In an important sense this is what the pedagogical struggle is all about: testing the ways we produce meaning and represent ourselves, our relations to others, and our relation to our environment. In doing so we consider what it is we have become, and what it is we no longer want to be. We also enable ourselves to recognize, and struggle for, possibilities not yet realized.

Some Cautions on the Way to Rethinking the Popular

Rethinking the notion of the popular is a difficult and hazardous task. Briefly, we wish to share our sense of some of these difficulties.

Popular cultural practices display a wide variety of differences, which in part are organized by the struggles inherent in existing gender, class, racial and ethnic, age, and regional relations. As long as such differences are used to establish and maintain disadvantage and human suffering, we need in any discussion of pedagogy and popular culture to register the notion of difference clearly and loudly. Our preference then is to eliminate the singular and always speak about popular cultural *practices*. It is also important to stress that we view such practices as lived processes, as part of the way in which everyday life is experienced and responded to differently by different groups. Of course, there is a danger here of reducing particular students to simple reflections of some putative characteristics of group membership. This is a path of classism, sexism, and racism. However, it is equally objectionable to avoid consideration of the social construction and regulation of both knowledge and desire.

We think it is important to retheorize the term "mass culture" in any analysis of popular culture. The agenda is not to simply assert the homogenization and domination of everyday life. We do not wish to conflate those forms which are mass-produced and distributed as products (toys, books, films, records, television programs) with popular culture. Of course, we are interested in those forms both as they offer and give form to (but not mechanically impose) the practices which organize and regulate acceptable styles and images of social activity and individual and collective identity. However, we think it is a mistake to reduce the discussion of popular culture to a discussion of products. If we want to sustain the notion of popular culture as a terrain of possibilities, not just of threat and profane desire, then we require other ways of conceptualizing the term. One alternative consistent with our emphasis on popular cultural practice is to consider commodities in their circuits of distribution focusing on the commodity not as text but as event. In other words, this means considering both the structured occasion of engaging a commodity and the ways in which a product is employed or taken up (Radway, 1984).

In making this suggestion we are stressing that popular cultures are constituted not just by commodity forms but by practices which reflect a creative and sometimes innovative capacity of people. Popular culture may contain aspects of a collective imagination which make it possible for people to surpass received knowledge and tradition. In this sense, popular culture may inform aspects of a counter-discourse which help to organize struggles against relations of domination. As Tony Bennett has written:

> A cultural practice does not carry its politics with it, as if written upon its brow for ever and a day; rather, its political functioning depends on the network of social and ideological relations in which it is inscribed as a consequence of the ways in which, in a particular conjuncture, it is articulated to other practices. (Bennett, 1986, p. xvi)

This notion was recently illustrated for us in an essay written by a woman teacher participating in a Masters of Education course on the relation of pedagogy and popular culture. In this paper she was reflecting on her fondness of the persona of Marilyn Monroe as expressed in both Monroe's films and public imagery (Rowe, 1987). On the one hand, a given popular cultural practice (the event of watching Monroe's movies) may feed into existing forms of domination (in this case, patriarchy). However, at the same time such forms can be an acknowledgment of the nondeterministic subjective side of social relations in which human beings are characterized by an ideal or imaginary life, where will is cultivated, dreams dreamt, and categories developed. This teacher's paper showed that, for a young girl growing up amid the patriarchal relations of a traditional rural farm family, such forms can provide a type of counter-discourse which is, in part, a promise of possibility. To ignore this possibility is to fail to understand that our material lives can never adequately reflect our imaginary lives. It is imagination itself that fuels our desire and provides us with the energy to reject relations of domination and embrace the promise of possibility (Fitting, 1987).

This view is not naively romantic. We cannot suppress those aspects of popular culture that we may see as regressive; rather we must face them for what they are and attempt to move beyond them. Fascism was and still is viable as a particular practice of popular culture. We must not forget there will always be a moral project associated with particular cultural practices and we need to understand and assess the relation of such practices to the commitments we hold as educators and citizens. It is important to reemphasize popular culture as a terrain of struggle infused with practices that are both pedagogical and political. Since consent has to be won for popular forms to be integrated into the dominant culture, popular culture is never free from the ideologies and practices of pedagogy. Similarly, popular forms have to be renegotiated and re-presented in order to appropriate them in the service of self- and social empowerment. This suggests a critical pedagogy operating to disrupt the unity of popular culture in order to encourage the voice of dissent while simultaneously challenging the lived experiences and social relations of domination and exploitation. Adam Mills and Phil Rice capture the complexity of these issues and are worth quoting at length:

> "Popular culture is always a threat": by always occupying the subordinate, illegitimate pole in the field of cultural relations the values embodied in the practices and representations there are antithetical to, what are by definition, the minority values of "elite" cultures. Of necessity those discourses and forms which originate in the dominant cultural institutions, as Stuart Hall suggests, must activate the "structural contradiction which arises whenever a dominant culture seeks to incorporate" and include, within its boundaries, the people. They must raise, in other words, even if it is only an attempt to neutralize, the spectre of oppression and subordination. That certain forms are popular must then require of analysis a recognition both of the means by which consent is won for those dominant discourses, and the way in which those discourses, by presenting themselves as popular, re-present yet connect with the lived practices and experience of subordinate social classes. This suggests that the popular is a site of political and ideological struggle, first and foremost over the formation of what is given as "popular," and beyond that over the formation of "the people." But more than this, it suggests that cultural forms can no longer be regarded

as coherent, expressive unities, or even that popular forms are no more than one-dimensional commodities functioning as standardized and stupefying cultural narcotics for the masses. What is implied is that cultural forms comprise a contradictory and uneven balance of elements, both dominant and subordinate —those which connect with "popular" social life, and those dominant elements which attempt to close or constrain alternative meanings and which attempt to mute the voice of dissent. (Mills & Rice, 1982, pp. 24–25)

A pedagogy which engages popular culture in order to affirm rather than mute the voice of the student is not without its difficulties. Michel Foucault in the first volume of *The History of Sexuality* (1980a) comments on "the pleasure of analysis": the pleasure of discovering and exposing the secrets of human pleasure. The teacher engaged in a pedagogy which requires some articulation of knowledge forms and pleasures integral to student everyday life is walking a dangerous road. Too easily, perhaps, encouraging student voice can become a form of voyeurism or satisfy a form of ego-expansionism constituted on the pleasures of understanding those who appear as "other" to us. This is why we must be clear on the nature of the pedagogy we pursue. Popular culture and social difference can be taken up by educators in either of two ways: as a pleasurable form of knowledge/power which allows for more effective individualizing and administration of forms of physical and moral regulation, or alternatively as the terrain on which we must meet our students in a pedagogical encounter that enables rather than disables human imagination and capacities in the service of individual joy, collective prosperity, and social justice. Dick Hebdige (1982) warned us when he reported the words of a young male member of a subculture he was studying: "You really hate an adult to understand you. That's the only thing you've got over them, the fact that you can mystify and worry them." Contemporary youth have cause to be wary of giving up their anonymity, of making their private and lived voices the object of public and pedagogical scrutiny.

There is yet one more caution to raise. We think it important to question the notion of what it means to put popular cultural practice into play in the context of a pedagogical encounter. Does it mean to make such practices topical as curriculum content, to put such practices "up" for discussion? Would doing so not fundamentally change their character? Iain Chambers (1985) has written quite explicitly about this question and his admonition should be pondered:

High culture, with its cultivated tastes and formally imparted
knowledge, calls for particular moments of concentration,
separated out from the run of daily life. Popular culture, mean-
while, mobilizes the tactile, the incidental, the transitory, the
visceral. . . . It does not undertake an abstract aesthetic research
amongst already privileged objects of cultural attention, but
invokes mobile orders of sense, taste, and desire. Popular culture
is not appropriated through the apparatus of contemplation but,
as Walter Benjamin put it, through "distracted reception". . . . To
attempt to explain fully. . .would be to pull back [popular culture]
under the contemplative stare, to adopt the authority of the
patronizing academic mind that seeks to explain an experience
that is rarely his or hers. A role as Barthes has said that "makes
every speaker a kind of policeman". . . .The vanity of such a
presumed knowledge runs against the grain of the popular
epistemology I have tried to suggest: an informal knowledge of
the everyday, based on the sensory, the immediate, the concrete,
the pleasurable. . . .These [are] areas that formal knowledge and
its culture continually repress. (Chambers, 1985, p. 5)

The Practice of Critical Pedagogy

The issue, in this case, is how does one make popular culture
an object of pedagogical analysis without undermining its privileged
appropriation as a form of resistance. How can popular culture become
part of a critical pedagogy that does not ultimately function to police
its content and forms?

A pedagogy which takes popular culture as an object of study
must recognize that all educational work is at root contextual and
conditional. Such a pedagogy can only be discussed from within a
particular time and place and from within a particular theme. This
points to a larger issue concerning the nature of critical pedagogy
itself: doing critical pedagogy is a strategic, practical task, not a
scientific one. It arises not against a background of psychological,
sociological, or anthropological universals (as does much educational
theory related to pedagogy), but from questions such as: How is human
possibility being diminished here?

We are deliberately offering an expanded and politicized notion
of pedagogy, one that recognizes its place in multiple forms of cultural
production, and not just in those sites which have come to be labeled
"schools." Any practice which intentionally tries to influence the
production of meaning is a pedagogical practice. This includes aspects

of parenting, film making, theological work, social work, architecture, law, health work, advertising, and much else. These are all forms of cultural work. There are possibilities for pedagogy in any site: schools, families, churches, community associations, labor organizations, businesses, local media, and so forth. All work in such sites must begin with naming and problematizing the social relations, experiences, and ideologies constructed through popular forms that directly operate within such sites as well as those that emerge elsewhere but exercise an influence on those who work within them. A good part of the political work of pedagogy includes the articulation of practices not only within sites but also across them. Indeed, one of our long-term tasks as educators must be to define a framework that is helpful in articulating what critical pedagogies would be possible in a variety of sites of cultural work. This point is essential. The practical efficacy of our own commitments rests with the possibility of constructing an alliance between different forms of cultural work.

In what follows we want to bring our discussion to bear more directly on classroom reality by presenting a list of problems that have been raised by students and a diverse group of educators (elementary and secondary school teachers, university professors, literacy workers, health care professionals, artists, and writers) in the process of sharing their own cultural work as well as their readings of various articles and books. In many ways, the questions and the issues they raise make clear that the journey from theory to pedagogical possibility is rarely easy or straightforward. At the same time, the problems being raised suggest new and alternative directions for rethinking pedagogy as a form of cultural politics supportive of a project of hope and possibility. Such problems are symptomatic of the fact that a critical pedagogy is never finished; its conditions of existence and possibility always remain in flux as part of its attempt to address that which is "not yet," that which is still possible and worth fighting for.

Curriculum Practice

Of course, a critical pedagogy would be sensitive to forms of curriculum materials that might be implicated in the reproduction of existing unjust and inequitable social relations (e.g. sexism, racism, classism, heterosexism). But just what does this "sensitivity" imply? Does it lead to a legitimate form of censorship of material? The other side of censorship is the exclusionary choice we all make as to what set of materials we will use in our teaching during any particular period of time. What forms of authority can be invoked to make such choices? How should we make such choices? Can we employ reactionary material in the service of a progressive pedagogy? If one argues that we should include materials that (while reactionary) are integral to the dominant mythos of the community and hence "ripe" for critical analysis, in what ways would the material chosen for use be similar or different in the southern United States, in the northern United States, in English Canada, in French Canada, in England, in Australia, etc.? What balance and integration should be given to the interrogation of global and regional social cultural forms?

Critical pedagogy always strives to incorporate student experience as "official" curriculum content. While articulating such experience can be both empowering and a form of critique against relations that silence, such experience is not an unproblematic form of knowledge. How can one avoid the conservatism inherent in simply celebrating personal experience and confirming that which people already know? In other words, how can we acknowledge previous experience as legitimate content and challenge it at the same time (Giroux, 1988). How do we affirm student "voices" while simultaneously encouraging the interrogation of such voices (Giroux, 1988; McLaren, 1988).

Popular memories and "subjugated knowledges" (Foucault, 1980b) are often discussed as useful forms of critique of dominant ideologies. How can one draw on such knowledges in one's pedagogy (Giroux, 1988)? Since, as we have suggested earlier, this means working with the knowledge embedded in the forms of sociality, communities of discourse, and the popular forms students invest with meaning, what should be done to avoid making students who live outside of dominant and ruling forms feel that they are being singled out as the marginal "other" when we take seriously the knowledge organized within the terms of their everyday lives? Furthermore, how do we confront forms of resistance by students to what they perceive as an invasion by the official discourse of the school into private and nonschool areas of their lives?

Cultural Politics, Social Differences, and Practice

In planning and enacting a pedagogy whose central purpose is directed at enhancing human possibility and establishing a just and caring community, how do we know that what we are doing is ethically and politically right? How can we keep from slipping from a vision of human possibility into a totalizing dogma?

Many teachers want to help students identify, comprehend, and produce useful knowledge—but what constitutes useful knowledge? Is it the same for all students no matter what their gender, class, race, ethnicity, age, or geographic region? If not, then how can I cope intellectually, emotionally, and practically with such diversity and social difference? What if the teacher's view of useful knowledge differs from what students and their families think? What should happen to the teacher's vision of education? How far can you go in doing critical pedagogy if people are not interested in your agenda or see it as suppressing theirs? Do democratic forms of curriculum making ensure a critical pedagogy?

What can we or should we know about the basis of students' interest or disinterest in the topics and materials of our pedagogy? How can such knowledge make a difference to our practice? What would it mean to understand ignorance as a dynamic repression of information (Simon, 1984)? Is there a form of ignorance that is produced as a defense against hopelessness?

What does it mean to work with students in different class, racial, and gendered positions with regard to privilege? Why would those whose interests are served by forms of oppression want to change the situation? Is this structural conflict inevitable in our present society? Are there not issues and values that could mobilize broad interest in social transformations (e.g. ecology, peace, health)?

Guarding Against Hopelessness

Sometimes when students and teachers engage in a critique of existing social practices or forms of knowledge, a feeling of powerlessness comes over the group. Doing critical pedagogy can turn an educational setting into a "council of despair." How can one guard against the production of hopelessness when you take up an agenda of critique and social analysis? Given all the limitations of teaching and schooling, how can we effectively empower people (Aronowitz & Giroux, 1985; McLaren, 1986; Simon, 1987)?

Working with students to make clear the social contradictions we all live is an important aspect of critical pedagogical practice (Simon, 1987). However, will not raising contradictions in students' lives simply threaten them (Williamson, 1981–1982)? Will not pointing to social contradictions lead to cynicism and despair? Furthermore, if the value of understanding "ideology" is to stress that what is often taken as natural and inevitable is historically constructed and morally regulated, will not ideology critique produce a destabilization of identity and a paralysis of action. If you start questioning the givens of everyday life, won't this simply be overwhelming?

The Work of Teaching

How can we understand the constraining effects of the administrative and economic contexts within which we work? How should one take into account the realities of state regulation and the limitations imposed by a corporate economy? Should these always be seen as limits?

For those of us who work within public education, why should a teacher act in a way that might be contrary to school board policy or directive? When would a teacher be justified in doing so? What would be the consequences? Should teachers be accountable to specific groups or an organized public sphere? In practice, how would/should this be done?

Given the fact that the practice of critical pedagogy requires a substantial personal investment of time and energy, does it require the near-abandonment of a teacher's "private" life? How can one cope with the moments of depression and emotional disruption that come from a continual concern with the extent of injustice and violence in the world? How can we develop forms of collegial association that might support our efforts?

Conclusion

Posing these questions should not suggest that they have not been addressed either historically or in contemporary forms of social and educational theory. In fact, much of our own work has developed in response to many of the issues and questions we have listed above. They are questions that emerge at different times from diverse voices under widely differing educational contexts, and need to be constantly reconstructed and addressed. The notion of critical pedagogy begins with a degree of indignation, a vision of possibility, and an uncertainty that demands that we constantly rethink and renew the work we have done as part of a wider theory of schooling as a form of cultural politics. Defining the connections between popular culture and critical pedagogy is only one part of this ongoing task, and our introductory comments on this issue have attempted to sketch our view of the work that lies ahead. We will have been successful if we have stimulated the search for new ways of thinking about the notion of popular culture, the issues to be addressed by critical pedagogy, and the relationship that a critical theory of education might have to a pedagogy of possibility.

Notes

1. Portions of this paper draw extensively from the following work: Henry A. Giroux and Roger Simon (Eds.), *Popular Culture and Critical Pedagogy* (South Hadley, MA: Bergin & Garvey, 1988); Roger Simon, "Empowerment as a Pedagogy of Possibility," *Language Arts, 64* (April 1987), 370–382; and Roger Simon, *The Critical Pedagogy Networker* (Volume 1, Australia, 1988).

References

Aronowitz, S., & Giroux, H. A. (1985). *Education under siege*. South Hadley, MA: Bergin & Garvey.

Bennett, T. (1986). Popular culture and the turn to Gramsci. In T. Bennett, C. Mercer, & J. Woolacott (Eds.), *Popular culture and social relations* (pp. xi–xix). London: Open University Press.

Bloom, A. (1987). *The closing of the American mind*. New York: Simon & Schuster.

Chambers, I. (1985). Popular culture, popular knowledge. *One Two Three Four: A Rock and Roll Quarterly*, pp. 1–8.

Clifford, J. (1981). On ethnographic surrealism. *Comparative Studies in Society and History*, No. 18, pp. 539–564.

Clifford, J., & Marcus, G. E. (Eds.). (1986). *Writing culture: The poetics and politics of ethnography*. Berkeley: University of California Press.

Fitting, P. (1987). The decline of the feminist utopian novel. *Border/Lines*, No. 7/8, pp. 17–19.

Foucault, M. (1980a). *History of sexuality: Volume 1, An introduction*. New York: Vintage Books.

Foucault, M. (1980b). Two lectures. In *Power/Knowledge* (C. Gordon, Trans.). New York: Pantheon.

Giroux, H. A. (1988). *Schooling and the struggle for public life*. Minneapolis: University of Minnesota Press.

Grossberg, L. (1986). Teaching the popular. In C. Nelson (Ed.), *Theory in the classroom*. Urbana: University of Illinois Press.

Hall, S. (1981). Notes on deconstructing "the popular." In R. Samuel (Ed.), *People's history and socialist theory* (pp. 227–240). London: Routledge & Kegan Paul.

Hebdige, R. (1979). *Subculture: The meaning of style*. New York: Methuen.

Lewis, M., & Simon, R. I. (1986). A discourse not intended for her: Learning and teaching within patriarchy. *Harvard Educational Review, 56*, 457–472.

Lusted, D. (1986). Introduction: Why pedagogy? *Screen, 27*(5), 2–14.

McLaren, P. (1986). *Schooling as a ritual performance: Towards a political economy of educational symbols and gestures*. New York: Routledge & Kegan Paul.

McLaren, P. (1988). *Life in schools*. New York: Longman.

Mills, A., & Rice, P. (1982). Quizzing the popular. *Screen Education*, No. 41, pp. 15–25.

Morgan, R. (1987). *English studies as cultural production in Ontario, 1860–1920*. Unpublished doctoral dissertation, Ontario Institute for Studies in Education, Toronto.

Radway, J. (1984). *Reading the romance: Women, patriarchy, and popular literature*. Chapel Hill: University of North Carolina Press.

Rockhill, K. (1987, February). *Literacy as threat/desire: Longing to be somebody*. Unpublished paper, Ontario Institute for Studies in Education, Toronto.

Rowe, E. (1987, January). *Desire and popular culture: The ego ideal and its influence in the production of subjectivity*. Unpublished paper, Ontario Institute for Studies in Education, Toronto.

Ryerson, E. (1868). Summary of a speech at the Ontario Literary Society. *Journal of Education* (Ontario), *21*, 72.

Simon, R. I. (1984). Signposts for a critical pedagogy: A review of Henry A. Giroux's *Theory and resistance in education*. *Educational Theory, 34*, 379–388.

Simon R. I. (1987). Empowerment as a pedagogy of possibility. *Language Arts, 64*, 370–382.

Williamson, J. (1981–1982). How does girl number 20 understand ideology? *Screen Education*, No. 40, pp. 80–87.

Critical Mathematics Education: An Application of Paulo Freire's Epistemology

Marilyn Frankenstein

Knowledge of basic mathematics and statistics is an important part of gaining real popular, democratic control over the economic, political, and social structures of our society. Liberatory social change requires an understanding of the technical knowledge that is too often used to obscure economic and social realities. When we develop specific strategies for an emancipatory education, it is vital that we include such mathematical literacy. Statistics is usually abandoned to "experts" because it is thought too difficult for most people to understand. Since this knowledge is also considered value-free, it is rarely questioned. In attempting to create an approach to mathematics education that can lead both to greater control over knowledge and to critical consciousness, it is important to have an adequate pedagogical theory that can guide and illuminate specific classroom practices. I want to argue that Paulo Freire's "pedagogy of the oppressed" can provide the theoretical foundation for that practice.

Freire's educational theory is complex. In this article I will focus on the problems he poses that are particularly pressing for teachers in schools in the United States. For this reason, I will not treat his theory on why revolutionary party leaders must also be educators, or his assumptions (historically grounded in the reality of the various Third World countries in which he has practiced) that these leaders would come from the bourgeoisie, "committing suicide as a class in order to rise again as revolutionary workers" (Freire, 1978, p. 16). Instead, I want to investigate his epistemology, his theory about the relationship between education and social change, and his methodology for developing critical consciousness. Because of Freire's argument that critical education involves problem posing in which all involved are challenged to reconsider and recreate their prior knowledge, this presentation should be seen as an exploration intended to help extend our thinking, not as "Freire's definitive formulas-for-liberation." A discussion of my own experience teaching urban working-class adults[1] basic mathematics and statistics for the social sciences demonstrates ways in which Freire's theory can illuminate specific problems and solutions in critical teaching, and ways in which mathematics education can contribute to liberatory social change.

The Problems Freire Poses To Teachers In The United States

What is Knowledge?

Freire's epistemology is in direct opposition to the positivist paradigm currently dominant in educational theory. Positivists view knowledge as neutral, value-free, and objective, existing totally outside of human consciousness. Further, knowledge is completely separate from how people use it. Learning is the discovery of these static facts and their subsequent description and classification (Bredo & Feinberg, 1982). Giroux's (1981) critique of positivism in educational theory focuses attention on what is omitted from that paradigm.

> Questions concerning the social construction of knowledge and the constitutive interests behind the selection, organization, and evaluation of "brute facts" are buried under the assumption that knowledge is objective and value free. Information or "data" taken from the subjective world of intuition, insight, philosophy and nonscientific theoretical frameworks is not acknowledged as being relevant. Values, then, appear as the nemeses of "facts," and are viewed at best, as interesting, and at worst, as irrational and subjective emotional responses. (pp. 43–44)

Paulo Freire insists that knowledge is not static: that there is no dichotomy between objectivity and subjectivity, or between reflection and action: and that knowledge is not neutral.

For Freire, knowledge is continually created and re-created as people reflect and act on the world. Knowledge, therefore, is not fixed permanently in the abstract properties of objects, but is a process where gaining existing knowledge and producing new knowledge are "two moments in the same cycle" (Freire, 1982). In addition, knowledge requires subjects; objects to be known are necessary, but they are not sufficient.

Knowledge. . . necessitates the curious presence of subjects
confronted with the world. It requires their transforming action
on reality. It demands a constant searching. . . . In the learning
process the only person who really learns is s/he who. . . re-
invents that learning. (Freire, 1973, p. 101)

Knowledge does not exist apart from human consciousness; it is
produced by us collectively searching and trying to make sense of our
worlds.[2]

So, for Freire, the world is "giving" rather than "given" (Collins,
1977, p. 82), and subjectivity and objectivity are not separate ways
of knowing.

To deny the importance of subjectivity in the process of transforming the world and history is. . . to admit the impossible: a
world without people. . . . On the other hand, the denial of
objectivity in analysis or action. . . postulates people without a
world. . . [and] denies action itself by denying objective reality.
(Freire, 1970a, pp. 35–36)[3]

Because of the unity between subjectivity and objectivity, people
cannot *completely* know particular aspects of the world—no knowledge
is "finished." As humans change, so does the knowledge they produce.
But, through constant searching and dialogue, we can continually
refine our understanding in the sense that we can act more effectively.

This action and the reflection upon it that leads to new action
are not separate moments of knowing. Reflection which is not
ultimately accompanied by action to transform the world is meaningless, alienating rhetoric.[4] Action which is not critically analyzed cannot
sustain progressive change. Without reflection, people cannot learn
from each other's successes and mistakes; particular activities need
to be evaluated in relationship to larger collective goals. Only though
praxis—reflection and action dialectically interacting to re-create
reality—can people become subjects in control of organizing their
society. Moreover, this praxis is not neutral. Knowledge does not exist
apart from how and why it is used, in whose interest. Even, for
example, in the supposedly neutral technical knowledge of how to
cultivate potatoes, Freire asserts that:

there is something which goes beyond the agricultural aspects
of cultivating potatoes. . . . We have not only. . . the methods of
planting, but also the question which has to do with the role of

those who plant potatoes in the process of producing, for what we plant potatoes, in favor of whom. And something more. It is very important for the peasants. . .to think about the very process of work—what does working mean? (Brown, 1978, p. 63)

For Freire, the purpose of knowledge is for people to humanize themselves by overcoming dehumanization through the resolution of the fundamental contradiction of our epoch: that between domination and liberation.

An additional concept that illuminates Freire's epistemology by helping unpack the objective and subjective forces that shape knowledge and the reflective and active moments in knowing is the dialectic. Giroux (1981) defines this concept as:

a critical mode of reasoning and behavior. . .(that) functions so as to help people analyze the world in which they live, to become aware of the constraints that prevent them from changing that world, and, finally, to help them collectively struggle to transform that world. (pp. 114, 116)

The central categories of Giroux's formulation of the dialectic— totality, mediation, appropriation, and transcendence—detail the various dimensions of a Freirean critical knowledge of reality. Totality involves understanding any fact or situation in its historical, socio-economic, political, and cultural context. So as we come to know a particular aspect of the world, we must be concerned with its causal relationships, with its connections to other phenomena, with who benefits from its continuance, and with how it relates to our humani-zation or dehumanization. As we explore these questions, the answers we formulate are mediated by the institutional structures of society, by our individual and class histories, by our depth psychology, by our current relationships, and by the specific details of the concrete moment in which we are involved. The category of mediation challenges the "taken-for-granted" by helping us unravel the layers of objective and subjective forces through which we make meaning. The category of appropriation focuses our attention on human agency —on how people's actions both continue and challenge the relations of domination which mark our society. Therefore, critical knowledge involves uncovering the limits and the possibilities of our actions for transforming the world. Finally, transcendence unites commitment with theory, insisting that we refuse to accept domination as a "fact" of existence and that we use our knowledge of the world to reconstruct society so that it is "free of alienating and oppressive social institutions and life forms" (Giroux, 1981, p. 122). Thus, the dialectic as a mode of analysis not only clarifies the critical nature of knowledge, but also points to the connections between critical knowledge and emancipatory social change.

Education and Liberatory Social Change

Although Freire insists that "There is no such thing as absolute ignorance or absolute wisdom" (1973, p. 43), he also maintains that in an oppressive society people's knowledge is at different levels. People with the most dominated, "semi-intransitive" consciousness have a fragmented, localized awareness of their situation and are unable to think dialectically about it. Therefore, they view their condition as caused by their own failure and/or by "God." People living in more open societies naturally develop "naive transitive" consciousness where they begin to see causes in a broader context, but are still convinced that "causality is a static, established fact" (Freire, 1973, p. 44) and, therefore, not susceptible to change through their actions.

One of the major obstacles that the "pedagogy of the oppressed" must overcome is the participation of the oppressed in their own domination. Freire explores the structural, emotional, and cognitive factors behind this "culture of silence." In Brazil, the people had internalized their lack of participatory democratic experience under Portuguese imperialism. This emotional identification was strengthened by the myths the oppressors created that the status-quo represented the only possible situation because the oppressed were completely ignorant and powerless, while the rulers were omniscient and omnipotent. In such situations, the oppressed tend to fatalistically adjust to their condition. Since the relationships they have experienced and internalized involve the oppressor-oppressed division, their visions for a better life were very individualistic and focused on joining the oppressors rather than eliminating them.

However, as Freire insists, "the concept of semi-intransitivity does not signify the closure of people within themselves, crushed by an all-powerful time and space. Whatever their state, people are open beings" (1973, p. 17). One very important aspect of this hope for Freire is people's *conscientização*—their development of critical consciousness —which he maintains can only emerge through dialogical, problem-posing education. Since action cannot be dichotomized from reflection, and critical education develops critical knowledge, Freire views education as vital in helping people to become subjects involved in liberatory social change.[4]

An analysis of how education in the United States can lead to people's *conscientização* involves a focus on overcoming what Freire has called "massified," as opposed to semi-intransitive, consciousness. People with massified consciousness understand that humans change and control the world. But they believe that each individual acts from rational free choice rather than from a complex interplay of choice and manipulation. In *Cultural Action for Freedom* Freire begins an analysis of how the massified consciousness typical of advanced technological societies becomes the major factor in people's participation in their own domination:

> The rationality basic to science and technology disappears under the extraordinary effects of technology itself, and its place is taken by myth-making irrationalism. . . . People begin thinking and acting according to the prescriptions they receive daily from the communications media rather than in response to their dialectical relationships with the world. In mass societies, where everything is prefabricated and behavior is almost automatized, people are lost because they don't have to "risk themselves." . . .Technology. . .becomes. . .a species of new divinity to which [people] create a cult of worship (1970b, pp. 49–50).

Both the (apparent) complexities of technology and the (superficially) wonderful concrete changes it has made in daily life, from washing machines to word processors, convince people that control over our high-tech society must be left to "experts." Critical education in the United States, therefore, must counter this belief by showing people that they can understand how technology works, and in whose interest. Also, critical education must challenge and expose the contradictions in this society's definition of "progress" and "the good life."

The meaning of "massification" in highly industrialized societies is illuminated by the concepts of ideology and hegemony. These concepts can sharpen the analysis of how a massified consciousness is developed and perpetuated and point to ways in which education could help break it open. Kellner (1978), drawing on the work of Karl Korsch and Antonio Gramsci, develops a theory of ideology-as-hegemony and of "ideological regions," which demonstrates how ideology contains "anti-capitalist and oppositional moments—contradictions that produce space for ideological struggle and social change" (p. 59). For Kellner, ideological knowledge, in contrast to critical thought:

tends to suppress reflection, and resists changing its core ideas in the light of recalcitrant experience. . . . Nonideological thought and discourse exercises consistent and systematic reflection and critique on its methods, presuppositions, doctrines, and goals. It continually tests its ideas in practice, remaining open to experience, flexible, and capable of critique, self-critique, and revision (p. 54).

The ideas and images about "the way the world is" that constitute an ideology become hegemonic when they serve to preserve the status quo, presenting it as "natural, good, and just" (p. 50). Hegemonic ideologies, however, are not simply *imposed* by the ruling classes and believed by the "duped" masses—these ideologies are constructed through negotiation so as to incorporate people's ideas in such a way that they are not dangerous to the ruling classes. This process leaves hegemonic ideology with contradictions and open to challenge.

In order to focus on these contradictions and challenges, Kellner refines his theory to detail various "ideological regions"—economic, political, social, cultural—"which reproduce in thought the practices, institutions, and relations in each realm of existence so as to legitimate it and achieve hegemony" (p. 58). Tensions among ideologies in different realms (e.g., the hedonistic consumer ethic vs. monogamy and the family), contradictions between hegemonic ideology and reality (e.g., the ideological notion of equality vs. institutional racism), the fact that there is no *one* unifying hegemonic ideology—these all help to create an opening for education to develop critical theory which can in turn foster liberatory social change.

Content and Methods for Education for Critical Consciousness

In developing a critical pedagogy we must consider both content and methods. Emancipatory content presented in a nonliberatory way reduces critical insights to empty words which cannot challenge students' taken-for-granted reality and cannot inspire commitment to radical change. Humanistic methods without critical content can make students "feel good," but cannot help them become subjects capable of using critical knowledge to transform their world.

Freire is adamant that the content of an education for critical consciousness must be developed by searching with the students for the ideas and experiences which give meaning to their lives (1970a, p. 118). These "generative themes" should be organized and "re-presented" dialectically so that the links between them, their relationship to the totality of ideas, hopes, values, and challenges of the epoch, their historical context, their relationship to the community, and their raison d'être, are all clarified. Only as people come to know these themes critically, as they realize how these themes support or contradict the dominant ideologies, do they see that "dehumanization, although a concrete historical fact, is *not* a given destiny but the result of an unjust order" (Freire, 1970a, p. 28). And only then are they motivated to intervene to transform that order.

Literacy becomes an important part of a liberatory curriculum because reading enables people to gain distance from the concrete immediacies of their everyday lives in order to understand more clearly how their lives are shaped by and in turn can shape the world (Freire, 1983, p. 11). Further the study of language is vital because:

> the object of the investigation [of generative themes] is not people (as if they were anatomical fragments), but rather the thought-language with which people refer to reality, the levels at which they perceive that reality, and their view of the world, in which their generative themes are found. (Freire, 1970a, p. 86)

Apple's (1979) analysis of labeling points to the value, in this context, of studying the language used to discuss the condition of the oppressed. He argues that the labels used in educational settings work against the development of critical consciousness by mystifying the situations and relations which they describe, so that causality and complexity are hidden. Labels tend to focus blame on the "victims" and encourage solutions directed solely *at* them, while simultaneously directing attention away from the broader social, economic, and cultural factors which created the conditions being labeled.

Since dominant language can distort people's ability to know reality critically, and illiteracy can prevent them from objectifying the world in order to gain a nonfragmented, socio-historical under-standing of it, some fundamental themes may not emerge from the people. Freire sees no problem with teachers suggesting additional themes, since the dialogical nature of critical education must respect teachers', as well as students', ideas. The central theme that Freire and his team added in their work was "the anthropological concept of culture":

> the distinction between the world of nature and the world of culture;. . .culture as the addition made by people to a world they did not make; culture as the result of people's labor, of their efforts to create and re-create;. . .the democratization of culture;

the learning of reading and writing as a key to the world of written communication. In short, the role of people as Subjects in the world and with the world. (Freire, 1973, p. 46)

With this understanding, people realized they already engaged in many actions which transformed nature into culture, and, "by understanding what culture is, [they] go on to understand what history is. If we can change nature which we did not make, then why can't we change the institutions which we did make?" (Freire, 1982).

A central theme which Apple (1979) suggests for inclusion in the curriculum in the United States is "the nature of conflict." He theorizes that a significant block to transforming massified consciousness into critical consciousness is the ideology that in our pluralistic society the interests of all groups (e.g., business, labor, unemployed) are the same, and that policy and institutions are formed by consensus.

A basic assumption seems to be that conflict among groups of people is *inherently* and fundamentally bad and we should strive to eliminate it *within* the established framework of institutions, rather than seeing conflict and contradiction as the basic "driving forces" in society. (p. 87)

Apple goes on to argue that by studying the positive aspects of conflict, such as its role in promoting creative change and in bringing attention to injustice, students will develop the critical insight that society is not static.

Whatever themes emerge as the content of a liberatory curriculum, Freire's theory insists we pay equal attention to the methods by which people and teachers co-investigate these ideas. Although his methodology was developed for peasants in various Third World countries, his focus on problem posing in contrast to problem solving— together with his commitment to dialogical rather than "banking" education—is also important for teachers in the United States.[5]

When Freire's teams discussed the generative themes with the people, they posed as problems what they had learned from their investigation. These problems did not have the clear-cut answers typical of textbook exercises, but were intended to challenge students and teachers to respond through dialogue and collective action. Traditional problem-solving curricula isolate and simplify particular aspects of reality in order to give students practice in certain techniques. Freirean problem posing is intended to reveal the interconnections and complexities of real-life situations where "often, problems are not solved, only a better understanding of their nature may be possible" (Connolly, 1981, p. 73).

In addition, Freirean problem posing is intended to involve the students in dialogue and co-investigation with the teachers. Freire insists that people cannot learn through "banking"—expert teachers depositing knowledge in the presumably blank minds of their students, who memorize the required rules in order to get future dividends. He stresses that this dialogue does not involve teachers' pretending ignorance. Since no one is omniscient and people each have different experiences related to the themes under investigation, teachers and students can truly learn from each other. Especially since the "Literacy Crisis" is being replaced in the mass media by the "Critical Thinking Crisis" in American education (Daniels, 1983, p. 5) we need to stress Freire's point that, "Our task is not to teach students to think—they can already think; but, to exchange our ways of thinking with each other and look together for better ways of approaching the decodification of an object" (1982). However, Freire is equally insistent that his concept of dialogical education does not mean teachers are merely "passive, accidental presences" (1982). They listen to students to discover themes which teachers then organize and present as problems challenging students' previous perceptions. Teachers also suggest themes they judge as important. Teachers can be strong influences without being "superiors" who totally control the learning environment.

> The opposite of manipulation is not an illusory neutrality, neither is it an illusory spontaneity. The opposite of being directive is not being non-directive—that is likewise an illusion. The opposite both of manipulation and spontaneity is critical and democratic participation by the learners in the act of knowing, of which they are the subjects (Freire, 1981, p. 28)

The aspects of Freire's theory that I have discussed above speak to teachers searching for ways to unite their classroom practice with struggles for social change. In order to develop a "pedagogy of the oppressed," Freire contends that we need to explore the nonpositivist nature of the knowledge we are teaching, and the ways in which producing such knowledge deepens commitment and involves action to transform the world. The next section of this paper relates my experiences using Freire's theory to teach mathematics. The specific details are presented to provide a case study of how Freire's theory can inform critical teaching. They also support the belief that critical knowledge of statistics is vital to transforming our massified technological society.

Freire's Theory for Mathematics Teachers

All people reflect on their practice to some degree; mental and manual labor can never be completely divided. Even mathematics teachers who have never heard of Polya (1957, 1981) or Freire will think about problems such as how to explain the "sampling distribution of the mean" so that students do not confuse it with a distribution of scores within one sample. However, studying theory deepens the nature of these reflections; in particular, I believe that a theoretical framework changes the depth and types of questions one considers when thinking about one's practice. Freire's theory compels mathematics teachers to probe the nonpositivist meaning of mathematical knowledge, the importance of quantitative reasoning in the development of critical consciousness, the ways in which math anxiety helps sustain hegemonic ideologies, and the connections between our specific curriculum and the development of critical consciousness. In addition, his theory can strengthen our energy in the struggle for humanization by focusing our attention on the interrelationships between our concrete daily teaching practice and the broader ideological and structural context.

Freire's Epistemology and the Meaning of Basic Mathematics and Statistics Knowledge[6]

The mass media, most academic social scientists, and "common sense" assume that mathematical knowledge consists of neutral facts discovered, not created, by people through their interactions with the world. Cynics claim statistics are all self-serving lies. A Freirean analysis, different from both of these approaches, directs our reflections to the relationship between subjectivity and objectivity in producing mathematical knowledge.

A course such as "Statistics for the Social Sciences" affords many opportunities for examining how subjective choice is involved in describing and collecting data, and in making inferences about the world. For example, Max (1981) and Greenwood (1981) show how the government makes military spending appear smaller by including funds held "in trust," such as Social Security, in the portion of the federal budget going for social services; and, counting war-related expenditures such as the production of new nuclear warheads, the space program, and veteran's programs, as part of various nonmilitary categories like the Department of Energy budget (the warheads!) and Direct Benefit Payments (veterans' income). The government calculates that 25% of the budget goes for "National Defense"; Max's and Greenwood's calculation give a figure of 57% of the budget going to pay for "Past, Present and Future Wars." Atkins and Jarrett (1979) show how significance tests, one of the most commonly used techniques in inferential statistics, can be used to "provide *definite* and *apparently objective* decisions, in a basically *superficial* way" (p. 103). One reason this occurs is because a 'favorable' numerical result in a significance test gives no assurance that the measurements used in the study are *meaningful*. In 1925, for example, Karl Pearson, an important figure in the development of modern statistical theory, found "statistically significant" differences in Jewish children's physical characteristics and intelligence—leading him to conclude they should not be allowed to immigrate into Great Britain (pp. 101-102). But, what *substantive* significance does this have when these characteristics are so clearly environmental? Also, the nature of probability *requires* statistical inference to be uncertain—a research hypothesis tested "significant at the .05 level" gives the impression of certainty, whereas it means there is a 5% chance that the hypothesis is false. Events with low probabilities sometimes do occur; significance tests only allow researchers to be reasonably (say, 95%) certain that the event described by their hypothesis is *not due to chance*. Moreover, the tests cannot determine which of many possible theories explains the event. For example, R.A. Fischer, author of a widely used modern statistics text, uses results from a chi-square test, showing a statistically significant greater frequency of criminality among monozygotic than among dizygotic twins of criminals, to conclude that this happens because of genetic factors. He ignores any other possible explanation, such as people's treatment and expectations of identical versus similar-looking twins (Schwartz, 1977, p. 28).

Freire's concept of critical knowledge further directs us to explore not merely how statistics are non-neutral, but why, and in whose interest. It is certainly not accidental that official statistics are much more useful to conservatives than to radicals. Nor is it accidental that, in spite of the technical weaknesses of significance tests, many standard social science computer packages lack convenient procedures for estimation, an alternative to significance tests that can be evaluated by statistical and *other* criteria and can facilitate comparison among investigations.

On the other hand, the thousands of government workers and university social scientists who produce this statistical knowledge are not *forced* to use methods whose outcome will uniformly support the ruling classes. An examination of the history of statistics can help explain how statistical knowledge "naturally" arises from the conditions of our society in such a way that its production is controlled by the ruling classes. Shaw and Miles (1979) trace its development to the expansion of commerce and the changing needs of the state. In 16th-century London, the crowded conditions of towns, which arose from the growth of markets, created the climate for widespread epidemics which led to the first collecting of mortality statistics. As these statistics were refined, they became more useful to the ruling classes. For example, William and Mary's government paid for loans to conduct the war against France with life annuities whose value was calculated using statistics on life expectancies of people in various age groups. In the 19th century, the rise of industrial capitalism led to the state's assuming a large role in providing conditions under which private industry could thrive, including the expansion and centralization of statistical knowledge. One consequence of this was that in 1832, the Statistical Department of the Board of Trade was charged with gathering and organizing material concerning British "wealth, commerce and industry."

Giroux's (1981) category of mediation extends this historical analysis by calling our attention to the combination of structural and individual factors which inform the production of this knowledge. One factor involves organizational "efficiency," which results in certain statistics being produced as by-products of administrative systems existing mainly for other purposes. For example, in England unemployment statistics are based on records kept by employment exchanges, so the workers who fail to register are omitted from the official reports (Hyman and Price, 1979). Another factor involves pressures on social scientists from journals that only accept articles which report statistically significant results, and from universities which grant tenure only to widely published professors. This "naturally" results in an underreporting of results that are *not* statistically-significant. Thus, one researcher by *chance* may produce and publish a statistically significant finding, while many others researching the same problem find no statistical significance, but since their work is not published, no conflicts among results can be detected (Atkins & Jarrett, 1979). Next, Giroux's category of appropriation focuses attention on how, in spite of the many factors resulting in what he calls a "selective affinity" for people to produce statistical knowledge to support the interests of the ruling classes, people can still learn from statistics. This is possible because statistical knowledge can be analyzed critically by examining its underlying interests and methods of collection, description, and inference, and by considering historical, philosophical, and other theoretical insights along with the statistical knowledge. Finally, Giroux's category of transcendence insists that we not only criticize existing statistics, but that we also explore what new knowledge might be produced consistent with humanization. Along this line, Griffiths, Irvine, and Miles (1979) suggest that new statistical techniques for collecting data can be developed. For instance, interactive surveys could, instead of treating the respondents as isolated, passive objects, make them participants in analyzing how they can use the information gathered to improve their lives. Further, Shaw and Miles (1979) hypothesize that in a liberatory society:

> we would replace accountancy in terms of money and profit by accountancy in terms of social needs. We would replace the definition of social goals by those at the tops of the bureaucratic pyramids, by democratic self-control over all collective activities. We would then require new ways of measuring our needs and goals, which expressed their great variety rather than reduced them to money values or standards imposed from above. (p. 36)

Mathematics Education and Liberatory Social Change

Applying Freire's theory to mathematics education directs our attention to how most current uses of mathematics support hegemonic ideologies, how mathematics education also reinforces hegemonic ideologies, and how critical mathematics education can develop critical understanding and lead to critical action.

A significant factor in the acceptance of this society's hegemonic ideologies is that people do not probe the mathematical mystifications that in advanced industrial society function as vital supports of these ideologies. A mathematically illiterate populace can be convinced, for example, that social welfare programs are responsible for their declining standard of living, because they will not research the numbers to uncover that "welfare" to the rich dwarfs any meager subsidies given to the poor. For example, in 1975 the maximum payment to an Aid for Dependent Children family of four was $5,000 and the average tax loophole for each of the richest 160,000 taxpayers was $45,000 (Babson & Brigham, 1978, p. 37). Also in 1980, $510 million of our tax money paid for new airports so that private pilots would not land their planes at large commercial airports (Judis &

Moberg, 1981, p. 22). Further, people's misconception that statistical knowledge is objective and value-free closes off challenges to such data. As Marcuse (1964) argues:

> in this society, the rational rather than the irrational becomes the most effective vehicle of mystification. . . . For example, the scientific approach to the vexing problem of mutual annihilation —the mathematics and calculations of kill and over-kill, the measurement of spreading or not-quite-so-spreading fallout. . . —is mystifying to the extent to which it promotes (and even demands) behavior which accepts the insanity. It thus counteracts a truly rational behavior—namely, the refusal to go along, and the effort to do away with the conditions which produce the insanity. (pp. 189-190)

Traditional mathematics education supports the hegemonic ideologies of society, especially through what Giroux calls "structured silences." Even trivial math applications like totaling grocery bills carry the ideological message that paying for food is natural and that society can only be organized in such a way that people buy food from grocery stores. Also it is rare that students are asked to evaluate their own understanding of math. My students are convinced that they are cheating if they check their own work using an answer key or with other people, and they have no experience analyzing which specific topics are giving them difficulty. In the past, when they could not do an assignment, they just expressed general confusion and gave control of their learning to the teacher to "diagnose" what they needed to review. This reinforces the hegemonic ideology of "expertise"—that some people have (i.e., own) a great deal of knowledge which can only be obtained from them and which they will impart *only* if you "follow the rules."

One of the obstacles that critical mathematics education must overcome in the United States is people's math "anxiety." Since, as Freire, stresses people who are not aware of the raison d' être of their situation, fatalistically "accept" their exploitation, teachers and students must consider the causes behind math "anxiety" as part of developing critical mathematics education. The immediate pedagogical causes of the situation—such as meaningless rote drill, taught so that it requires extensive memorization, and unmotivated applications which are unrelated to the math one actually uses in everyday life—create a situation where people "naturally" avoid mathematics (Hilton, 1980). Discussions with students helped me to re-conceptualize these pedagogical causes in terms of misconceptions about learning. One misconception concerns the group process in learning. Students often feel they must be able to solve a problem on their own before they can contribute to the group. They do not realize that collectively a group can solve problems that individual members working alone could not solve. Another misconception is the idea that 'a wrong answer is totally wrong, nothing can be learned from analyzing it' (Frankenstein, 1983).

Understanding the deeper causes of math "anxiety" involves an examination of how the structures and hegemonic ideologies of our society result in different groups being more affected than others by this "anxiety." It also involves recognition that, to some extent, people participate in their own mathematical disempowerment. Considerable research (summarized in Beckwith, 1983) has documented that:

> sex differences in mathematical training and attitudes. . .are *not* the result of free and informed choice. . . .They are the result of many subtle (and not so subtle) forces, restrictions, stereotypes, sex roles, parental-teacher-peer group attitudes, and other cultural and psychological constraints. (Ernest, et al., 1976, p. 611)

Further research needs to be done. In particular we need to investigate how differential treatment based on race and class interacts with mathematics "anxiety" and avoidance. We also need to explore why the research on math anxiety has focused only on the relationship between sex and mathematics learning.

In addition to the effects of sexism, racism, and classism, the hegemonic ideology of "aptitudes"—the belief, in relationship to mathematics, that only some people have a "mathematical mind"— needs to be analyzed. Women's belief that men have more "mathematical aptitude" has been explored. Tobias (1978) discusses research investigating the hidden messages in math textbook content and images; Beckwith (1983) summarizes studies of media influence on children's perceptions of boys' allegedly superior math abilities. However, Apple's (1979) discussion of labeling suggests that more research needs to be done on the contradictory effects of the term "math anxiety." Students are initially relieved that their feelings about mathematics are so common that educators "have a name for them." But in fact this label focuses the problem, and therefore the solutions, on individual failure rather than on the broader societal context which plays such a significant role in producing personal "math anxiety." Bisseret (1979) demonstrates how language functions ideologically to support the belief that "a difference in essence among human beings...predetermines the diversity of psychic and mental phenomena" (p. 2). Her analysis illuminates the role which this ideology of aptitudes plays in people's beliefs that the given structure of society is "natural" and "inevitable," and suggests further research to be done in uncovering the complex factors behind the ideology of a "mathematical mind." Bisseret argues that this ideology results in class-specific language; we need to consider how this language encourages dominated groups to believe and act as if they have "nonmathematical minds."

Critical mathematics education can challenge students to question these hegemonic ideologies by using statistics to reveal the contradictions (and lies) underneath the surface of these ideologies by providing learning experiences where students and teachers are "co-investigators" and where math "anxious" students overcome their fears. Further, critical mathematics education can link this questioning with action, both by illustrating how organized groups of people are using statistics in their struggles for social change and by providing information on such local groups as students may wish to join. Above all, critical mathematics education must take seriously Marcuse's (1964) injunction that:

> the trouble is that the statistics, measurements, and field studies of empirical sociology and political science are not rational enough. They become mystifying to the extent to which they are isolated from the truly concrete context which makes the facts and determines their function. This context is larger and other than that of the plants and shops investigated, of the towns and cities studied, of the areas and groups whose public opinion is polled or whose chance of survival is calculated.... This real context in which the particular subjects obtain their real significance is definable only within a *theory* of society. (p. 190)

Content and Methods in Critical Mathematics Education

In order to apply Freire's theory to critical mathematics education we need to consider what mathematics knowledge is implied by, and would clarify, our students' "generative themes." In most school settings, teachers cannot get to know their students as well as Freire's teams got to know the communities in which they taught. However, teachers can ask students about the issues that concern them at work, about the nonwork activities that interest them, about topics they would like to know in more depth, and so forth. These discussions can indicate the starting point for the curriculum. Then the teacher's contribution can be to link up the students' issues with an investigation of the related hegemonic ideologies. Any topic can be so connected; for example, art can lead to an exploration of such areas as the ideology of "high status" knowledge, the ideology of "taste," and the commodification of culture.[7]

In addition, almost all of the basic math and statistics skills and concepts, as well as the critical nature of statistical knowledge, can be learned in the context of working on applications which challenge the contradictions involved in supporting hegemonic ideologies.[8] For example, Max and Greenwood's critique of the official statistics on the military portion of the federal budget can be used to learn percents and circle graphs. In addition, students can discuss how they would decide to present the critique, and what aspects of this research and presentation they control. Would they choose to present their critique using raw data, percents, or graphs? Do they agree with Max that the space program should be considered part of the cost of "Past, Present and Future Wars"? Discussing how to present the statistics to demonstrate that the United States is a welfare state for the rich can include practice of arithmetical operations; students need to divide in order to describe the tax loophole data as "each of the richest 160,000 taxpayers got nine times as much money as the maximum AFDC grant for a family of four." This same data helps students learn about the meaning of large numbers; they can consider the services that the total taxes not paid by these rich 160,000 ($7,200,000,000 = $7.2 billion) could have provided if this money were included in the federal budget. For a final example, Gray (1983) presents positive uses of statistical techniques (such as chi-square and regression analysis) in legal cases. In one situation, such techniques were used to show that in jury selection "a hypothesis of random selection, that is, of no discrimination, is so improbable as to make it likely that some other process must have been at work" (p. 72).

Not only can math skills and concepts be learned in the classroom from applications which challenge the hegemonic ideologies, but interested students can also work with the many groups uniting reflection about statistics with action for social change. The Coalition for Basic Human Needs, in Boston, uses statistics (for example, those showing that actual shelter costs in every major Massachusetts city exceed the AFDC welfare grant) to fight for decent conditions for (poor) welfare recipients. The International Association of Machinists had a statistician prepare a report on "The Impact of Military Spending on the Machinists Union" (Anderson, 1979), which documents that "as the military budget goes up, and procurement contracts rise, Machinists' jobs in military industry steadily decline" (p. 1). Counter-Information Services (CIS), a London-based group of journalists, trade unionists, and statisticians, reconceptualizes information in official corporate reports, at the request of workers at the companies involved. CIS issues "Anti-Reports" which present a critical analysis of the company's statistics. CIS's Anti-Report on Ford (1978), for example, used that company's data to show that Ford had been exaggerating the profitability of its West German operation and understating that of its British plants. Since the United Kingdom workers were more militant in their demands than the German workers, Ford used its doctored statistics to threaten the UK workers with their alleged poor performance. For another example, CIS's Anti-Report on Rio Tinto Zinc (RTZ) Corporation (1972), used RTZ's data that 42% of its profits were made in South Africa, whereas only 7.7% of its assets were located there, along with additional information CIS researched, to support its charge that these high profits came directly from the low wages paid to RTZ's black miners.

As these math examples challenge students to reconsider their previously "taken-for-granted" beliefs, they also deepen and increase the range of questions they ask about the world. Once the idea of comparing the results of military vs. civilian spending on jobs is introduced, one can then ask that same question of other government spending. For example, are more jobs created through spending on energy conservation or nuclear power? Further, by learning and re-creating a theory of math education and social change with their teachers, students can develop their ability to critique ideology in general.

Freire's methodology shares much in common with humanistic ideas on student-centered teaching but his ideas go beyond those methods in terms of their *intent*. They are not merely the techniques that any dedicated teacher who respected his or her students might use. Instead, they are intended to be part of the process of developing new social relations in the struggle for humanization. Freire's methodology directs math teachers' attention to how students with large gaps in their mathematical background can in practice co-investigate the statistical aspects of their "generative themes." It also directs teachers to consider how students can become independent at decoding the problems coded in the barrage of quantitative data encountered in their lives.

By exploring the statistical aspects of students' themes in such a way that the mathematics involved starts at a very basic level, and by having students pose problems about the data even if they cannot yet solve those problems, teachers and students are *truly* co-researchers. Since math teachers will probably not have previously investigated many of the suggested themes, students are likely to ask questions that teachers will not be able to answer and which students and teachers will have to research together. For example, the following chart can be used to start a dialogue with students who have previously suggested the theme of racism:

TABLE 1

Median Income of Black and White Families 1969–1977

	1969	1972	1974	1975	1976	1977
Black	$5,999	6,864	8,006	8,779	9,242	9,563
White	9,794	11,549	13,408	14,268	15,537	16,740

Source: Census Bureau, Current Population Reports, P-60 Series

Students can initially be asked to describe what the main point of the chart is—an exercise in which they can practice such skills as comparing numbers, subtraction, or finding what percent one number is of another number. As the investigation deepens, students and teachers are equals in problematizing what other statistics would clarify the theme of racism (e.g., comparisons by race of maternal mortality rates; comparisons by race of unemployment statistics; comparisons of latinos with blacks and whites). The importance of statistics in revealing institutional patterns, in contrast with personal instances of racism, is also brought out by this research. Further depth is added to the investigation by students and teachers jointly finding and considering various social science studies which use more advanced statistical techniques to clarify the theme. Reich (1978), for example, uses correlation coefficients between various statistical measures of racism and white incomes to show that racism results in lower wages for white, as well as black, workers and higher profits for the capitalist class. Finally, any thematic investigation must include more than just statistical data. As Reich comments, in this case:

the simple economics of racism does not explain why many workers seem to be so vehemently racist, when racism is not in their economic self-interest. In noneconomic ways, racism helps to legitimize inequality, alienation, and powerlessness—legitimization that is necessary for the stability for the capitalist system as a whole. . . .Through racism, poor whites come to believe that their poverty is caused by blacks who are willing to take away their jobs, and at lower wages, thus concealing the fact that a substantial amount of income inequality is inevitable in a capitalist society. (p. 387)

The above example also illustrates how a dialogical analysis involving the interpretation of statistical data helps students practice the slow, careful thinking necessary to produce any critical knowledge. This practice, combined with opportunities to reflect on the learning process, helps students to become independent learners. Many such opportunities come from involving students in evaluation. For example, as students work on review problems they can answer keys which pose questions about potential errors. Thereby, students are encouraged to pinpoint their own misunderstandings and determine how well they understood each problem. They can be asked to choose between "wrong answer because confused about _____"; "correct answer but unsure of method"; and "understand well enough to teach others." Students can also learn a lot about posing problems by evaluating the clarity, the difficulty, and the interest, of other students' and teachers' problems. Finally, having students keep a math journal is another method of having them reflect about their learning process. Journals can be vents for students' feelings about math and can act as a concrete record of progress for students who too often belittle their successes and focus on what they cannot do. The journal helps students realize that they can now accomplish what one month ago they thought was impossible. It helps them clarify which learning techniques worked best and why, and can give them personal feedback from the teacher and/or other students offering encouragement and alternative perspectives. The journal is also another way for students to be involved with the teacher in planning the curriculum, as their comments about their learning and their reactions to the class are considered in future lessons. Following is an example from one of my students' journals:

Class #6: I know that I ended my last entry into this journal as saying that: "I am ready to tackle the next class," but I wasn't. I was very tired and became bored at the very start of class. I have to learn to control my feelings of being critical of other

people's problems in Algebra. I found myself thinking of the
questions that some of the others asked as being elementary.
I just assumed that if I understand, everyone should. Some of
the problems I did have a little difficulty doing them, but I did
not mention it in class because I felt that I would sound stupid
or should I say unable to comprehend what was being said.
Finally I began to fight the feelings that I had about other
people's problems and started being more attentive of what was
being asked. I began to understand more and more and at one
point, the questions that I wanted to ask were answered so, it
wasn't so stupid after all.

My comments in the margin noted that it is hard to be patient with
others' problems, but that after all, you want others to be patient with
your problems. I suggested that it might be more interesting for her
if she tried to answer the other students' problems, helping them to
see exactly what was confusing to them. I also challenged her use
of the label "stupid," and praised her insight into the learning process.
I ended by asking if she would read this entry to the entire class as
a way of introducing a discussion on what we can learn from collective
work. This journal entry taught me about the importance of such
discussions in helping everyone understand how much can be learned
whenever anyone poses a problem.

Conclusion

The context in which we are working in the United States is
quite different from the culture-circle context in and for which Freire
developed his theory. In this article, I have attempted to convince
people working in U.S. schools that Freire's theory contains many
insights which we can use to inform our practice. Here I want to pose
some problems arising from practice in our context that suggest areas
of Freire's theory we need to develop further. These include the roles
and responsibilities of students, the pressures on teachers, the
complexities of moving students from massified to critical consciousness, and the tenuousness of the link between an emerging critical
consciousness and radical social change.
    Freire focuses on the responsibilities of teachers to challenge stu-
dents' taken-for-granted beliefs, while simultaneously insuring that
students become their "co-investigators" in this process. What responsibilities, then, do students have? How do we deal with the daily
concrete reality of adult students whose work and family commit-

ments make it difficult for them to do their "homework" or even attend class? How do we work within the enormous tensions created in our society between students' desire for individual "advancement" and our radical vision of collective progress?

Teachers of course, are also affected by the pressures of daily life and the structures of our workplace. Freedman, Jackson, and Boles (1983) have shown how the conditions that elementary school teachers encounter in their day-to-day school situation—conditions such as the overwhelming emphasis on quantification (both in scoring children and in keeping records), the growing lack of control over curriculum (separating conception from execution), the isolation from their peers, the condescending treatment by administrators, and the massive layoffs of veteran teachers—"naturally" produce the frustration and anger that the mass media labels as "burn-out." In what struggles must we engage in order to change these conditions and sustain our energy to teach?

It is often tempting to abandon dialogical education, because of these pressures on students and teachers, because students have internalized misconceptions about learning and about their intellectual abilities from their previous schooling, and because we can get such quick positive feedback and (superficial) positive results by "banking" humanistically. But students' desire for "banking" education in an academic setting does not mean that they are not independent learners in many other situations. Freire discusses how in the transition from semi-intransitive consciousness, myths from the former stage remain even as the consciousness becomes more critical and open to new ideas (1970b). In addition to this overlapping of levels of consciousness, my practice calls attention to the nonlinear character of the levels of consciousness, and poses the problem of how to make a bridge from the critical insights my students have in some areas to their developing an overall critical approach to knowledge. My students' journals show how difficult it is for them to maintain a totalizing movement; entries show frequent "ups" and "downs" in self-image, and move between critical insight and myth. It seems clear that if the dialogical classroom experience is isolated and students are treated as objects in most other situations, then only fragments of critical consciousness can develop.

Further, these fragments are often theoretical, unconnected with practice. In both my experience and that of others (Rothenberg, 1983), the critical use of quantitative data can crack open hegemonic ideologies and students do become angry and intellectually committed to social change. But that does not necessarily mean they then join organizations working against oppression. Some even take jobs in business after getting their degree. Critical individual change does occur—when students overcome their math anxiety and learn math, they have a concrete, deep experience that *"things can change."* They also develop the ability to critique and they increase their questioning of the conditions in which they live. It may be that the most critical collective change that a pedagogy of the oppressed can bring about in our circumstances is a subtle shift in climate which will aid the progress of liberatory social change.

Understanding the limits of our situation can increase our energy to focus on the radical possibilities of education as a force to promote emancipatory change. Using Paulo Freire's ideas as the theoretical foundation for our classroom practice situates that individual practice within the larger ideological and political struggle for humanization. We become more deeply committed as we realize how our actions are connected to this collective struggle. Using the term "militants" for people committed to justice and liberation (1978, p. 73), Freire argues that:

> militancy forces us to be more disciplined and to try harder to understand the reality that we, together with other militants, are trying to transform and re-create. We stand together alert against threats of all kinds. (1978, p. 146)

Notes

1. The students at my school are adults who have a clear commitment to work in public or community service. Their average age is 35, about 70% are women, and about 30% are people of color.

2. Matthews (1981) traces Freire's emphasis on the social nature of thought to Karl Mannheim's philosophy that strictly speaking it is incorrect to say that individuals think; it is more correct to insist that they participate in thinking further what others have previously thought.

3. One of Freire's first comments at the Boston College course he taught (July 1982) concerned his debt to the many American women who wrote to him praising *Pedagogy of the Oppressed* but criticizing his sexist language. He has changed his language; I therefore, change his quotes in this respect.

4. Freire's writing on the details of how critical consciousness leads to radical social change (e.g., "This pedagogy makes oppression and its causes objects of reflection by the oppressed, and from that reflection will come their

necessary engagement in the struggle for their liberation" (1970a, p. 33))
leaves him open to Mackie's critique that by ignoring "the political economy
of revolution in favour of an emphasis on its cultural dimension. . .[Freire's]
talk of revolution. . .tends to become utopian and idealized" (Mackie, 1981,
p. 106). However, Freire's comments at his 1982 Boston College course (e.g.,
"in meetings like this we cannot change the world, but we can discover and
we may become committed") convince me that he recognizes the limitations
as well as the possibilities of education in bringing about liberatory social
change. His writing, possibly, concentrates on the role of human consciousness
in changing the world as a counter to overly determined structuralist theories
of revolution.

5. For a discussion of the specific conditions in Brazil under which Freire
developed his theory and practice, see "Imperialism, Underdevelopment and
Education" by Barnard (1981). For a detailed presentation of Freire's
methodology, see Freire, 1973, pp. 41–84.

6. Although this paper focuses on basic mathematics and statistics,
Freire's theory can also illuminate other areas of mathematics knowledge.
Some of these connections are suggested by the ideas about the nature of
abstract mathematical knowledge in Gordon (1978) and Kline (1980). In his
introduction, Kline quotes Hermann Weyl, one of the most prominent
mathematicians of the 20th century, " 'Mathematizing' may well be a creative
activity of man, like language or music, of primary originality, whose
historical decisions defy complete objective rationalization" (p. 6).

7. Any topic can be connected to mathematics also: there are always
statistics about that topic. In this case, there are even a number of
contemporary artists whose work is based on specific mathematical structures
(Frankenstein, 1982).

8. For more basic mathematics examples, see my article which focuses
on content and methods (Frankenstein, 1981). For more statistics examples,
see Horwitz and Ferleger, 1980.

References

Anderson, M. (1979). *The impact of military spending on the machinists union.*
    Lansing, Michigan: Employment Research Associates (400 South
    Washington Ave., Lansing, MI 48933).

Apple, M.W. (1979). *Ideology and curriculum.* Boston: Routledge & Kegan Paul.

Atkins, L. and Jarrett, D. (1979). The significance of "significance tests." in
    J. Irvine, I. Miles, & J. Evans (Eds.), *Demystifying social statistics.* London:
    Pluto Press.

Babson, S., & Brigham, N. (1978). *What's happening to our jobs?* Somerville, Massachusetts: Popular Economics Press.

Barnard, C. (1981). Imperialism, underdevelopment, and education. In R. Mackie (Ed.), *Literacy & revolution: The pedagogy of Paulo Freire.* New York: Continuum.

Beckwith, J. (1983). Gender and math performance: Does biology have implications for educational policy? *Journal of Education, 165,* 158–174.

Bisseret, N. (1979). *Education, class language and ideology.* Boston: Routledge & Kegan Paul.

Bredo, E., & Feinberg, W. (Eds.) (1982). *Knowledge and values in social and educational research.* Philadelphia: Temple University Press.

Brown, C. (1978). *Literacy in 30 hours: Paulo Freire's process in Northeast Brazil* (Alternative Schools Network, 1105 W. Lawrence, Rm. 210, Chicago, Ill. 60640).

Collins, D. (1977). *Paulo Freire: His life, works and thought.* New York: Paulist Press.

Connolly, R. (1981). Freire, praxis and education. In R. Mackie (Ed.) *Literacy and revolution: The pedagogy of Paulo Freire.* New York: Continuum.

Daniels, H. (1983). Notes from the interim: The world since CLAC. *Conference on Language Attitudes and Composition, 8,* 2–7. (Illinois Writing Project, P.O. Box 825, Elmhurst, Ill. 60126)

Ernest, J. et al. (1976). Mathematics and sex. *American Mathematical Monthly, 83,* 595–614.

Ford anti-report. (1978). London: Counter Information Services (9 Poland Street, London W 1).

Frankenstein, M. (1981). A different third r: Radical math. *Radical Teacher,* No. 20, 14–18.

Frankenstein, M. (1982). *Mathematics patterns and concepts that can generate art.* Unpublished book proposal.

Frankenstein, M. (1983). *Overcoming math anxiety by learning about learning.* Unpublished manuscript, University of Massachusetts.

Freedman, S., Jackson, J., & Boles, K. (1983). The other end of the corridor: The effect of teaching on teachers. *Radical Teacher,* No. 23, 2–23.

Freire, P. (1970a). *Pedagogy of the oppressed.* New York: Seabury Press.

Freire, P. (1970b). *Cultural action for freedom.* Cambridge: Harvard Educational Review.

Freire, P. (1973). *Education for critical consciousness.* New York: Seabury Press.

Freire, P. (1978). *Pedagogy in process.* New York: Seabury Press.

Freire, P. (1981). The people speak their word: Learning to read and write in Sao Tome and Principe. *Harvard Educational Review, 51,* 27–30.

Freire, P. (1982). Education for critical consciousness. Unpublished Boston College course notes, taken by M. Frankenstein, July 5–15.

Freire P. (1983). The importance of the act of reading. *Journal of Education, 165,* 5–11.

Giroux, H. (1981). *Ideology, culture and the process of schooling.* Philadelphia: Temple University Press.

Gordon, M. (1978). Conflict and liberation: Personal aspects of the mathematics experience. *Curriculum Inquiry, 8,* 251–271.

Gray, M. W. (1983). Statistics and the law. *Mathematics Magazine, 56,* 67–81.

Greenwood, D. (1981). It's even worse. *In These Times,* June 17–30.

Griffiths, D., Irvine, J., & Miles, I. (1979). Social statistics: Towards a radical science. In J. Irvine, I. Miles, & J. Evans (Eds.), *Demystifying social statistics.* London: Pluto Press.

Hilton, P. (1980). Math anxiety: Some suggested causes and cures: Part 1. *Two-Year College Mathematics Journal, 11,* 174–188.

Horwitz, L., & Ferleger, L. (1980). *Statistics for social change.* Boston: South End Press.

Hyman, R., & Price, B. (1979). Labour statistics. In J. Irvine, I. Miles, & J. Evans (Eds.), *Demystifying social sciences.* London: Pluto Press.

Judis, J., & Moberg, D. (1981). Some other ways to cut the budget. *In These Times,* (March 4–10).

Kellner, D. (1978). Ideology, marxism, and advanced capitalism. *Socialist Review,* No. 42, 37–65.

Kline, M. (1980). Mathematics: The loss of certainty. New York: Oxford University Press.

Mackie, R. (1981). Contributions to the thought of Paulo Freire in R. Mackie (Ed.) *Literacy and revolution: The pedagogy of Paulo Freire.* New York: Continuum.

Marcuse, H. (1964). *One-dimensional man.* Boston: Beacon Press.

Matthews, M. (1981). Knowledge, action and power. In R. Mackie (Ed.), *Literacy & revolution: The pedagogy of Paulo Freire.* New York: Continuum.

Max, S. (1981). How to make billions for arms look smaller. *In These Times,* (May 27-June 3).

Polya, G. (1957). *How to solve it.* New York: Doubleday.

Polya, G. (1981). *Mathematical discovery: On understanding, learning, and teaching problem solving.* New York: John Wiley & Sons.

Reich, M. (1972). The economics of racism. In R. C. Edwards, M. Reich and T. F. Weisskopf (Eds.), *The capitalist system.* Englewood Cliffs, New Jersey: Prentice-Hall, Inc.

Rio Tinto zinc anti-report. (1972). London: Counter Information Services.

Rothenberg, P., et al. (1983). Teaching "racism and sexism in a changing society": A report. Unpublished manuscript.

Schwartz, A. J. (1977). The politics of statistics: Heredity and IQ. In Ann Arbor Science for the People, *Biology as a social weapon.* Minneapolis: Burgess Publishing Company.

Shaw, M., & Miles, I. (1979). The social roots of statistical knowledge. In J. Irvine, I. Miles, & J. Evans (Eds.), *Demystifying social statistics.* London: Pluto Press.

Tobias, S. (1978). *Overcoming math anxiety.* Boston: Houghton Mifflin Company.

Writing Pedagogy: A Dialogue of Hope

Anne-Louise Brookes and Ursula A. Kelly

October 2, 1988

Dear Anne-Louise,

I begin this letter in that hazy state which is fatigue mixed with longing and hope. I am tired, yes. And it is a tiredness which, tonight, I can name as coming from a struggle, embodied for weeks now, of how to teach using what Paulo Freire and Ira Shor (1987) call the dialogical method of critical and reflective teaching—what Roger Simon (1987) calls critical pedagogy. My longing is part nostalgia. I recall during our one year teaching together at Memorial University, how we supported and nurtured each other through various stages of growth and change in our teaching. My hope in reaching out to you in this letter is that we might begin to construct a different space for that dialogue. During our graduate studies together, we often talked of creating a collective piece on pedagogical practices. I now recover that dream to begin envisioning and sharing with you.

Being involved in teacher education is, more often than not, an incredibly exhilarating experience for me. It's truly exciting (for both them and me) that these students get a chance at the beginning of their BEd program to observe and critique teachers in action. It's invaluable data for their work and for mine. Such "situated research" (Shor & Freire, 1987) is fundamental to their evolving understandings of their work as teachers who, hopefully, are committed to social change. I enjoy the tiny moments of political import where I see a student begin to get beneath the "taken-for-granteds" of schooling and thrill at the insight gained through analysis. At the same time I can see them struggle to articulate a practice of difference and egalitarianism, of empowerment and critique. These are young women and men who will, some of them, work with upward of 150 or more students in the run of a school day. Their struggles are my struggles, just as mine are theirs, to some extent. Let me give you an example.

Yesterday, a young woman in my class stopped me in the library to tell me of an article she had found by Peter McLaren. This same woman, who has an MA in English, is also in my English Studies class—another in her repertoire was by John Willinsky—so she gets a double dose of such ideas and practices. Her eyes shone as she pointed out these writings to me. Suddenly, though, the shine dimmed somewhat. "You know, I've been thinking this week about what I see when I'm out in the schools observing teachers working with students. It occurred to me that the way I want to do things clashes with just about everything everyone is doing out there. It's really discouraging." We talked, then, about the notion of a politics of hope and the need to create, nurture, and sustain a solid community of politically like-minded workers.

Throughout these beginning classes, I have struggled to break down some of the firmly entrenched attitudes and presuppositions about teacher education. Of course, the fact that I don't lecture was cause for suspicion at first. We spent the first class sharing stories of positive and negative moments in our student lives. The discussion followed on the themes of disempowerment, anger, silencing, and then, on mutual respect, solidarity and caring. In retrospect, I realize that this discussion was crucially important groundwork for further dialogue and reflection.

Yet, Anne-Louise, I'm overwhelmed with the task at hand. To confront my needs and the needs of these young women and men in our gendered, classed, and raced practices—to struggle with them to find alternative forms of practice in schools where the ideologically dominant is rarely questioned and to remain hopeful amidst the everyday struggles—demands all my energies. I'm thankful that I'm building a dialogue of trust with so many of my students. But with few around me who share my politics, I'm sometimes lonely in this work. So, I turn to you, dear friend, for solace, for hope, for nurturing in this commitment to teaching which we share.

I just recently read an article by Ira Shor and Paulo Freire (1987), "What is the 'Dialogical Method' of Teaching?," which helps me think through some of these struggles. I have always reaped much from the work of both of these men. Yet I find myself uncomfortable with some of their assumptions and omissions. I'm enclosing a copy of this article. I hope we can critique the work of Shor and Freire in our dialogue of hope, our rewriting of pedagogy. What do you think?

En/vision and Hope,
Ursula . . .

October 24, 1988

Dear Ursula,

How good it was to hear from you. Your invitation to write a collaborative piece on pedagogical practices delights me. I'm excited by the idea of writing letters to each other as a way of talking about our respective pedagogical practices from within a perspective which you so aptly term a *politics of hope.*

In my work as a Sociology of Education teacher I too am sometimes lonely in my attempts to *do,* and theorize about, critical pedagogy. I welcome the opportunity to talk with you about the hopes and frustrations which organize our respective work. I especially like the idea of using Ira Shor's and Paulo Freire's article "What is the 'Dialogical Method' of Teaching?" as a focus for our writing.

The problem of how to *do* critical pedagogy is, too, central to my work as a university teacher. I'm interested in the problem of how to teach students from a perspective located in what Shor and Freire term the dialogical method of *situated* teaching and learning. Motivated by this work, as well as by the work of Magda Lewis and Roger Simon (1986) and others, I nonetheless resist some of the assumptions which organize these works. My aim in this letter is to begin talking with you about some of the assumptions which inform my resistance. Explicit in the Shor-Freire article is the assumption that "talking with students," in very particular ways, is a *better* method of teaching students than is the method of lecturing, or talking at, students. While I agree with this assumption I resist their less explicit assumptions about what it means to dialogue.

Explicitly Shor writes that "Dialogue is a moment where humans meet to reflect on their reality as they make and remake it" (p. 13). Theoretically, I agree with this statement. Practically, I know the difficulties involved in organizing a learning space within which students and teachers can actually begin to learn in transformative ways—ways which will enable all to reconsider that which is so often thought to be obvious, normal, and natural. Given the *vested* and varied versions of reality which students and teachers bring to any learning situation, creative exchanges between students and teachers demand something important of everyone involved. They must bring to the exchange either the understanding of, or the willingness to consider, the view that all knowledge, what it is we "know" about our world, is socially constructed. Students, like myself, oftentimes unknowingly work from assumptions situated in a less than critical or, more specifically, a normalized or naturalized view of reality.

Let me be more explicit. This term I'm teaching a course called "Gender and Society." Ostensibly, it's a seminar course geared to run most effectively with, say, 25 students or so. This term, due to increased enrollments and teacher cutbacks, 50 students were admitted into this class. This makes it difficult for me to work closely with the number of written critiques I expect students to do. It also makes it hard for me to facilitate a climate of trust in which the students can discuss openly how it is they, as women and men, take up differing social practices defined as feminine and masculine.

To encourage lively and emotional discussions about those aspects of our lives so often termed private, I use autobiographical writings and novels which I juxtapose with so-called theoretical essays. This term, I requested that students critique, from their perspective as women and men, the term *misogyny* as it might explain the relationships of the protagonist to various men in William Gough's novel *Maud's House* (1984). In their written critiques, the women in the class tended to accept the term and depict the practices of men in the novel as misogynistic. The men students, however, both verbally and in their written work, responded to the use of this term with considerable hostility. They refused to consider the possibility that the male characters in the novel disliked Maud because she was a woman. Instead, they argued that the men treated Maud badly because she was calling into question the dominant values and assumptions which organized this particular community. From their perspective this did not constitute male hatred of women. One male student suggested that my use of the term misogyny was manipulative. According to him, in introducing the term misogyny as a way of analyzing the social relations which organized Maud's daily life, I was forcing him to accept a woman's view of reality which was quite unacceptable.

Polarized around the problem of whether or not the concept misogyny could be used to describe effectively social practices, some students were silenced. I tried to move the class from this polarization through to a discussion of how it is that gender inequalities are socially constructed, and I tried to examine why the male characters in the novel, unlike the female characters, were not hated when they called into question the dominant rules of this community. But the initial responses created a tension in the class which is not yet fully resolved. Despite attempts to confront these reactions openly and honestly, I'm finding it difficult in this particular class to create an atmosphere conducive to open discussion. In this atmosphere of tension and fear, I find it tempting to "fall back" on a *lecture mode* of teaching, a not-at-all satisfactory solution, as you might imagine.

As a teacher interested in doing critical pedagogy, and as a teacher who works hard, and well, to facilitate class discussions, I am always unsatisfied when a class "does not work." Knowing that this is sometimes the case, and even knowing why, does not satisfy me. Like yourself, I enjoy those moments when students "begin to get beneath the *taken-for-granted* of schooling" and learn from analyses situated in differences. Unhappy with my initial assumption that many of the male students refused to take up the notion of misogyny, I want to consider further my responsibilities in the *silencing* which occurred. I want to find ways to examine the dynamics of this situation. With respect to my ongoing struggle to understand, let me talk further about an insight which I gleaned recently from my rereading of an article by Magda Lewis and Roger Simon (1987).

I respect Lewis's and Simon's efforts in this article and their decision to keep separate their respective female and male voices. In particular, I applaud their attempts to get at the differences which organized their "common" work as student and teacher in a shared classroom context. Equally, I applaud Lewis's attempts to refuse the kind of silencing which she and other women students experienced in the class, and Simon's attempt to understand his own "complicity in the practice of gender domination" (p. 460). In contrast with Shor and Freire, the aim of Lewis and Simon is not to "provide a dialogue but to juxtapose our differences as the ground on which we could formulate a reconstructed practice that would counter patriarchy" (p. 458). I agree with their intent to speak from a place of articulated differences—differences which clearly make it difficult for them as student and teacher, woman and man, to hear and learn from one another. At the same time, I resist their further assumption that the concept *patriarchy* can explain structurally the social relations which make it difficult for them to dialogue as equals.

From my perspective, what is lost through the use of this term is a more concrete examination and description of how relations of power actually work. In other words, I think that in this case a premature use of a theoretical concept, patriarchy, works to mystify, rather than to illuminate, the situation being analyzed.

How different, I then wondered, is the way in which I used the concept *misogyny* from the way in which Lewis and Simon use the concept *patriarchy*? Do we both not create situations in which it becomes difficult to understand the practices which organize the concepts we're trying to explain? Do you think that Shor and Freire use the concept *dialogue* in a similar manner? Is it possible that I actually normalized and naturalized male hatred of women through my premature use of the concept misogyny? In beginning from a concept seemingly set in stone, do I not preclude creating the atmosphere of trust so necessary to the conditions of dialogue? On the other hand, how do I (and the women students) explain our understanding of our collective readings of Maud's experience which we have come to know as male hatred?

Is it possible, Ursula, to make and remake reality in a society so definitively organized to empower and to reproduce a masculine perspective (a perspective well described by Dorothy Smith, 1987), within the terms described by Shor and Freire? Within these terms, I want to underline the complexities involved in actually attempting to *do dialogue*—especially when it takes place between genders as demonstrated by Lewis and Simon. Plagued by my resistance, I welcome your comments. As you know, I value your ongoing support of my struggle to teach in better ways.

Love, Hope, and Solidarity,
Anne-Louise

October 26, 1988

Hello Anne-Louise,

Thank you for your letter. I was struck, while reading it, by the degree of struggle which is teaching, especially in a situation like yours where you are teaching large numbers of students and using a method whose effectiveness surely diminishes with the numbers involved. This is one very real way in which the conditions of schooling nip radicalism in the bud and perpetuate the relations of the status quo. In your classroom the gendered conditions of silence are compounded by the capitalist organization of undergraduate education at a large university. As Shor points out, "the right to have a small [group] discussion begins as a *class* privilege" (p. 12). I believe the fact that you're trying to overcome such inequality is a crucially important aspect of your practice.

Now I want to focus on these aspects of struggle and silence both to comment on your work and to point to what I feel are gaps in Freire and Shor's dialogical account of the dialogical method. Implicit in their account, I believe, is a particular understanding of the politics of reading, the ways in which meanings are produced within, and are productive of, social relations (Kelly, 1988). I fundamentally disagree with that understanding. Freire argues that "dialogue is the sealing

together of the teacher and the students in the *joint* act of knowing
and re-knowing the object of study," while Shor argues that "the
teacher selecting objects of study knows them *better* than the students
as the course begins but the teacher *re-learns* the objects through
studying them with the students" (p. 14). Shor's premise is problematic
for me. In this case, I would suggest that the teacher may well know
the object of study *in a certain way,* or *differently* than the students,
but I balk at the hierarchization overtly captured in "better." In such
a context of hierarchization, I would argue that a student is left in
a position where s/he must *defend* a version of reality rather than
explore it. S/he must do so always unsuccessfully, because the teacher
ultimately, despite the relearning, is seen as holding the "truth."

I believe a key starting place in the dismantling of such destructive ideology is in your insistence on a meeting place for students and
teacher where "all involved bring to the exchange either the understanding of, or the willingness to consider, the view that knowledge,
what it is we 'know' about our world, is socially constructed." Clearly,
this expectation can best be lived out in a situation of trust. I would
suggest that this trust might be negotiated through practices, at the
very beginning, which point to the historicity of versions of reality
so that students might then feel safe to express their own. There are
many examples from which to draw, such as the work of Catherine
Belsey (1985) on Renaissance drama, Michel Foucault (1979) on the
history of sexuality, and Gary Kinsman (1987) on sexuality in Canada.
Such examples need not imply that the teacher knows "better" the
object of study. It does explicitly require, however, that the teacher
make clear the framework out of which s/he is working, *how* it is s/he
knows the object of study. S/he must also make clear that that
framework, that knowing, too, is a site of contestation, of struggle.
"Struggle" is a word rarely used by either Freire or Shor, although
"empowerment" is. Empowerment isn't something we give students;
it is, rather, struggled into existence, and in that struggle, we find
as teachers that our own versions of reality are also contested. Of
course, strains of elitism in Freire's and Shor's arguments show
elsewhere, too. The separation of the intellectual community in "we
intellectuals first describe concepts while the people first describe
reality, the concreteness" (pp. 19-20) offends me. It sets up a class and,
yes, gendered either/or, us/them, mental/manual which I find both
theoretically unacceptable and antithetical to a dialogical method.
With such divisions in place, where might we speak together?

This brings me to my second point. You have probably already
noted the silence surrounding gender in the Freire and Shor article.

The "silent dominant" male voice is clearly in place in this dialogue. They do not address adequately the question of silence and, in fact, approach gender unproblematically in their discussion of dialogue. This is where I find the Lewis and Simon work important. While I agree with your critique of the structuralism of Lewis and Simon, I do find important the discussion of dialogical space as it is occupied differently by women and men. As you point out in your previous letter, Freire and Shor inadequately address this, leaving their notion of dialogue unproblematic in this respect. Yet our experiences as women students and teachers strongly reinforce the living out of these social relations. Where men and women occupy mutual dialogical space, men often dominate that space, for all sorts of reasons, as Lewis and Simon point out. There are just so many ways in which men can police space, ways in which women often collude. It is that point which I want to use to lead into a discussion of your class on misogyny.

Let me first of all say that as women teachers who work in dialogical spaces shared with women and men students, we must be keen strategists. I imagine it is no more useful to tell a man he is misogynistic than it is to tell a woman she is oppressed. Perhaps we as teachers can facilitate alternative discourses in which alternative versions of reality might be produced which incorporate such understandings. Again, historicizing is important here. Yet I get the impression that, in this case, your class was polarized around whose version of reality was "correct." The women could more easily accept your version, explicated in the introduction of the notion of misogyny, for it empowered them against the perceived "enemy." However, it's unlikely that men will concede, passively accept this construct and then examine their reality through it. Pedagogically, I think, it might have been more fruitful to explore the dynamics of Maud's rejection by the male community of George's Cove and, through such dialogue, then arrive at a theoretical notion of misogyny which, even then, *could still be contested.* By drawing on other social and historical examples, you might well strengthen your argument. To acknowledge that meaning is always plural and always contested is to allow student and teacher to dialogue apart from the tyranny of absolute truth. I find this is a more compassionate space, and as you well know, it's a space where the most insistent often confront their own contradictions. Instead, in the space of your classroom, one male student used his power to refuse dialogue to dispel dialogue, for polarized positions do not dialogue make! I feel this is where Freire has a valid point: "Dialogue does not exist in a political vacuum. It is not a 'free space' where you may do what you want. Dialogue takes place within some kind of program and context" (p. 16). Part of that program is that very requirement that everyone listen and hear, as you point out. I believe dialogue was sabotaged in the case of the discussion on misogyny. It was sabotaged because the negotiated conditions of dialogue were forsaken and the struggle over the word, over meaning, became demands of truth. What could have been fluid, constructive tension became irrevocable and destructive tension. An acknowledgement of this violation might possibly have reclaimed the dialogical space.

I have encountered similar problems in my own teaching. Much of it I now can relate to what I understand to be the struggle for always-ever-multiple meaning. In the dialogue around any text—a student's experience, a "literary" text, an article—the struggle for meaning is always evident. Various versions are offered, discussed, and proclaimed. I've come to cherish this diversity and even now I resist moving toward even the slightest closure, for there seems always to be some tyranny in closure. Unmistakably, though, and especially where women and men share the same dialogical space, divergent meanings arise which have similar strains, experiential patterns, or historical consistencies. In such cases I find it useful to try to move the dialogue around to these shared strains of meaning and to question the conditions of which such meanings are possible effects. It is a form of "consciousness raising" over class, race, and gender, and at times it has been successful for me. I say this to in some way address the despair you proclaim at your inability "to get at the differences which the women and men differently experience in their reading of [*Maud's House*]." An understanding of the social construction of knowledge necessitates a politics of reading. That is what I'm advocating. I'll talk more about that in my next letter.

Now, in my ending, let me talk once again about hope. The fact that we even ask the questions we ask, and examine our teaching practices in the ways we do, is hopeful. We must not be too hard on ourselves in this questioning. With integrity, we do the best we can, always wary of our weaknesses. But there is such glory for me in knowing that you persist, against such odds, to teach compassionately and justly. I salute you. The words of Kathleen Weiler (1988) come to mind at this time:

> I think it is vital that feminist and other progressive teachers remember the power that social forces exert on themselves and on their students and that they recognize the limits of what is possible to accomplish in a classroom. But by recognizing the

limits of what is possible, teachers (and all of us) should recognize the value and importance of *doing* what is possible. (p. 153)

You are important. You do important work. Nolite te bastardes carborundorum.

En/vision and Hope,
Ursula . . .

November 11, 1988

Salute Ursula,

As so often occurs in our letter exchanges your responses help me examine aspects of my teaching practices that are not always obvious to me. Your responses encourage me to look afresh at problems which I share with you in a way which helps me to move from an individual to a social analysis. Through dialogue, you work in good teacher manner to help me understand *differently*. In sifting my problems, reactions, and assumptions through your reading of the situation, I'm encouraged to critique the problem at hand in multiple ways—in this case through our multiple rereadings of Shor and Freire. In so doing, I learn (as I assume you do) in and through our respective discussions, rather than because I am presented a correct or truthful perspective. This kind of learning requires a great deal of trust, I've discovered.

More specifically, in your critique of Shor's and Freire's use of the term *better* to describe an assumed hierarchy of learning between student and teacher, your attention to language practices encourages me to examine how assumptions can produce teaching practices in which students find themselves *defending* a version of reality, rather than exploring one. In pointing this out, you enable me to reconsider my use of the term misogyny as a starting place—a place decided by me as the teacher. It created a situation in which the social relations which I was attempting to describe remained unexplored, because the men felt it necessary to defend themselves against the supposed assumption that "all" men hate women. The discussion of misogyny evolved into a battleground rather than an exploration site. As you so ably point out, to begin from this place is akin to telling a woman she is oppressed—a place highly resisted by women students. Thank you, Ursula, for helping me to relearn the obvious!

As a teacher, I now see how in this instance I began from neither a *better* place than students, nor from a place where we were able as a class to relearn specific material. In other words, I learned once again that I cannot begin from the elitist assumption that I, as a teacher, am always in a position to know better than students. Rather than, in Freire's terms, putting "the object to be known" (p. 14)—in this case, gendered relations—on the table for examination, I mistakenly tried to measure the conceptual fit between the term *misogyny* and the gendered relations in *Maud's House*. Dialogue did not occur for a number of complex reasons, not the least of which was my decision to begin in a particular place—a place which proved inappropriate. For this reason, I continue to struggle with how to create a classroom context which makes possible liberating kinds of dialogue, which begin where students are and extend from there, through dialogue. As a woman teacher who knows some of the difficulties involved in meeting across gender divisions, I do work from the assumption that it is neither easy, nor at times even possible, for women and men to begin to speak from a place of equality.

My assumption that women and men are not always able to begin to talk from a place of equality brings me to your second point. Here, you quite astutely point out the "silence surrounding gender" (p. 2) in the Shor and Freire article: It is here that I, too, find the article by Lewis and Simon much more helpful. Shor and Freire implicitly assume that it is *not* fundamentally important to problematize gender in any discussion of dialogue between women and men. I want to respond to this perceived silence in two ways. Firstly, I will discuss Freire's statement that "a dialogical situation implies the absence of authoritarianism" (p. 16) and secondly, I will discuss Shor's assumption that "in situated pedagogy we discover with students the themes most problematic to their perceptions" (p. 17).

In order to "uncover" my resistance to these two statements I want to speak briefly about recent research suggesting that women's *learning* and *developing* are shaped to an alarming extent by male violence, sexual abuse, incest, and sexual harassment. Research indicates that most women in North America experience sexual harassment, and that a majority of women experience some form of sexual abuse (Belenky et al., 1986; Brookes, 1988; Rockhill, 1987). In their study of women in Canadian universities, Anne Innis Dagg and Patricia J. Thompson (1988) note that:

> Sexual harassment and violence against women are the most obvious manifestations of the sexist attitude present in Canadian universities. Although many women do not become victims of these crimes during their university careers, all university women are subject both to the threat of sex-specific physical

violence and to the more subtle sexism that creates an uncomfortable ambience. This atmosphere can affect women students' ability to concentrate, hamper their freedom to work, and destroy or thwart the creation of a supportive environment. (p. 94)

This is important research. These findings, I suggest, must be considered when analyzing any kind of learning experience which involves relations between women and men. Significantly, research indicates that sexual abuse, in its myriad of forms, is extremely disruptive to women's development and learning, making it difficult for women to relate equally to figures of authority. As victims of sexual abuse, women internalize, often at a precognitive age, the authority of the other, the violator. This internalizing of the authority of another through abuse makes it extremely difficult for abused women to relate healthily to any authority figure, but particularly to male authority figures (Brookes, 1988). Similarly, women who fear or anticipate male violence will internalize the authority of the abuser. Women have found it difficult to publicly discuss abuses done to them in private because of disbelief, fear, social reprisal, and socially enforced taboos— taboos which work to keep such topics out of legitimate classroom discussions—and the result is that many women are effectively silenced. They can neither describe the conditions of their reality, in Shor's terms, bring "themes problematic to their perceptions" (p. 17) to situated pedagogy, nor, alternatively, work in a context described by Freire as an "absence of authoritarianism" (p. 16). For abused women, it is difficult to erase this kind of authority and, hence, it is difficult to work from a relationship of equality in any classroom context.

If we take seriously the current research compiled by a number of feminist scholars, the problem of how to take up socially constructed gender differences shaped by male violence against women is complex. In a classroom context designed to create critical dialogue, are the predominantly male teachers interested, willing, and able to contend seriously with the conditions of many women's lives? I recently discussed this problem with a male colleague. This man is perceived as an excellent teacher, a teacher who works in innovative ways with students. He relayed to me a story about the immense discomfort which he experienced when lecturing recently to an audience composed of women and men. In the context of speaking about prisons in North America, he chose to speak about rape. The audience reaction took on a degree of emotionalism and discomfort, and as a result he experienced anxiety. His response to this felt anxiety was to conclude that such sensitive topics should be left to women academics. And I've discovered that his response is not uncommon. Many male academics even tell me these kinds of topics do not constitute serious academic research.

In my own classroom, I quite often problematize sexual abuse. Invariably, in taking up this problem, I invite highly charged and emotional learning contexts which I must be prepared to contend with. This is particularly true when women students report experiences of abuse, most often in their written work. It's also hard to learn how to respond when men dismiss violence against women and dismiss the idea that abuse can affect and shape women's way of knowing (Belenky et al., 1986). Women's difficulties in a male-organized university structure are similarly dismissed (Dagg & Thompson, 1988). Simon (in Lewis and Simon, 1987), in critiquing his own male-organized teaching practices, very consciously discusses some of the privileges accorded to male academics. From your perspective, Ursula, how necessary is it for both women and men to begin to problematize gender? In taking up this question could you speak more explicitly than I have in this letter about relations of power between women and men in the classroom context?

Lastly, I want to take up your third point, your more explicit discussion of my class on misogyny. I quite agree with your assumption that "dialogue was sabotaged" in this situation through the polarization created by differing groups defending *positions of truth*. Working from a notion of *correctness*, neither group was able to hear or learn from the other. Drawing from this insight, I want to state my deep appreciation for the work of Shor and Freire. From a perspective of critique, however, I would ask that they seriously consider further the importance of addressing the problem of gender, not as a sub-theme but, rather, as a problem which is immediately central to any work situated in critical pedagogy. Their work, I suggest, is much too important to go unnoticed by those who begin from a more explicit analysis of socially constructed gender differences. In taking up this work, and through our discussion of misogyny, I am relearning once again how easy it is to fall into a dichotomous (either-or/true-false) perspective, despite my "intellectual" understanding that knowledge is socially constructed.

You mentioned that you would speak about a politics of reading in your next letter. Given my ongoing struggles to read beyond the obvious, I look forward to hearing from you. Your letters bring me hope and help me always to consider more clearly alternative ways of thinking about, and doing, teaching. In this hope, I imagine that social change can occur in and through the everyday practices of women and men.

Love, Hope, and Solidarity,
Anne-Louise

December 3, 1988

Dear Anne-Louise,

Thank you so much for your letter. I was especially enthused by these responses both to me and to the ideas of Shor and Freire because I believe you make a crucially important breakthrough. I think your question of "how to take up socially constructed gender differences shaped by male violence against women" is especially insightful, because it points to what I consider to be a major problem with the dialogical method that Shor and Freire advocate. I deeply appreciate the arguments of these two men but I insist that their presentation of the notion of dialogue and the conditions of dialogue are largely unproblematic. I believe this because of the gender blindness which you pointed out in their dialogue and their discussion of the dialogical method itself. Beyond that, I see in their discussion a lack of attention to what I've called a politics of reading the world, social relations, as text (Kelly, 1988). I want to attend to these points here.

Fundamentally, what I want to argue is that Shor and Freire, in their presentation of the dialogical method, were unsuccessful in attending to (and, even, perhaps, were unable to attend to) gender differences in any significant way. In other ways, they failed to "read" the conditions of women's silence in classrooms. This is so, partially, I believe, because of the ways in which their own readings are formed, and, in parts, limited by their social differences as men and, even, their social differences as first and second world men, respectively. Here, I do not mean any "essential" sorts of differences but, rather, differences which exist in and through the ways in which they (do not) speak of dialogue in classrooms. Let me try to be clearer.

You will notice that in their article there is an important section on "Class and Empowerment." While I would never argue that gender oppression is separate from class oppression, I am always astounded that men still talk about class oppression without ever taking up the issue of gender differences and gender oppression. On this point, I want to respond to your story of your male colleague and his decision to leave "sensitive topics" such as (what I assume was male) rape in (male) prisons to women academics. The obvious sexism in that remark is one thing, but there is another issue there, as well. Without knowing the context or the content of his discussion, I assume it might have been an opportunity to examine the relations of power which constitute homophobic practices. But that, like the issue of gender in Shor and Freire's discussion, is not one which deeply affects your male colleague. Thus he could easily forsake it, in fact, might not have even "read" it as such. The silent dominant have difficulty reading marginally, and I do not expect such men to discuss the problems of women or gay men or lesbians. What I do expect of them, though—in fact, what I demand of them—is that they examine their own positions of power as *effects of* and as *affecting* oppressed *others*. In answer to your question, "How necessary is it for both women and men to begin to problematize gender?" I would respond, "Not how necessary, but how?"

It is out of such a position that I critique the work of Shor and Freire. While Shor, for example, claims that "dialogic inquiry is situated in the culture, language, politics and themes of the students" (p.18) and Freire claims that "my insistence on starting from their daily life experiences is based in the possibility of starting from concreteness, from common sense, to reach a rigorous understanding of reality" (p. 20), they don't acknowledge the forces that come to form these *readings*, these understandings. In short, they don't discuss why these readings exist, and why students might even have chosen them in order to satisfy certain desires. Nor do they acknowledge the politics surrounding a *voicing of these readings*, which you so clearly pinpoint. Without this knowledge, rereadings (which, it seems to me is what the dialogical method is about creating) are still further mystifications. The determinants of race, class, gender, sexuality, age, and region in reading practices, readings of the world, have to be always, and overtly, on the agenda in the dialogical classroom and in any discussion of method in dialogical teaching.

In this respect, I want also to address a little more the insistence by Freire that "a dialogical situation implies the absence of authoritarianism" (p. 16). I think I agree with this principle, and I respect Freire and Shor's shared commitment to disavowing authoritarianism. But students bring into the dialogue patterns of learned behavior, and deeply internalized understandings of power differentials. These, again, are "readings" of the world which, as you point out, the *apparent* absence of authoritarianism will not completely dispel. The absence of authoritarianism does not, indeed, cannot, guarantee the absence of power struggles. The production of meanings, of understandings, of readings of the world in any context is a contentious practice fraught with struggle, contradiction, and politics. The subject/reader is a gendered subject/reader and these struggles embody these gendered differences. Any outline of the dialogical method cannot ignore this; where it does, as in the case of Freire and Shor, it is a practice of the politics of gender oppression which I find unacceptable.

Given these convictions, Anne-Louise, I find it increasingly more pressing to attempt to imagine how it might be possible, in and through our pedagogical practices, to create spaces in which these struggles over the word and over the world might be waged more positively. What I call empowerment is the recognition of subject agency in the transformation of the subject in the transformation of the world. Yet the obstacles to subject transformation are tremendous as the world inhabits the subject, inhabits the classroom. I want to nudge at the silences, recall the erasures, cry "foul" within the male-formed structures of voicing, of dialogue. I consider our efforts to be part of these resistances. Thank you for being part of the struggle.

En/vision and Hope,

Ursula. . .

References

Belenky, M. F., Clinchy, B. M., Goldberger, N. R., & Tarule, J. M. (1986). *Womens ways of knowing: The development of self, voice and mind.* New York: Basic Books.

Belsey, C. (1985). *The subject of tragedy: Identity and difference in Renaissance drama.* London: Methuen.

Brookes, A.-L. (1988). *Feminist pedagogy: A subject in/formation.* Unpublished doctoral dissertation, Ontario Institute for Studies in Education, University of Toronto.

Dagg, A. I., & Thompson, P. J. (1988). *MisEducation: Women in Canadian universities.* Toronto: OISE Press.

Foucault, M. (1979). *The history of sexuality, Vol. 1* (R. Hurley, Trans.). London: Allen Lane.

Gough, W. (1984). *Maud's house.* St. John's: Breakwater Books.

Kelly, U. A. (1988). *Marketing 'place': Regional readers reading—Capitalism, patriarchy and culture.* Unpublished doctoral dissertation, Ontario Institute for Studies in Education, University of Toronto.

Kinsman, G. (1987). *The regulation of desire: Sexuality in Canada*. Montreal: Black Rose Books.

Lewis, M., & Simon, R. (1986). A discourse not intended for her. *Harvard Educational Review, 56*, 457–472.

Rockhill, K. (1987, March). *Violence against wives*. Paper presented at the School of Social Work, University of Toronto.

Simon, R. (1987). Empowerment as a pedagogy of possibility. *Language Arts, 64*, 370–382.

Shor, I., & Freire, P. (1987). What is the "dialogical method" of teaching? *Journal of Education, 169*(3), 11–31.

Smith, D. (1987). *The everyday world as problematic*. Toronto: University of Toronto Press.

Weiler, K. (1988). *Women teaching for change: Gender, class & power*. South Hadley, MA: Bergin & Garvey.

Contributors

Madeleine Arnot (previously McDonald) teaches in the Department of Education at the University of Cambridge. She has published widely in the fields of sociology of education and educational policy, particularly on class, gender, and race issues. Her recent publications include *Race and Gender: Equal Opportunities in Education*, and two coedited collections with Gaby Weiner, *Gender and the Politics of Schooling* and *Gender Under Scrutiny*.

Deborah P. Britzman is an Associate Professor in The School of Education and Human Development at the State University of New York at Binghamton. There she teaches courses in multicultural education and English education. Britzman is the author of *Practice Makes Practice: A Critical Study of Learning to Teach*.

Linda Brodkey is an Associate Professor of English at the University of Texas at Austin, where she teaches undergraduate and graduate courses on writing and writing pedagogy. She is the author of *Academic Writing as Social Practice* and numerous articles on literacy in theory, research, and practice.

Anne-Louise Brookes is an Assistant Professor in the Department of Sociology and Anthropology at St. Francis Xavier University, Antigonish, Nova Scotia. Her most recent work is *Feminist Pedagogy: A Subject In/Formation*. She is currently working on a project in which she uses the primary teaching methods of Sylvia Ashton-Warner to teach university students how to read and write in critically informed ways.

Cleo Cherryholmes is a Professor of Political Science at Michigan State University and has been interested in curriculum issues since teaching high school American Government. He is presently interested in pragmatism, curriculum, and public policy. He has published in the *American Journal of Education, Journal of Curriculum Studies, Journal of Education, Theory and Research in Social Education*, and *Social Education*. His most recent book is *Power and Criticism: Poststructural Investigations in Education*.

Michelle Fine is an activist involved with urban education and grass-roots feminist organizing as well as a Professor of Psychology in Education at the University of Pennsylvania. Her books include *Framing Dropouts: Notes on the Politics of an Urban High School*, *Women with Disabilities: Essays on Politics, Culture and Psychology* (co-edited with Adrienne Asch), *Reconstructing Silence and Privilege* (co-edited with Lois Weis), and *Disruptive Voices: The Politics of Feminist Psychology*.

Michèle Foster is an Associate Professor of Education at the University of California at Davis. Between 1989 and 1991 she was on leave at the University of North Carolina at Chapel Hill where she was a Carolina Minority Postdoctoral Scholar, and concurrently a National Academy of Education Spencer Postdoctoral Fellow. Her articles have appeared in *Language in Society*, the *Journal of Education*, and the *NWSA Journal*. She is also editor of *Readings in Equal Education. Volume 11: Qualitative Investigations into Schools and Schooling*.

Marilyn Frankenstein has taught mathematics to junior high school, high school, and young adult students in New York City and New Jersey, and since 1978 has been teaching mathematics to adults. She currently heads the Department of Applied Language and Mathematics at the College of Public and Community Service, University of Massachusetts, Boston. She is the author of *Relearning Mathematics* (London: Free Association Books, 1989) and numerous articles on the teaching of mathematics. She is co-founder with Arthur Powell and John Volmink of the Criticalmathematics Educators Group and is a member of the *Radical Teacher* editorial collective and the *Science for the People* editorial board.

Henry A. Giroux is a Professor and Renowned Scholar in Residence in the School of Education and Allied Professions at Miami University and Director of the Center for Education and Cultural Studies. He is the author of numerous works including *Ideology, Culture and the Process of Schooling, Theory and Resistance in Education, Teachers as Intellectuals,* and *Schooling and the Struggle for Public Life,* and co-author with Stanley Aronowitz of *Education Under Siege* and *Postmodern Education.*

Maxine Greene is a Professor of Philosophy and Education and William F. Russell Professor of Foundations of Education (emeritus) at Teachers College, Columbia. Her major publications include

The Dialectic of Freedom and *Landscapes of Learning*. She has published extensively on art and curriculum and is currently working in the areas of gender and multicultural issues.

Ursula A. Kelly is an Assistant Professor in the Faculty of Education at Saint Mary's University, Halifax, Nova Scotia, where she teaches courses in English Studies, Gender and Education, Critical/Feminist Pedagogies, and Media Studies. Her research focuses on post-structuralist investigations into gender, subjectivity, culture, and schooling.

Cameron McCarthy is an Assistant Professor of Social and Political Foundations in the Department of Education at Colgate University. He is the author of *Race and Curriculum* and has written extensively on the politics of film and theater and popular culture, as well as critical analyses of neo-Marxist writing on racial domination in education.

Laurie McDade received her doctorate in Educational Anthropology from Rutgers University in 1987. During the school year 1987–1988 she was an Assistant Professor in the Department of Educational Leadership, Miami University, Oxford, Ohio. Her areas of interest included gender studies and ethnography. She published articles in the *Journal of Education, Anthropology and Education Quarterly*, and the *North Dakota Quarterly*. The article published here drew from her dissertation, *Community Responses to Teenage Pregnancy and Parenting: An Ethnography of a Social Problem*. Laurie McDade died on June 15, 1988.

Thomas S. Popkewitz has written widely on the problems and issues of educational reform and research in the United States and Europe. His co-authored work, *The Myth of Educational Reform*, addresses current issues of educational reform; he has also written about the sociology of educational research in the United States and the Soviet Union in *Paradigm and Ideology in Educational Research* and in various journals. He is a Professor of Curriculum and Instruction at the University of Wisconsin/Madison and a Faculty Associate at the Wisconsin Center for Education Research. His most recent book, *A Political Sociology of Educational Reform: Power/Knowledge in Teaching, Teacher Education, and Research*, investigates the discourse of contemporary education reform as part of historically formed changes in social regulation in society.

Roger I. Simon is an Associate Professor in the Department of Curriculum at the Ontario Institute for Studies in Education. He teaches and writes extensively in the areas of critical pedagogy and cultural studies. He is currently working on his next book, *Teaching Against the Grain: A Pedagogy of Possibility.*

Index